PRAISE FOR
RETHINKING
BRANDING

'This is one of the best books to come out in recent years on the changes and elevations of branding in marketing and society today, through to their mythic aspects. Bravo!' **Professor Robert Kozinets, Schulich School of Business, York University, Toronto**

'*Rethinking Prestige Branding* describes in an entertaining way today's marketing paradigm of prestige and luxury brands. It's an absolute must-read for any marketer working within the prestige or luxury industries.' **Atissa Tadjadod, Director Global Communications, Piaget (Richemont International)**

'I was fascinated by the authors' approach, and highly encourage you to read this book.' **Dr G Clotaire Rapaille, author of *The Culture Code*, and Founder-CEO, Archetype Discoveries Worldwide**

'This book made me reflect on the Moleskine brand in a radically different way. There is much to learn from its innovative approach.' **Maria Sebregondi, Co-founder, Moleskine**

'This book sets a clear compass, balancing the mystery of magic and distance with the importance of purpose, meaning and customer delivery.' **Jenny Ashmore, President, Chartered Institute of Marketing (CIM), UK**

'To escape price competition there are not many routes: one can adopt the luxury strategy... Another one, seemingly related yet different, is to build brands that endow their buyers with prestige in the eyes of their tribe – based on an extensive benchmarking this book unveils the seven major clues explaining the success of these brands. This is a much welcome book for all marketing VPs.' **Professor Jean-Noël Kapferer, HEC Paris, author of *The Luxury Strategy*, *Kapferer on Luxury* and *The New Strategic Brand Management***

'Thoughtful and probing, the authors expertly delve into the marketing alchemy of 'Ueber-Brands' beyond superficial catchphrases and generic notions. A fresh and comprehensive work. Definitely worth the read.' **Deryck J van Rensburg, President, Global Ventures, The Coca-Cola Company**

'Schaefer and Kuehlwein find the rules of luxury have changed once again. This book is a great read for managers charged with building and maintaining prestige brands.' **Professor Scott Galloway, NYU Stern, Founder of Red Envelope and L2**

'An essential and timely meditation on the nature of brands, luxury, and the relationship between ownership and identity. The authors have given us a book that reflects deeply on the interconnectedness of material culture and the most ethereal aspects of human nature. An unlikely and very rewarding investigation into core human values.' **Dr David LaRocca, director of documentary *Brunello Cucinelli: A new philosophy of clothes*, author of *Emerson's English Traits and the Natural History of Metaphor***

'*Rethinking Prestige Branding* is very timely. In a rapidly changing world where prestige brands are facing explosive growth and incredible challenges, Wolfgang and JP provide a framework to understand and develop "Ueber-Brands".' **Professor Srinivas K Reddy, Academic Director, LVMH-SMU Asia Luxury Brand Research Initiative, Singapore Management University**

'A thoroughly enjoyable read. The well researched and insightful principles provide a new framework to define prestige branding in the socially connected landscape. And in a world where creating an aspiration brand is more about high values than high value and demands a connection to the consumer's mindset versus their wallet.' **John Goodwin, Chief Financial Officer and Executive Vice President, Business Enabling, LEGO**

'*Rethinking Prestige Branding* provides a thorough understanding of the often paradoxical rules for successful premium brand management. This book presents a complete and information-packed resource covering every aspect of this mythical sector.' **Professor Christiane Beyerhaus, Program Director, Global Brand and Fashion Management, International School of Management, Germany**

'A compelling, enlightening and fascinating translation of the language of luxury. The authors have thoughtfully analysed and carefully defined a subject matter that has been overlooked in its significance to culture and contribution to inno-vation.' **Gwen L Whiting and Lindsey J Boyd, Co-Founders, The Laundress**

'I enjoyed reading the book because the authors do not restrict themselves to luxury brands but explain concepts from multiple and varied industries. They have chosen carefully companies which are not only well-known but are mak-ing news in their respective industries and categories.' **Professor Ashok Som, Founding Director, ESSEC-IIMA Global Management Program on Luxury and Retail**

'You have to be able to make your customer dream and love your product .... The authors help professionals and people who are about our industry to dig in some of its "secrets".' **Christian Foddis, Managing Director, Greater China, Salvatore Ferragamo**

'As these authors demonstrate, anyone can be everything to everyone but to become a seductive Ueber-Brand, nothing is as volatile as a dream.' **Patrick Hanlon, CEO, Thinktopia, author of *The Social Code* and *Primal Branding***

'With this book and the "Ueber-Brand" concept we are all stimulated to put a new energy to our brands as conditions for success in the contemporary world. Easy reading and not only academic but rich with real examples of success.' **Fabrizio Penta de Peppo, Professor of Luxury Marketing Management, Instituto Europeo di Design**

Rethinking Prestige Branding
Secrets of the Ueber-Brands™

Wolfgang Schaefer
and JP Kuehlwein

KoganPage

LONDON PHILADELPHIA NEW DELHI

First published in Great Britain and the United States in 2015 by Kogan Page Limited

2nd Floor, 45 Gee Street	1518 Walnut Street, Suite 1100	4737/23 Ansari Road
London EC1V 3RS	Philadelphia PA 19102	Daryaganj
United Kingdom	USA	New Delhi 110002
		India

www.koganpage.com

© Wolfgang Schaefer and JP Kuehlwein, 2015

The right of Wolfgang Schaefer and JP Kuehlwein to be identified as the authors of this work has been asserted by them in accordance with the Copyright, Designs and Patents Act 1988.

ISBN   978 0 7494 7003 6
E-ISBN 978 0 7494 7004 3

British Library Cataloguing-in-Publication Data

A CIP record for this book is available from the British Library.

Library of Congress Cataloging-in-Publication Data

Schaefer, Wolfgang.
  Rethinking prestige branding : secrets of the ueber-brands / Wolfgang Schaefer, J. P. Kuehlwein.
    pages cm
    ISBN 978-0-7494-7003-6 (paperback) — ISBN 978-0-7494-7004-3 (ebk)   1. Branding (Marketing)
2. Brand name products.   I. Kuehlwein, J. P.   II. Title.
  HF5415.1255.S392 2015
  658.8'27—dc23

                                                                                           2015008794

Typeset by Amnet
Print production managed by Jellyfish
Printed and bound by CPI Group (UK) Ltd, Croydon, CR0 4YY

CONTENTS

Principle 5: Behold! – the product as manifestation 145

Principle 6: Living the dream – the bubble shall never burst 173

Principle 7: Growth without end – the ultimate balancing act 203

PREFACE, OR WHAT DO A RED BULL AND A GREY GOOSE HAVE IN COMMON?

It all started with a glass of beer and a simple observation: some brands have gained almost mythical status – seemingly beyond any price or performance considerations.

We had been working with each other for a while, JP as Brand Director for Procter & Gamble, the consumer goods behemoth, I as Chief Strategy Officer for SelectNY, a renowned global brand and communication agency. We were having an after work drink when one of our bar mates cut through our conversation, ordering a 'Supercharger' (aka Vodka Red Bull), triggering a spiral of questions: Why do people flock to a 'gourmet vodka' like Grey Goose, where vodka is mostly liked for being flavour neutral? What keeps Red Bull cool after all those years? And isn't the mystery around taurine, its famous ingredient, eerily similar to that of skin care brand Crème de la Mer's miracle broth? Such different brands with different targets at vastly different price points, but both applying similar strategies and demanding a significant premium in their respective categories...

Both of us have extensive experience with branding ranging from the mass to class tier and across many categories. We had discussed the differences many times, but somehow this time we got into a heated debate, raising question after question culminating in the ultimate: what makes a brand prestige in the 21st century?

The deeper we dug, the clearer it became that the answers aren't as simple anymore. Prestige is accrued in many more ways than it used to be. Its marketing rules are in flux. And, perhaps most importantly, it is flourishing these days across pretty much all tiers and categories – from a US $2 soft drink to multi-million dollar jewellery. Just like we all have come to blend designer with high street in our daily outfits, so are marketers growing more and more inclusive in their ways to exclusivity. Classic notions are shattered and reshuffled. Which is why we quickly felt uncomfortable using the established terminology and started talking about 'modern prestige' or finally 'Ueber-Brands'. Because this newly emerging breed of prestige brands thrives on paradoxes, breaks with branding traditions and inspires us with an innate sense of mission paired with often very counter-intuitive commercialization strategies. They understand that purpose beats performance and that price is often rather a catalyst than a barrier to purchase. They've taken the insight to heart, that the best way to sell is often not to sell and that function can be really emotional – if you wrap it in a story. They know that devotion needs distance, but they know also that both are built differently in the digital age. They appreciate that slow can be fast and small is often much bigger, that it takes true dedication to instil the same in others and, above all, that marketing must be much more mythical if you want to become a brand of such proportions. In one word, they are Ueber – above and beyond their competition not only in standing and their ability to make their price premium an afterthought, but mostly in courage and conviction. Perhaps (hopefully) they will lead the way into a new kind of marketing for the new millennium.

The idea for this book was born, and a couple of years of intense research and synthesis ensued which finally yielded this book.

In developing and validating our thinking we approached the subject from a multitude of angles, speaking with countless practitioners as well as experts ranging from store managers to shoppers, designers to marketing executives, supply chain strategists to touch point planners, founders and CEOs to investors and many of the specialists, journalists and academics who study them. We owe all of them immeasurable gratitude for their time, wits, smarts, patience and encouragement. We can't possibly mention them all, but we'll give it a try at the end of the book. A special 'thank you' at this point to all our colleagues at SelectNY, Frédéric Fekkai, Smith & Norbu and P&G who allowed us to experience and learn so much through the years. To Shona Seifert and Dominic Pettman who graciously took on the daunting task of fighting their way through the first manuscript. To Sasha Duravcevic and Galerie Stefan Roepke for the wonderful artwork. To Isabelle, Leo and Max who generously handed over the keys to the house while we finalized the manuscript… And to all our partners, supporters and clients throughout the years, especially the last one. We are (almost) always happy to hear from you at authors@ueberbrands.com

Wolf and JP

 To access videos and other materials referenced in the book as well as bonus materials, please scan this QR code or visit our blog 'Ueber-Brands' on wordpress.com.

A note about the photographs:

The photographs introducing each of the seven principles are of 'Untitled', 2012, a sculpture in the r/e collection by renowned American-Montenegrin artist Aleksandar Duravcevic. You will find his work in many public collections including the Metropolitan Museum of Art, NYC, the San Francisco Public Library, the Lyrik Kabinett, Munich and representing Montenegro at the Venice Biennale 2015.

aleksandarduravcevic.com; photo credit: Simon Vogel

ACKNOWLEDGEMENTS

We would like to thank all those who have enriched and encouraged, inspired and enlightened, helped and supported us over the years, particularly in writing this book. Without your knowledge, insights, time, patience and generosity this would have never been possible. We are especially indebted of course to all those brands, friends, colleagues, experts, marketers and artists who shared their experiences and donated their time, art and talent in making this book as illustrative but also instructive as it hopefully turned out to be. Thank you to:

Alan Sutherland (Dyson), Allie Tsavdarides (TOMS), Andrea Davey (Tiffany & Co), Andrew Keith (Lane Crawford), Andy Janssen (Natura), Angelica Cheung (Vogue), Anna Berkl (Red Bull), Antoine Delgrange (Rochas/P&G), Arnaud De Schuytter (Vertu), Atissa Tadjadod (Piaget), Benoit Ams (Smith & Norbu), Dr Brigitte Walz, Caroline Duke (method), Caroline Gibbons (PortiCo), Cheewee Tam (SK-II/P&G), Chris Lansing (Naked Emerging Brands/PepsiCo), Christian Doose (Swarovski), Christian Foddis (Salvatore Ferragamo), Christophe Archaimbault (Diesel), Clara Lin (Shang Xia), Claudia Mayer-Santos, Clemmie Nettlefold (Innocent), Clotaire Rappaille (Archetype Discoveries Worldwide), Dr Cordula Krueger (&Equity), Corinne Dauger, David LaRocca (State University of New York), Davide Nicosia (NICE), Debi Feinman, Deryck van Rensburg (The Coca-Cola Company), Diane Duperret (Nespresso), Dominic Pettman, PhD (The New School, NYC), Dorothee Boivin (P&G), Elizabeth Holder Raberin (Ladurée), Elizabeth Isenegger (Freitag), Fabio Stefani (Max Factor), Florent Bayle-Labouré (Cirque Du Soleil), Florian Weik (BMW Group), Franzrudolf Lehnert (NICE), Frederic Derreumaux (Kellog), Frédéric Fekkai, Frederic Guiral (Aigle), Ghislain Devouge (Egon Zehnder), Gwen Whiting (The Laundress), Heike Haag (Madame), Herwig Preis (SelectNY), Ian Ginsberg (C.O. Bigelow), Inge Heinsius (Godiva), Isabelle Pascal (Wu Hao), Jason Beckley (Dunhill), Jean Zimmerman (Ba Yan Ka La), Jean-Noël Kapferer (HEC Paris), Jess Clayton (Patagonia), Jill Kluge (Mandarin Hotel Group), Joanne Crewes (SK-II/P&G Prestige), Joe Doucet, Johan Buelow (Lakrids), John Goodwin (LEGO), John Habbouch (Elizabeth Arden), John Scharffenberger (eponymous chocolates and sparkling wines), Judith Azoulay (P&G), Juliana Hendershot (Chanel), Kathy Kilz (Zucker Kommunikation), Kirk and Kelsey Graham (TOMS), Kyle Garner (New Chapter), Lena Fissler (Freitag), Leonora Polonsky, Lindsey Boyd (The Laundress), Lito German (BMW Group), Maartje Kardol (Red Bull), Makie Prager (Betones), Marc Brulhart (marc & chantal), Marc Pritchard (P&G), Marco Bevolo, Marco Parsiegla (P&G Prestige), Dr Marco Wehr, Maria Sebregondi (Moleskine), Markus Strobel (Braun/P&G Prestige), Mathilde Delhoume (P&G), Matteo

Martignoni (Aesop), Max Kater (Murchison-Hume), Michael Moszynski (LONON), Michela Ratti (P&G), Nancy Swanson (P&G), Noel Estrada and Stefan Roepke (Galerie Roepke), Olga Gutierrez de la Roza (P&G), Olivier Rose van Doorne (SelectNY), Patrick Hanlon (Thinktopia), Paul Husband, Paul Smith, Raymond Dulieu (Freecaster), RC Menard (Cirque Du Soleil), Reuben Carranza (Luxury Brand Partners), Richard Hsu, Robert Kozinets (York University), Sandra Pickering (opento.com), Sandrine Huguet (La Maison Du Chocolat), Sara Riis-Carstensen (LEGO), Sasha Duravcevic, Scott Galloway (New York University), Seth Box (LVMH), Shona Seifert, Srinivas Reddy (Singapore Management University), Stephan Kanlian (Fashion Institute of Technology), Stijn Augustynen (Nespresso), Sue Gill (Icebreaker), Sumit Basin (P&G Prestige), Susan Plagemann (Vogue), Tanzawa-san (Hoshino Resorts), Tarane Yuson, Thomas Delabriere (Innocent), Tina Adolfsson (Ralph Lauren), Tom Jarrod (Ralph Lauren), Tyler Brule (Monocle), Vivian (Yuan Soap), Werner Domittner (Diageo), Wes Tsang (Ermenegildo Zegna), and the fine team at Kogan Page.

PART ONE
Rethinking prestige branding

When we started this book, our goal was fairly easy and straightforward: share our insights and learnings on how prestige brands function, how they are being built and what makes them secure in their comfortable position on the upper end of their categories, relatively sheltered from price sensitivity. Now, almost four years later and after hundreds of expert interviews and a countless number of case studies things are not so clear-cut anymore, largely because the parameters of prestige have become increasingly blurred: What defines prestige brands today and what distinguishes them from their non-prestige counterparts? Does prestige the way we know it, or used to know it, even still exist? Or is the concept completely outdated? Have we all 'traded up' (Silverstein and Fiske, 2003) to the point where there's no difference anymore and everything is prestige – or nothing? Where the attempt to classify prestige vs other brands seems totally futile, where luxury has 'lost its lustre' (Thomas, 2007) and become completely subjective?

We think not. The concept of prestige will always exist as it is baked into our human need for distinction as well as aspiration. But it's time to take a closer look again. It seems we are in the midst of a big shift in how this need for prestige manifests itself, which role brands play in this and how. We, that is the marketing world and all of us partaking in it – professionally or privately – are seeing old rules and behaviors still present but new ones starting to take their place. Classic categorizations like 'luxury', 'premium' or 'mass' are in flux and new, only recently 'inaugurated' ones like 'masstige' or 'super-premium' are almost on their way out again. We are living through times of change, creating and experiencing a lot of unclarity and contradiction in our market- and branding-dominated worlds – but also enormous excitement and intrigue.

Based on all the analyses we did and all the conversations we had – and confounded not the least by our daily experience as practitioners – it seems there is a new kind of prestige emerging. And in its wake there's a new kind of marketing taking hold, new mantras and mechanisms that are becoming common ground, a new language that seems to be establishing itself. Of course most of these changes are less revolution than they are evolution, but many of them are yet a revelation. There's a healthy mixing and merging of the tried and true with the new and breakthrough, partially enabled only recently through new technologies or driven by a generally evolving marketscape and consumer consciousness. The prestige rules, while by no means all reinvented are being reshuffled and redefined. Which is why we thought it important to revisit them.

Modern prestige brand founders (clockwise from top left): Johan Buelow (Lakrids), Lindsey Boyd and Gwen Whiting (The Laundress), Benoit Ams (Smith & Norbu), Maria Sebregondi (Moleskine), Adam Lowry and Eric Ryan (method)

Courtesy of the respective brands

All this is spearheaded by new brands appropriating patterns and strategies that until not long ago pertained exclusively to prestige or, as Jean-Noël Kapferer, one of the leading thinkers in this area would argue, only true luxury brands and their categories (Kapferer, 2009). But, there are also established luxury or premium brands acting in less expected ways, rethinking old musts with aplomb and venturing into previous no-go areas with gusto – like social media for instance. And that makes for a rather motley crew, living and breathing prestige in very modern ways – decidedly cross-generational, as some players are centuries old where others are newly minted, and enthusiastically cross-border, as they are growing in categories and at price points as diverse as possible. Which is why we coined the new term Ueber-Brands: their prestige is way beyond traditional notions and expectations and they set new standards for this very old concept that take our hearts and minds and their markets on a journey into the future. They are a cut above the rest, in standing but also in the way they guide our thinking – in a word, they are 'Ueber'.

What defines these brands, what unites them and how they build their business and their success is what this book is all about – culminating in the seven principles of modern prestige or Ueber-Brands and case studies featuring brands from long-established and rarefied Hermès to popular behemoth Red Bull, from small but high-minded Aēsop via activist Patagonia to rather fun and funky MINI or Freitag and others.

But before we get into the details of what we really mean by Ueber-Brands and what are their commonalities despite all their differences, we will first set the stage – if ever so briefly. This is what these following introductory pages are all about.

First we will lay out some of the key socio-economic and technical dynamics that are driving this change in our approach to prestige. 'The Times They Are a-Changing' maybe a somewhat pretentious or even preposterous title given the adoration that Bob Dylan and his anthem still command, but as we'll see, the changes we are going through seem to be little less profound than the ones in the sixties, when the human rights movement shook up our societal order.

For all readers that are not so versed in the evolution of our marketing world and the concept of brands, we will go through 'A Brief History of Branding', showing how what were once merely markers of quality have developed over the past century to become beacons of our culture and bellwethers of our collective myths.

Finally, in the third chapter, we will lay out some of the defining qualities of this 'New Kind of Prestige' that we see emerging: the three key dimensions of Ueber-Brands and how they enable their stellar position – from the importance of mission and myth to the new balance between connection and exclusion to their need for truth. We'll give you an overview of what constitutes modern prestige and how this new world is appropriating and remixing a lot of what used to be classic luxury strategies. And we will explain why it thus felt very apt for us to also re-appropriate an old term because it is of new-found relevance: 'What We Mean by Ueber-Brands'.

Welcome to *Rethinking Prestige Branding* – a quick tour of the dynamics that are driving and changing our marketing world and particularly our notions of prestige and how this leads to a bunch of new prestige rules and a new breed of brand for the 21st century: the Ueber-Brand.

The times they are a-changing

When Bob Dylan wrote his anthem of change in 1964 we were truly on the brink of a new societal order with the rise of the human rights movement and all that it entailed in terms of equality and the core values of our Western world. Whether the shifts we are currently experiencing will be anything as seismic as the ones in the second half of the last century remains to be seen. But one thing is already clear: where we were then talking mainly about the Western world we are this time looking at the entire globe.

A lot has been written about the global economy, our increasingly connected cultures, the digital revolution, how the world is getting smaller and flatter (Friedman, 2005) and what all this means for us people and the way we live, love and shop. We don't have the faintest ambition to go into depth on any of these issues – and neither would we have the authority to – but we feel it's important to at least remind ourselves of the key aspects that are shaping the way we interact, with each other as well as with the brands and products around us. Look at the major dynamics that have altered our economies as well as our behaviours – at least in brief. Because only then will the changes and new stratagems we discuss further on with regards to prestige brands make sense.

We see nine mega-trends relevant and noticeable in the context of our attitudes towards brands and marketing in general and prestige in particular.

Where's the magic?

More and more of us are recognizing that science can't answer all of life's questions and are starting to re-embrace the blurry lines towards mystery and magic. We understand that what we call truth may change from time to time, depending on the latest research, or may shift from culture to culture and certainly from person to person. We realize that our realities are to a large degree constructed, not just shaping but also depending on our world-view. And we grasp that despite all our best efforts in nano- and neuro-science there are still a lot, if not most of the important things, beyond our reach. On top of this, religion has been in decline for such a long time that strongly held and shared beliefs have become few and far between, at least in the Western world, which naturally leads to an overall loss of security and comfort and a vacuum of values.

All this has been fertile ground for a re-emergence of interest in the spiritual, mythical and magical. In New York for instance there is a burgeoning magical cabaret scene, complementing the well-established esoteric schools and institutions. Buddhism and yoga as 'spirituality-light' have become a cliché. And we've all enjoyed the magic-mystery tales of Harry Potter and Dan Brown's secret science and society thrillers. **In an age of change, instability and little truths, we are yearning to rediscover what's beyond the obvious, what's behind it all and what's at the core, holding everything together**. In other words, we are trying to reconnect our physical worlds with their metaphysical counterparts. And this is where myths, and more specifically brand myths come into play. Brands have become something akin to heroes in our contemporary culture. They are fixtures, not unlike those mythical figures in Greece, Rome or Egypt: things that we use to find orientation, direction, guidance. They are models in a lot of ways – supra-models so to speak – potentially linking us with higher powers and truths while very much being concerned with our earthly delights.

Culture, commerce – unite!

What once were polar opposites have become entangled in an ever-closer love affair. **The spheres of culture and commerce aren't so much fighting any more as they are recognizing their mutual interest and their interdependencies.** Here money and might, there praise and applause. Of course, the two have been mating ever since the time of the Medici, but their embrace has become tighter and more passionate than was imaginable even a few decades ago. There's hardly a prestige brand that doesn't act as patron saint to the arts and barely an artist or cultural arbiter that hasn't toyed with a commercial player. And, as Dr Clotaire Rapaille, the author of bestseller *The Culture Code*, pointed out in an interview with us, cracking that code and becoming part of a society's culture is key for a brand to achieve a superior market position and eminence. Since then, the importance of cultural resonance beyond individual relevance has become even more crucial in brand building. This is especially true now that all brands have to become their own medium, creating content beyond the products they provide for us to connect with them and each other in happily engaged shopping communities (see also a brief history of branding on page 11).

Capitalism, evolved

Just as commerce and culture seem to focus more on commonalities than differences lately, so have our capitalist system and our ethical one as a whole. We are still largely living in a shareholder world where the Milton Friedman concept of profit as singular focus of an enterprise rules, but there are a lot of cracks appearing in this concept. And more and more companies are using these cracks to make a business, one that is not solely profit driven but is also people conscious – environmentally aware, socially considerate and ethically minded. **Many economists already see the re-emergence of stakeholder capitalism as opposed to the all-prevailing shareholder one.** As Paul Polman, CEO of Unilever said: 'I do not work for the shareholder, to be honest; I work for the consumer, the customer... I'm not driven and I don't drive this business model by driving shareholder value' (*The Economist*, 2010).

Some call this new frontier 'Humanistic Capitalism'. Personally, we like to think of it as 'Enlightened Capitalism', a capitalism that is being reborn together with our culture and our worldview as they were during the Renaissance. Where making money isn't something to frown upon but neither is it something to glorify in and of itself. Where profit has to serve a purpose and greed is not good unless it *does* good – more than merely filling someone's pockets. Where creating value is not the opposite of having values and where any enterprise has to really undertake something worthwhile, something that is bigger than simply sustaining itself. As we will see, there are many very successful examples of this – creating a whole new kind of prestige and outstanding Ueber-Brands.

Consumerism, re-rooted

The craft brewery craze of the 1980s has grown into an ever-increasing part of the beer market, putting the giants under pressure and realizing a CAGR (compound annual growth rate) of almost 14 per cent in the United States alone from 2009–11 (Demeter, accessed September 2014). You can see the same trend in pretty much any category from chocolate to detergents, food to fashion, liquor to liquorice. It's partially what Michael Silverstein and Neil Fiske announced in their 2003 break-out hit book *Trading Up*. We are, certainly in the established markets, migrating to 'augmented' goods, replacing mere functional benefits with experiential ones and standard products with more refined and expensive ones, if for no other reason than that we can afford to. But there is more to it. It's not just our consumerist craving for better, bigger, more. Actually, it's the opposite that seems to be at work lately: consumerism re-rooted or rebooted. **Most of us have had so much that we are finally discovering that less can really be more.**

We are replacing quantity with quality, and in this we are showing a new, deeper concern and a more demanding attitude. We are looking for integrity and sincerity in what we buy, beyond quality and reliability. We are more drawn towards what is philosophically called the essence rather than meaningless iterations of it. We want the real thing, not just anything, which is why everything handmade or personally produced with soul and substance is on the winning side. And this is not just a matter of refinement and price, of 'trading up'. Very often it's actually the opposite: it's about 'trading down', down to the local, the simple, the unrefined but raw and 'true', as any green market can show you. Some see this already as a reversal of roles, where now products are becoming differentiators of brands rather than the other way around (Warc, 2013). We feel this is taking it too far, but a re-balance or re-calibration of product and brand relations is certainly happening.

The limits of money

Another aspect of consumers 'trading up' and the world of luxury bending over backwards to acquiesce to our desires and their shareholders' demands for growth, is the fact that price as a defining factor is losing importance. **In an age of 'affordable luxury', where pretty much anyone can and will have bits and pieces of high-priced brands, the distinguishing power of affordability has been eroding.** As Dana Thomas put it 'luxury lost its lustre' (Thomas, 2007), at least if it was a luxury whose value was primarily based on its cost. Pricing many 'out', so that few can feel 'in' doesn't work so well anymore. Even if a lot of luxury brands have started to course-correct and 're-tighten the reins', there are simply too many people with too much money to create a sense of exclusivity and aspiration simply by pricing up and out. Everybody can 'do expensive', so that the more advanced and sophisticated consumers have been looking for other ways to show their discriminating sense and set themselves apart – ways which money can't buy, or at least not that easily. Which brings us to...

The importance of knowledge

At least since the late '80s or early '90s everybody has realized that we are living in 'The Information Age': our economies are largely grounded on computing increasing amounts of information and data, and our societies have become knowledge-based and driven. Consequently, knowledge has become the new status driver. **Where it was 'having' that was the high road to social distinction and superiority during the industrial age, it is 'knowing' that has taken on this role today.** Being aware of something that others are not (yet) is what puts you apart and ahead – more than having it. It's the literal insider knowledge that differentiates between those 'in' (the know) and those not. This is how you show your trend-forwardness, your connectedness and your currency, and your cultural and social position as someone linked and leading rather than isolated and following.

The age of transparency

Certainly one of the politically most distinctive aspects of the digital revolution has been everybody gaining access to everyone and everything all the time. This new connectivity gives a heretofore unknown degree of transparency, which has played out in all kinds of civic engagements and uprisings from the Middle East to the 'Occupy' movement to local grass-root protests against gentrification or a new airport. In the commercial context this means that companies can't hide as well as they once could and that corporate responsibility or the lack thereof has become a non-negotiable factor in consumer behaviour.

The Cone Communications/Echo Global CSR study, one of the biggest of its kind with 10,000 respondents in the 10 largest global economies, concluded in 2013 that 'consumers across the globe resoundingly affirm CSR (corporate social responsibility) as a critical business strategy', with two-thirds of consumers saying they use social media 'to address or engage with companies around CSR' (Cone Communications, May 2013). **We want more nowadays than just a nice sneaker or an aromatic coffee: we want to be sure that no child labour was involved in producing them, our environment wasn't unduly harmed and that their – and our – trade was and is fair.** Or at least we don't want to know the opposite, because then we cannot and will not purchase with a clean conscience anymore, as numerous examples of boycotts, from Nike to coffee, have shown. And although we are all experiencing that web connectivity and transparency can also work against us, it seems that whistle-blowing and spontaneous wikileaks will be here to stay. Companies and brands are forced today to adhere to ethical, environmental and social standards just like any other public person or entity, or they live with a permanent threat of a sudden imbroglio all the way to annihilation.

One in a million

In around 2005, Chris Anderson brought the concept of long tailing to our cultural conscience and gave the internet a totally new spin: not just as a place where crowds and connectivity rule, but one which would equally serve and empower the individual. In short, the idea of 'long tailing' states that the internet, together with other digital and technical advances, will de-emphasize the importance of local penetration and allow even outliers and rarities to be produced and traded at scale. We've all experienced this in the meantime – finding that odd item we've been searching forever thanks to a collector and trader on eBay or getting a digi-print of an out-of stock book through Amazon. But even further, this has led to a resurgence of the custom-made – preferably in real time. It's become just as normal to mix your own organic muesli or create your personal cereal bar online and have it delivered to your breakfast table (mymuseli.com) as it is common practice to customize your sneakers, be they from Nike or New Balance. **Thanks to the internet, the mass-tailor made is on the rise**. This helps us to catch two of our most precious birds with one click: getting something that feels authentic, soulful and honest, made by ourselves for ourselves, and feeling like one in a million – though it's pretty clear that we are exactly just that, ie one *of* a million.

Together apart

Last, comes probably the most important aspect of the advance of our virtual world for what we call modern prestige: our social interactions. We people have always been and will always be driven by the need to balance being social with being individual. But the internet has opened new ways of doing this, or so it seems. **The borders of being together and apart have become more porous, permissive and have started to be re-drawn in the age of social media**. There's a growing number of people starting to question how 'social' social media truly is, and we can see an increasing number of younger people migrating again from Facebook to more 'intimate' or at least direct and temporary ways of communicating such as WhatsApp, Snapchat or Yik Yak. But there is a very noticeable shift or at least expansion of how we define 'having friends', being 'liked' and 'sharing' and 'connecting' with others. And that seems pretty irreversible, having a huge effect on marketing, evolving communication from mass monologues to multi-faceted dialogues, turning passive recipients into more active participants and making 'community building' every marketer's dream. For prestige brands this means that the known paths to exclusivity have opened up, that there are more – and more flexible – ways nowadays of making certain consumers 'stand out' while allowing them to be connected with the rest of us who admire them. But before we get into that in more detail (Principle 2), let's take a quick look at how branding has evolved over the past decades.

From marker to myth – a brief history of branding

Did it all start in the caves of our earliest ancestors and their sign language? Or was it in the Wild West where cowboys 'branded' their cattle? Or did Josiah Wedgewood invent the modern concept of branding when he marked his tableware to command a premium in the 17th century? There are many points of view on what defines the origins of branding, but in the widest sense it is as old as we people are, since it serves our human need for connection as well as distinction. And while our thinking about brands and the roles they play has evolved over more recent decades, most elements of them were there all along – they were just not being analyzed or consciously utilized. For instance, from the very early days a branded good has bestowed a certain aura of sophistication or status on its user. It just wasn't marketed this way then, but rather sold on the merits of its functional superiority. Because most customers were more interested in factual aspects during times when their functional needs weren't entirely satisfied yet.

Which brings us to an important point: the development of branding and marketing outlined below is by no means universal yet, nor is it irreversible. It relies on certain socio-economic conditions. Not only through Abraham Maslow's famous hierarchy of needs do we know that people don't migrate to the fulfilment of higher needs until their more immediate ones are met. The same holds true for the way we deal with brands. First of course, one must be in an economic position to indulge in 'higher order' products and brands. This is the case for many people in many developed societies, but certainly not for all. Also, historical and cultural differences play a big role. While, for instance, most of us in the West have been living in the 'experience economy' since the '80s (Pine/Gilmore, 1999, also Schulze, 1992), many people in Asia or other parts of the world are just recently entering that stage. It is only in times and cultures of material security or surplus that we become more concerned with the immaterial aspects of our consumption. Only when we have everything we need do we start wondering about what else we desire.

The following chronology thus shouldn't be understood as one idea of branding replacing the other: rather, they were layered on top, living and working in parallel – as they still are today. Which of them takes priority can switch very easily, depending on socio-economic realities or even from person to person and moment to moment, depending on levels of involvement or psycho-social context. We will all sometimes look at a brand as a mere quality guarantor while in other situations and categories happily engage more emotionally, becoming completely enamoured by their myth or loving them as a medium for connecting with others.

Brand as quality guarantor

One of the first companies to establish today's idea of marketing and brand building through rigorous go-to-market plans and communication strategies was arguably Procter & Gamble. 'All thy garments smell of myrrh and aloes and cassia, out of the ivory palaces whereby they've made thee glad' (Psalm 45.8) was supposedly the inspiration for Harley Procter in naming 'Ivory Soap'. And as a very devout, proud and shrewd man it doesn't surprise that he took God as the ultimate, though indirect (and unpaid we might add) endorsement, while his overall marketing strategy was completely down-to-earth, focused on the functional and rational. '99 and 44/100 per cent pure' was what we today would call his promise, benefit or USP – Unique Selling Proposition – and 'floats in water' was his RTB – Reason To Believe – because 'only what is so pure' is lighter than water (Ivory Soap, Wikipedia, accessed August 2013).

And that's the point: **When Harley Procter – and with him others like Coca-Cola or The Quakers (of Oats fame) – started what we now call 'branding' in the commercializing world of the early 20th century, their focus was on exactly this: functional benefits**. Brands for them were first and foremost a way to signify and guarantee superior quality. The idea was to physically distinguish their product from the competition and build a quality reputation, which would allow them to charge a premium.

The consumer relationship, if that term is even appropriate for those early days, was thus one that was supposed to be based on trust. They tried to build a trust bias, an emotional shortcut to stir purchase decisions and to ensure customer preference and loyalty. The interesting thing is that today, in many ways, we are closing the circle and getting back to exactly the same point – albeit on a higher level, as we saw in the previous chapter and discuss in more detail in Principle 5. It's like T.S. Eliot says in *Little Gidding*: 'And the end of all our exploring will be to arrive where we started and know the place for the first time' (Eliot, 1943/71).

Brand as badge

Thorstein Veblen had already discussed the idea in his groundbreaking 1899 work *The Theory of the Leisure Class* (Veblen/Banta, 2009), but it wasn't until the middle of the last century that a lot of focus was directed towards the social aspects of branding. In 1950 the economist Harvey Leibenstein published an article in the *Quarterly Journal of Economics* entitled 'Bandwagon, snob and Veblen effects in the theory of consumer demand', and kicked off a deluge of research, theories and talks, which shape our thinking around brands and branding, especially in the prestige world, to this very day (Leibenstein, 1950).

Then came the 1960s and their passion for cultural theory with two of the most prominent proponents, Ernest Dichter, also known as the father of motivational research, who supposedly coined the term 'focus group', (Dichter, 1964) and Vance Packard with his blockbuster *The Hidden Persuaders* (Packard, 1957/87). This was more or less the birth of looking particularly at prestige brands as status symbols or badges. In fact, 'badge value' as well as Veblen's original moniker 'conspicuous consumption' became so popular they entered our public language and conscience – ironically, as the theory was all about the powers of the sub- or unconscious.

The idea is in essence quite simple: what we consume says something about who we are – or at least who we would like to be. Of course this had been true from the very beginning of branding, and actually it's even true beyond branding. It simply means that all our choices and actions, and particularly our consumptive ones, have a social or personal dimension. For marketers and branding experts this thought opened a whole new playing field: positioning and marketing brands for their social currency, triggering and leveraging so-called extrinsic motivations, and overly promising the gain of social prestige beyond a product's functional benefit. It became about putting brands in aspirational contexts or situations to create the impression of them leading to or at least having the aura of a more sophisticated, desirable life. The big concept of lifestyle branding was invented – and hasn't left us since.

Brand as building block

Closely connected to the above idea of brands as social badges or signifiers of a certain prestigious lifestyle, but expanding this concept, is the idea of brands as building blocks – the next evolutionary step in brand theory.

It started around the same time as the social perspective came into view, but it took on steam a little later, in the '70s and particularly in the '80s – the 'me'-decade, when everything became bigger and better, including brands. The difference: beyond the external value, the social relevance of a choice, there's a myriad of other powers, but mainly also internal or intrinsic motivational ones that brands can hold and leverage. They can do so much for a consumer – they are a value in their own right, hence we marketers also often speak of 'added value': beyond the actual product value there is the added value of the brand.

Brands quickly started overtly promising everything from might to sexiness, happiness or youth, a sense of adventure or one of control... it was a whole new world and the opportunities were endless, because it wasn't only that brands could make me appear a certain way; they actually could make me feel this way, or at least so the theory goes. **Brands weren't just badges anymore, they became building blocks, building blocks of my sense of self, of my identity... heck, of my whole world.** This was the time of the big advertising icons and campaign ideas like the Marlboro Man and his 'taste of freedom and adventure', some of which survive today, even if only in our collective conscience.

This was also the time during which it became clear that the true owners of brands aren't the companies who invent them, but the consumers who cherish – or despise – them. It is in their heads and hearts that the ultimate meaning and value of a brand is being constructed. As they embrace brands to construct their selves they assess and create the value that these particular brands hold. And they can just as easily de-construct or devalue those brands, which of course didn't keep companies from trying to measure and define the value of 'their' brands, ideally in monetary terms, thus creating the concept of brand equity.

Brand as medium

As if those three tasks – quality guarantor, badge and building block – weren't already enough for a brand we have recently added two more. Again, we shouldn't even say 'add', as these dimensions were there all along. It's really more that we expanded our perspective yet again and re-focused our attention on two other powers that brands possess – or through which they possess us.

In the first case of 'brand as medium' we look pretty much back to the early days of modern brand building, the soap opera – the radio or TV formats initially launched and produced by Procter & Gamble to tell stories around their products and promote their brands. In those days, the brand was message and medium at the same time. You didn't buy media space to place your message in an attractive context – you created the context yourself. Or better yet, you merged the two and produced what we nowadays call 'content', something for people to rally around and love – with your brand in the centre and hopefully smack in the middle of your audience's interests and thoughts.

And that's exactly what marketing and brand building in the 21st century is about again. The only difference is that we've gone interactive. TV and radio have lost their lustre because communication and content aren't one-way streets anymore. The audiences have become actors themselves: they've started talking back and taking things into their own hands.

But the principle remains, and is regaining popularity: with once-captive audiences having liberated themselves through remote controls, DVRs and the internet, not to mention mobile devices, you cannot rely on borrowed or bought interest anymore – you must become interesting again yourself. **Brands can no longer force their way into existing content or discourse, they must become the content and initiate the discourse themselves, attractive enough for people to rally around, connect and engage with.** In other words they must become their own media for communities of like-minded people to rally around, just like we once gathered around the radio to follow the latest soap opera. Today, this idea is called Community Marketing – inspiring conversations and a fan-like community of followers.

A brand that has been spearheading this despite its heritage and age is Coca-Cola. Actually, they've always been at the forefront of marketing. In the 1920s they created Santa Claus as we know him today, and they were one of the first to objectify men as sex symbols in the United States with their infamous 'Window Washer' advertisement for Diet Coke in 1998. Today they arguably set the tone when it comes to creating 'ideas that do' (see more in Principle 3, Walk the Talk). One of the most ingenious examples of late is their 'Happiness' campaign. At first, Coca-Cola installed so-called 'Happiness Machines', ATMs that dispensed US $100 to passers-by who promised to use the money to make someone else happy – by buying them food, serenading them or giving them a backrub. In 2012 they turned this into the 'Happiness for Couples Machines', where you had to testify to your love to get two cokes for free. Lately they've evolved this even further, into making political connections, asking Pakistanis and Indians to 'share' a coke in Kashmir, the region they are perennially fighting over (Coca-Cola .com, accessed May 2014). Apart from engaging people, the brand shows on the spot what it means by 'the joy of Coca-Cola'. They don't just tout the benefits of their products, they prove them then and there, turning marketing into a beneficial 'user experience'.

Brand as myth

The last dimension of brands that has been unfolded, and the one that sits at the core of our seven principles of what modern prestige is about, is the idea of brands elevating themselves into a myth by pursuing a clear mission and sharing and expanding this through legendary tales. Since we will talk about this at length throughout the book, starting with the next chapter, let's stick to a brief overview here.

There are various ways this idea is being talked about. In some discussions you'll find it as 'Ethical Branding' or 'Ideological Branding'. Roy Spence, one of the leaders in this field of thinking, simply calls it 'having purpose' (Spence, 2009) and Simon Sinek, another authority, makes it about 'starting with why' (Sinek, 2009). What all these theories share is the high importance they place on the fact that brands need a reason for being. They must stand for something in order to connect with people and ultimately guide them, in their decision-making but potentially also in life in general.

One of the main reasons for this is the fact that brands need to regain respect. Consumers have become disillusioned and cynical, yet also more demanding, as we saw earlier. **Brands need to re-prove themselves as not just 'empty' marketing shells but reliable holders of meaning.** The starting point for this is a clear, definite point of view (POV). Having values and convictions beyond making a buck, and communicating those beliefs openly and credibly, is the beginning of every relationship. Transparency helps control in case of doubt, but it can never substitute for a clearly articulated and reliable standpoint as the basis for a shared commitment. And that's what brands must be and are in the best of circumstances: consensual communities driven by a core belief that attracts others who share this belief. This is how they achieve the trust bias, which gives them an edge against their competition and an 'up' in their commercialization.

Yet, a clear POV is only part of what's needed today. We have discussed the fact that brands need to be their own medium, create their own content to develop an ever-growing loyal community. And for that it's not enough to project a clear WHY and have a distinct WHAT: brands need to also translate these into an incomparable, fascinating and engaging HOW. They need to wrap their purpose in engaging stories that can easily be understood, taken to heart and shared. They need to elevate their mission into a myth, projecting a strong viewpoint onto the world, providing meaning and a clear moral compass, but in an enticing and entertaining narrative. They need to light the fire we can gather around, but they also need to keep us there with fascinating tales we can dream of in the dark hours. Brands must become storytellers with a purpose, which is why we called this latest stage 'Brand as Myth' and not just 'Brand as Mission'.

The evolving role of brands (and their benefit)

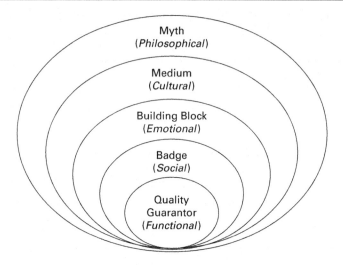

Myth
(*Philosophical*)

Medium
(*Cultural*)

Building Block
(*Emotional*)

Badge
(*Social*)

Quality
Guarantor
(*Functional*)

A new kind of prestige – or what we mean by Ueber-Brands™

As we saw in the first chapter 'The Times They Are a-Changing', there's a multitude of dynamics that are in the process of altering our ideas around prestige. We are looking for the metaphysical beyond the physical and want some magic. Culture and commerce are not clashing as much anymore but have united, and capitalism is evolving, taking a broader perspective with more ethical, social and ecological responsibilities, not least because the age of transparency has created increasingly vigilant consumers. But our desires are also shifting: we're re-rooting our consumerism and re-focusing on the real, the true and soulful. Money is reaching its limits as a status provider and knowledge has become much more important in separating those in (the know) from those not. Last, but not least, we are seeing technologically driven shifts: making the custom-made a mass opportunity to let all of us feel special and changing the way we interact and set ourselves apart while being more together than ever.

All this has led to prestige being slowly but unmistakably re-defined: less traditional through pricing up and celebrating yourself as rarified, but more so by evoking pride and aspiration through esteemed ideals and ideas wrapped in mythical storytelling. Less classical by building exclusivity through extreme restraint and scarcity, but by mixing these with a dose of inclusivity, sometimes even allowing for ubiquity, astutely balancing exclusion with connection. And third, less marketing-manipulated and more master- and truth-minded, living brand-specific convictions and radiating them from the inside out rather than glossing over uncomfortable realities and glamming it all up with a thin veneer of gold plating. Still telling stories of dreams come true, probably even more than ever, but not in the sense of faking it: more as truths enhanced and messages massaged.

We have termed the brands that exhibit this new kind of prestige Ueber-Brands, so as not to confuse and restrict our thinking by traditional notions, and to clearly communicate that these brands act differently and go above and beyond – mostly in three dimensions.

Ueber-Brands: three key dimensions, one stellar position

The first thing to note is the one that remains unchanged: modern prestige brands reside on top – top of recognition and top of price tier. Not necessarily top in terms of volume, though that's already becoming one of the things that are changing. And also not automatically top in profit, because the margins aren't always as exceptional as the high price points may suggest. Our analyses showed that the net margin of many prestige brands might hover at around 10 per cent rather than the 10–20 per cent that – often much larger – mass brands might achieve. But Ueber-Brands are Ueber-Stars. They reign supreme, in their categories and our culture at large, continuously managing to charge way above average and remain at the centre of our hearts and desires.

In all this Ueber-Brands are pretty much in line with traditional prestige brands. So what then makes them more modern? What's new? It's their behaviours, the ways in which they achieve these stellar positions, which are different. These ways or patterns can be devised into seven principles, which we will go through in Part 2. Overall, they address three overarching aspects:

1. The must of mission and myth

Allie Tsavdarides, Head of Marketing in Europe, Middle East and Africa for TOMS, the brand that invented what is now known as the 'One for One' giving model, put it this way when we spoke to her recently: 'We never approached people primarily with our product or our business proposition. We share our philosophy and our identity, and that's what people are buying into'. Key to this from the get-go was the brand's founder, Blake Mycoskie, sharing his legendary trip to Argentina where the idea was born, initially personally and nowadays through videos like 'TOMS 2.0' posted on YouTube (scan QR code in the Preface to get the video). And that's the point: modern prestige brands, and not just the new ones like TOMS but also long-_d ones like Hermès, who have retained their prestige and taken it 1st century, write their own story very intently, craft their own leg-_uild their own myth. And they root this self-created narrative in a _of commitment – towards themselves, their stakeholders as well as their environments. **Ueber-Brands are built on big ideas, often even ideals, and they express these with compelling storylines.** It is this combination of daring vision, self-determination and socio-ecological perspective that feeds their superior collective and aspirational power, very differently from their forbears. They know their story, they write it themselves (unerringly) and they make sure to take all their stakeholders, from employees to investors to trade partners and consumers, with them on their journey. In fact, they don't just take them along, they activate, engage and inspire them. And that's what makes them Ueber-Brands.

2. The balance between connection and exclusion

Millennials, the generation that hasn't known a world without the web and came of age around the millennium, have developed different ways of building social status. Ways where being a part is as important as setting yourself apart. The ultimate goal remains creating distinction, a sense of self and of superiority, but the means to achieve it have become softer, warmer and more accessible. **Ueber-Brands have taken this to heart and show extreme attention to balancing exclusivity with connection where previous prestige brands were singularly focused on the former.** They grow further than usually thought possible without diluting your sense of prestige. And they do so to a large degree by always sticking with or going back to their core fan base, the ones that personify their myth and their mission in the best possible way. Red Bull, the premium-priced energy soda that created its own category and turned itself into a super-success is a perfect example of this, as our case study in Principle 2 will show. Their event marketing and sponsorships are legendary and there can only be few who are unaware of it. Yet, they always strive to do better, re-charging their myth with hard-core 'energy' icons like the strato-jumper Felix Baumgartner. And that's what makes them an Ueber-Brand. They don't sit, guarded and protected, waiting to be adored. They engage and actively push, yet carefully create an irresistible pull at the same time. They make their fame self-perpetuating, as it must be in the age of online communities, crowd- and co-creation and word of mouth.

3. The need for truth

The other aspect of this digitally driven connectivity, and the third dimension of modern prestige or Ueber-Brands is truth. The will of one has been replaced by the wisdom of many and is currently morphing into the wisdom of mine. Single-source marketing has evolved into a multi-channel engagement game, with professional blogger recommendations already being more and more replaced by those from personal friends. Over-promising and under-delivering is thus being detected and scolded quicker than marketers can say 'new and improved'. Lapses in ethics or deficiencies in a company's culture are outed before the PR agency can even be briefed. And this is changing the way prestige has to be built. Not outside-in, but inside-out. Not through marketing that stimulates desires by gilding the lily, but by marrying style with substance. The best prestige brands have always done this, which is why they are still here and part of this book.

Modern prestige or Ueber-Brands have made this a must, taking great care to practise what they preach, under- rather than over-sell and generally stay understated than overrated. They try to attract their fans rather than attack them, giving them time to discover their 'truth' and building it slowly and gradually from cult to movement so the base can solidify and the whole doesn't turn into a bonfire. Yes, the products are wrapped in something bigger and this bigger something is what makes the brands shine stronger and brighter than others. But this can never be an excuse for a sub-par product, as Allie Tsavdarides from TOMS put it. It is just the opposite: it requires modern prestige brands to think broader, deeper and further than ever before.

To sum up: **Ueber-Brands are meta not mega. Where mega shouts power, meta means perspective. And that's the big difference.** Ueber-Brands and thus modern prestige are less self-important or aggrandizing than prestige used to be but more self-aware and self-reflecting. They don't take themselves super seriously, but they do their mission and their myth. They don't elevate their followers by putting others down, but by staying a step ahead and true to their core. And they shine not just around their products, but through them. And this is why Ueber-Brands can be of any size and come from any category at any price point. What puts them on a higher level and secures their stellar position is a sense of discrimination paired with dedication, and that is as priceless as it is progressive.

Ueber-Brands: an old term of new-found relevance

By now you've probably understood why we felt the urge to come up with a new term for what we see as modern prestige brands and also why we were drawn to the idea of 'Ueber'. But just in case, here's a bit more background for those interested in the etymology and why this word seems so fitting for marketing in the 21st century.

It was the German philosopher Friedrich Nietzsche who coined the term 'Ueber-Mensch' (over-man) in his 1873 masterpiece *Also Sprach Zarathustra*. The term over-man (or woman, one should add, as the German 'mensch' is decisively gender-neutral) describes someone who is willing to take risks for the sake of humanity as opposed to the common man, who's mainly concerned with his own comfort. He or she establishes his/her own values and thus affects and influences the lives of others, inspiring and guiding them to a higher or meta-level – self-determined, following self-chosen principles instead of being driven by external authority or sheer opportunity.

And that's exactly what strong brands do today, especially modern prestige ones – or Ueber-Brands as we have outlined above and will go through in the seven principles. Like it or not, they have ever-increasing social and cultural significance. They are no longer just beacons of status or building blocks of our identities; they are morphing more and more into mythical fixtures and leaders, sometimes creating movements not unlike political parties. They have created and become narrative constructs that inspire our public discourse, provide meaning to rally around or to reject – affecting, influencing and yes, often guiding our lives, not just materially or functionally but emotionally, ethically and even spiritually.

Apple is the Ueber-example, having built a cult not only around their superior design and innovative products, but ultimately based on their mission of making technology for 'the creative class', as it is called today. And they've enshrined this mission into a myth, starting with the iconic commercial '1984', which aired during Super Bowl XX and established Apple as the David against the then Goliath IBM. A hammer-swinging young blonde runs into a cinema filled with brain-washed lemmings enraptured by their Big Brother, and launches her hammer into the gigantic screen, shattering and crushing the whole aura and power of the establishment at the same time. This very instant, a countercultural icon was born. And although Apple has now become the establishment itself and most customers today don't even know about that infamous commercial anymore, the spirit of the brand still lives, beguiling and guiding us to 'Think Different'. During all its growth, Apple has done an outstanding job of maintaining and re-creating their iconoclastic attitude again and again, be it by starting the flagship store craze at a time when this was distribution sacrilege or by re-inventing the music industry with single-song downloads. They stayed true to their archetypal 'character' and that's why we have stayed true to them, enjoying the benefits of a well-catered lifestyle while still feeling a bit like the creative rebel-rousers we once were or always wanted to be. It's this spiritual or attitudinal promise that made Apple the ultimate Ueber-Brand and us loyal, paying much more for products that are arguably at best on-par in many aspects. They continue to inspire and guide us, at least for now, even though their whole point is that we should live unguided and self-inspired.

A good explanation for why all this is happening now, why prestige brands are morphing into cultural and ethical leaders and turning into Ueber-Brands, comes from a theory that US sociologist David Riesman developed in the 1950s and with a lot of foresight called 'The Lonely Crowd' – as if he'd known about the internet and our modern ways of connecting and separating ourselves through and with brands (Riesman, 2001). According to Riesman people and societies evolve in three stages.

First they are 'tradition-directed', bound by rituals, living their lives as prescribed by their forefathers, deeply engrained in social codes. This is followed by an 'inner-directed' phase, where people emancipate themselves from societal expectations and develop an internal compass to navigate through life. The last stage is 'other-directed': a fully-liberated and commercialized society where strong beliefs have given way to flexibility, situation-driven decisions and an overall desire to fit in and gain approval. Opportunism reigns, driven by an ever-changing world demanding an adaptable workforce. Everything is possible, all is relative, and uniting or guiding values are hard to find. Leadership has become almost impossible.

For Riesman, this was the end point. But it seems he may have been wrong and that history is reversing itself. We may have reached a tipping point where we are getting tired of being 'other-directed' and are starting to favour 'inner-directedness' once again. In the political, the theological and even the commercial we witness people searching for values, yearning for convictions, looking for clear ideas and ideals to hold onto. And that's what partially drives the evolution of modern prestige and the emergence of Ueber-Brands. **With their strong sense – and story – of self, Ueber-Brands provide guidance and principles, not to mention roots, in a life that is defined by constant change and upheaval with little to rely on.** They put stakes of absolute values in a more and more swampy ground of relativity. They allow us to nurture our own growing sense of self and provide something to aspire to or to reject, but in any case help navigate the wobbly world in which we live.

Where traditionally brands were the epitome of other-directedness, developed around a perceived consumer need – aiming to please, the more the better – modern prestige or Ueber-Brands build their power, their status and their allure in the exact opposite way. They are not so much product-driven as purpose-driven, less 'bossed around' by the consumer or the market in general, but more driven by their own convictions. At their core is a philosophy and a story that guides them – and in turn attracts us. When Steve Jobs famously declared marketing research as bollocks, following only a focus group with n = 1, meaning him, he took that to the top – and the brand with it. Taking charge, giving us the sense that he knows what we want, even though we might not know it ourselves yet. Guiding us blindly into a tomorrow of more fun and better lives, with our wallets open.

Of course, there have always been brands that were more vision-driven than marketing-driven, often founder-managed ones. And naturally, even Ueber-Brands still need to find a sufficient following to survive and will in that sense always be other-directed – especially as brands are created in the heads and hearts of their stakeholders anyway. But today's most successful and modern prestige brands project a sense of inner-direction, concerned with their own myth and mission rather than the needs of their constituencies, that reaches a new level – or goes back to the pre-market driven days. They build themselves confidently by putting an offer and a point of view out for a following to flock around rather than pursuing a supposedly underserved need or segment. They dare to be rejected instead of trying to please at all costs. Or, to quote Riesman 'they want to be esteemed... where the other-directed ones just want to be loved'. And that's what gives them prestige in a very modern way, making them Ueber-Brands in the truest, Nietzschean sense.

PART TWO
The seven secrets of Ueber-Brands

In developing, solidifying and validating the following principles or 'secrets' we didn't only rely on our combined 50 years of dissecting, shaping and marketing brands, we spoke to many industry leaders and experts from brand founders, CEOs, marketers to journalists and professors. We pulled together and analysed more than 100 case studies, looking at premium-priced players in dozens of categories and all sizes, from tiny soap brand start-up to long-standing financial services behemoth. We went beyond the usual suspects, because, as we outlined in Part 1, it soon became clear that prestige is not as narrowly defined as it used to be. Yes, there are still the venerable luxury houses we all know, but there are also many brands developed in the past few decades, some even just in the past few years, that have broadened our perspective and helped shape what we like to think of as 'modern prestige' or Ueber-Brands.

Our findings on what constitutes this 'modern prestige' pertain to three dimensions, as previously explained. Ueber-Brands are rooted in a mission and a mythical narrative; they connect with their constituencies by creatively balancing inclusion and exclusion; and they are – for the most part – built on integrity and sincerity, more than used to be the case in our marketing world. To better understand the 'real-life' implications of these dimensions or shifts we have translated them into seven principles, each one dealing with a specific aspect of brand building or marketing:

1 **Mission Incomparable**. This is about the core of any modern prestige brand, the belief on which it is built, its raison d'être. Setting new challenges for marketers as they not only need to worry about what they do and how, but more so why.

2 **Longing vs. Belonging**. Second most important: defining your audiences and how to connect with them, learning to balance inclusivity with exclusivity so consumers can continuously experience both – belonging but also longing.

3 **Un-selling**. The third point expands on the second: how to communicate and interact with your constituencies by mixing signals, proximity and distance specifically – to turn a sales-pitch into the art of seduction.

4 **From Myth to Meaning**. At the centre we talk about the ultimate objective of modern prestige brands. Explaining how going deep is the best way up – in individual relevance but more so in cultural resonance, and how that means crafting narratives that let people believe they know and know why they believe.

5 **Behold!** This is all about the importance of product. All fiction and no function works in prestige as little as anywhere else in life, even less so in its modern version. Because here products need to not just hold a promise, they must manifest a myth, making the intangible brand believably tangible.

6 **Living the Dream**. Perhaps the hardest task: how to make the dream come true. How to define the elements that are essential to a brand's myth and mission and radiate them from the inside out. How to create a culture and craft experiences that let the 'bubble' shimmer in all colours – but never burst.

7 **Growth Without End**. Last: how to deal with the age-old challenge of prestige brands in modern ways. Growing, but without undermining a sense of specialness. 'Killing' the competition, but softly, slowly and quietly.

Before we get into all these things in detail, three quick notes upfront:

It's practical – but also conversational

To ensure this book is not just theoretically but also practically and empirically sound and relevant it is all grounded in and illustrated with real-life cases. Throughout the book you'll find plenty of examples as well as insights from successful practitioners. At the end of each principle there is an extensive Ueber-Brand case study that we found particularly enlightening in the context of the chapter's thoughts, but also for the brand's way of applying the seven principles of modern prestige as a whole.

In all this we made sure to cover a broad range of categories, as modern prestige does, ranging from cars to skin care and from brands that have sprung up recently to those that have been around for decades and centuries, varying in size, price point and attitude. We also included examples from brands that aren't quite Ueber yet, but practise certain aspects of Ueber-Branding well. You'll find all the brands discussed listed in the index.

Each principle is summarized with 'How-To' Rules, and an extensive list of questions covering all seven principles at the end of the book allows for a very hands-on guide to building or reviewing your own Ueber-Brand.

The language is intentionally kept more conversational than educational, and the chapters are short, branching out into feature boxes for those who want to know more on a subject. We have read many books on marketing and brand strategy over the years, and apart from providing a

Ueber-Brands often build prestige in light-hearted ways – like
Mandarin Hotels with their fans like 'Dame Edna' and Barry Humphries

Courtesy Mandarin Oriental Hotel Group; Photo: Lord Lichfield

lot of shoulders to stand on, these reminded us again and again: it's not really fun to read 'textbooks' while you're waiting for your plane or your train is rattling into the night. Adding value doesn't mean you have to be heavy – as a lot of the modern prestige brands will show. Nothing in life and certainly in marketing is so serious that it couldn't be at least somewhat entertaining.

It's 'numerological' – how else to explain there are seven?

Is it sheer coincidence or divine intervention that we ended up with seven principles? Is all of this really empirically based on examples, experts, evidence and experience, or are we fulfilling a pre-written script unbeknownst to us? You do wonder, when you realize that you ended up with seven key points: not six or eight but seven. After all, seven is too perfect a number – unless you're Chinese. Especially when you're writing about making myths.

The world has seven seas and seven continents. It even used to have seven wonders and many claim it only knows seven narrative plots. The modern Western musical scale consists of seven notes; our week has seven days, with the seventh being the most special of all, for some closely connected to seventh heaven. And, speaking of which, more people were married on 7-7-2007 than on any other day in history. Seven is a big number indeed, the biggest arguably, not the least because it belongs to God, so to speak: there are seven candleholders in a Jewish menorah, Muslims believe in the existence of seven heavens and earths and Christians teach of the seven deadly sins. 777 is generally seen as a symbol of the Holy Trinity. And when asked by Peter how many times we need to forgive others, Jesus replies: 'I say to you not seven times, but seventy seven times' (Matthew 18:22).

Of course, the appeal of the number seven isn't lost in less celestial contexts either: a lot of companies have tried to harness the power and allure of the number, especially in the United States. Popular brands include 7-Eleven, 7-Up, Seventh Generation, Boeing 777, Mazda RX-7, Audi Q7 and 7 For All Mankind jeans. Not to forget 007, the world's most famous spy, longest acting super hero and biggest entertainment brand. But what really convinced us to stick with seven principles, despite or because of their magical connotations, was this: 'The number seven is the seeker, the thinker, the searcher of Truth. The seven doesn't take anything at face value... it knows that nothing is exactly as it seems and that reality is often hidden behind illusions' (Numerology.com, accessed May 2013).

It's symmetrical – with myth in the middle

Lastly, our seven principles aren't just practical or logical-magical – they are methodical, actually symmetrical, organized in a matrix between 'Vision' and 'Action', 'Relations' and 'Organization'. At the core sits the ultimate objective of any Ueber-Brand, reaching 'From Myth to Meaning'. The first three principles leading up to this core goal concern themselves mostly with the external relations of modern prestige brands, starting with their 'Mission Incomparable' through balancing 'Longing vs Belonging', all the way to 'Un-selling'. Principles five to seven on the other hand are about the internal strategies and culture of modern prestige brands; their organization, going in reverse from 'Behold!' through 'Living the Dream' leading (ideally) to 'Growth Without End'. All together they make for a 'Golden Star' like the one you see below.

And with that said we wish you an 'enlightening' read.

The 'Golden Star' of Ueber-Branding

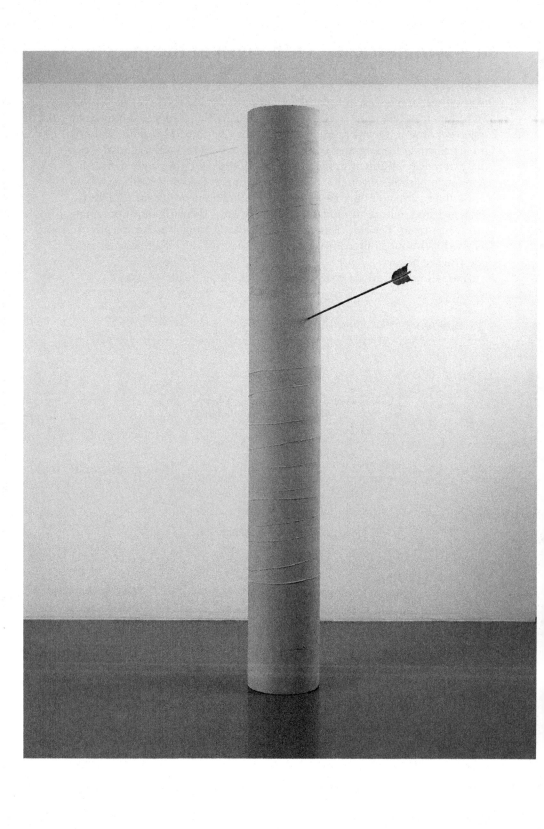

Principle 1
Mission incomparable
The first rule is to make your own

At the beginning there is an idea – or better yet an ideal. Something that itches, bothers or encourages – a challenge that ignites you to take action and undertake a change. The first principle of greatness is to think and dream big and move beyond what is to what could or should be. Have a vision and be crazy enough to pursue it. This holds true for all outstanding enterprises in life, and brands are no exception. Of course there are many very successful brands whose only goal in life is to be profitable. Or who simply want to follow in someone else's footsteps and live on someone's leftovers. But do you think they could achieve prestige status today? Would they be the ones that will be talked about, the ones we'd like to call Ueber-Brands? Most likely not. At least we have not found many examples for this, which is why the first principle of modern prestige is all about a brand's mission; ideally one that is incomparable and idiosyncratic if not iconoclastic.

This makes a lot of sense if you think about the role that Ueber-Brands play in our lives. As we laid out in Part 1, they are here to guide us and give us something we do not already have. They need to be – and make us feel – more than we are without them, and in order to achieve this, they must be ahead of us – or above us. Only then are they literally in a position to create desire and become, in marketing parlance, 'aspirational'. Only if they have a clear sense of self and strong convictions can they lead us and ideally turn us into their followers. And only then can they offer us something that we can identify with or better yet use as building blocks in crafting and re-confirming our own identities. **In one line: Ueber-Brands can only fulfil their mission if they have a mission.**

There are basically two ways for Ueber-Brands to get to this 'Mission Incomparable'. The first, 'Noblesse Oblige', talks about the holy grail of missions, often also called a purpose. This means making a socio-eco-political goal the core of your existence, with the commercial side of things, the products and services, sometimes being felt as a mere funding activity. A good example of this is Ben & Jerry's, the ice cream brand whose true reason for being was 'to see if it was possible to use the tools of business to repair society' (Page & Katz, 2012, accessed May 2014). Another, perhaps even more determined one is Patagonia, the big outdoor brand and one of the boldest and earliest crusaders in saving and protecting our environment, even or especially as we traverse and explore it. We will look at this most modern of ventures in detail and discuss the differences and opportunities between making 'doing good' a true part of your DNA and just 'green washing' yourself with an alibi CSR programme.

The second route to making your brand 'missionary' is arguably a less radical and substantial one, but one that nevertheless doesn't need to be less successful or convincing. We call it 'Reinvention': redefining a category and setting new standards that take you and your followers beyond the obvious and the known to a higher level – of existence as well as price. A great example of this way of rising to a challenge and beyond your competition is Starbucks, the company that gave America the Grande Latte and made it willing to pay US $5 for it while the cost of the average coffee hovered around US $1. Or Red Bull, the Thai-Austrian syrupy soda that established a whole new category – energy drinks – and managed to maintain a cool, counter-cultural vibe and a sexy price point despite the fact that in 2011 the company sold more than 4 billion cans in more than 160 countries (see case study Principle 2).

No matter which route you follow and what mission you'll make your own, the cardinal rule is to be daring and stand out. Don't just feed a need but listen to your heart and show guts. Never be afraid to alienate. Because despite popular opinion, most premium brands didn't get to where they are because they competed to be the best, but because they fought to be unique, best summed up as: *Quod licet Jovi, non licet bovi* – 'What's ok for Jupiter is not ok for the cow'.

Apart. Ahead. Above.

'Once upon a time... Johan dreamt of elevating liquorice to the level of a gourmet experience... to share the magical qualities of the mighty liquorice root and combine it with carefully selected ingredients...'. This is how the website of Lakrids by Johan Buelow opens, the Danish David who's about to trade up the next food category largely commoditized and dominated by multi-national Goliaths. It's a great piece of storytelling we recommend you read for inspiration (Lakrids by Johan Buelow, accessed August 2014). But what's interesting at this point is how clearly Johan lays out his and the brand's mission: eloquent and yet straightforward, magical and yet totally logical.

A sense of purpose

This clear and well-articulated sense of purpose is quite indicative of today's Ueber-Brands, the much-hyped digital start-ups as well as the sometimes more quietly growing 'traditionalists'. They all have a mission – way beyond filling or exploiting a perceived market gap and certainly way beyond just making a profit. They have (and show!) a very strong conviction of Why the world needs them, Why it would be a better place with them and Why they thus have a right to exist and to win. This Why has become the core of their brand and their marketing, and is much more important than the What in most cases, because the What (ie the product, its features or the services you provide) is often hardly, or if then only shortly, a point of difference or a true progress. **For modern prestige brands it's becoming less and less about what we buy and more and more about what we buy into.** The products are morphing from main event to means to an end, no longer the core around which all is built, but the medium through which we express and share an attitude. The Why makes the Ueber-Brand and is the reason we buy its products.

One of the most iconic examples in this field is certainly TOMS, the brand that single-handedly invented the 'One for One giving model', initially in shoes and now expanded to eyewear, coffee... and soon probably much more, given the recent mega-investment by Bain Capital (O'Connor, 2014). We spoke with Allie Tsvadarides, Head of Marketing for TOMS EMEA, about how TOMS built one of the most successful Ueber-Brands in recent memory, giving many impulses for modern prestige in the process. Allie freely admits that the product was actually 'quite poor' or at least 'more

Ueber-Brands are less about what you buy than about what you buy into. TOMS' 'One for One giving model' is a prime example

Courtesy TOMS, 'TOMS 2.0 video stills' (http://www.youtube.com/watch?v=zsmry84bARk)

symbolic' in the beginning, but it didn't matter as it was always the Why that was driving TOMS more than their What. This Why Blake Mycoskie found on a 2006 trip to Argentina, where he saw many children in need of shoes and all the problems this caused, from health to educational issues (for the whole story read Mycoskie, 2012). The 'Amazing Race' contestant and successful serial entrepreneur did what he'd done many times before and started a business, but this time not only for profit, more as a 'social enterprise': selling Argentina's national shoe, the Alpargata, and providing the same to the country's kids in need – one for one. For each pair of Alpargatas sold, TOMS was giving away one new pair, in the size and style needed, instead of traditional donations, which often accumulate goods of little use to those they are actually collected for. And so he still does today, as 'Chief Shoe Giver', only his venture has grown to a US $600 million business covering many countries and climates, supporting students in Africa with school uniform shoes as much as Syrian refugees with winter boots. He's perfected the model, working with select 'giving partners' as producers and distributors, providing 'last mile expenses' to ensure local organizations have the capital to get the shoes where they're needed (and not piling up at storage facilities) and allowing or rather encouraging employees to go on 'giving trips' to experience the good they are doing first hand. Speaking of people: they are and will always be the best 'advertising' for TOMS, as Tsavdarides says. TOMS hires only those who believe in their mission, and their passion works like a word-of-mouth wonder-machine passing the message together with the love of the product on and on and on. They create a community with a shared belief and a sense of purpose, which is exactly the point. Apart from this, the product has naturally become much better and more varied over time as well. It was always competitive, but today it's actually even seen by many as superior, because at the end of the day in modern prestige even if the Why is important you cannot win in the long run if you neglect the What. Doing good can never be an excuse for not making something well – in that even modern prestige is still as traditional as it always was (see also Principle 5).

TOMS' model has been so successful, and the concept of building a business on an ideal as well as an idea is so timely, that many have copied it, including Warby Parker, a US prescription eyewear company that became famous for what they call the 'buy a pair, give a pair' model. Other recent examples of 'Why' start-ups are Juniper Ridge, who claim to be 'the world's only wilderness fragrance distillery' (juniperridge.com). Or Shinola (shinola .com) a brand trying to build its reputation on US nostalgia and patriotism. It re-launched a legendary pre-war brand name (Shinola shoe polish) through manufacturing high-end watches and bicycles in Detroit, reviving a city and a workforce hard hit by economic evolution, and redefining 'Made in the USA' in terms of prestige. 'We wanted to create an accessory company and tell a "Made in Detroit" story', Shinola CEO Steve Bock told us at a recent L2 conference in New York. 'We believe in Detroit and we believe it is a differentiator in the marketplace'.

Conceptual consumption

We have reached a point in our market-driven society where entrepreneurs, employees and consumers alike are yearning for businesses and brands to make sense – particularly if they want to charge more than the average. Just making better products does not suffice anymore in a world where we have pretty much everything we could possibly want. It's about making it better *and* with less damage, making it more wholesome or more surprising. It's about finding new ingredients or twists that let something banal shine in totally new, fascinating ways. In short, it's about making a true difference. And that means that for most modern prestige brands it's more a matter of metaphysics than physics. It's the attitudes and philosophies, the intangible which is gaining ground in a world where the tangible has become a given for most of us. A phenomenon that Dan Ariely, professor of behavioral economics at Duke University, and Michael Norton, assistant professor of marketing at the Harvard Business School, termed 'Conceptual Consumption' (*The Annual Review of Psychology*, 2009).

It is widely accepted that brands are social and cultural signifiers. We use brands – and especially prestige brands – to say something about us just as much as we use them to 'label' others. We look at them to inspire our thinking and behaving as much as we find them helpful in constructing and structuring our everyday realities. Even those of us who explicitly reject specific brands do so to make a point, to themselves as well as to all of us. A great case is the stylish minimalist Japanese retailer Muji. Muji literally translated means 'No logo', and it's true: none of their products are overtly branded. Yet their wares are instantly recognizable, at least to the cognoscenti. It's like Paul Watzlawick, the great Swiss-German communication theorist and thinker once said: 'You cannot not communicate' (Watzlawick, Beavin and Jackson, 1969/85). And in our world this means: you cannot not communicate – with or without brands.

More than me

In order to play this role, prestige brands need to deliver on three levels. Not unlike good friends, they need to tell me that they 'like me', that they 'are like me' and that they are 'more than me'. The first function is basic for any relationship: you need a fundamental level of sympathy and trust. Only if a brand gives me the feeling it respects and appreciates me as a customer will I honour it with a certain level of interest. Only if a brand shows it cares about me will I potentially care about it in return.

Second, there must be a connection, a minimum overlap of interests and a sense of shared identity. A brand needs to 'be like me' to some degree, share my attitudes, values, style… my position in and perspective on life.

The third aspect, however, is the most important dimension and the one that is needed to turn brands into Ueber-Brands. In order to become aspirational,

Ueber-Brands need to be 'more than me'. They need to provide me with something I don't already have, or more precisely something I am not, because it's not so much about functional benefits but psycho-social ones. **A strong brand must inspire, enrich and elevate me and my life. It needs to make me feel bigger and, today more importantly, better than I am without it. It must allow me to at least temporarily shift the standpoint from which I relate to the rest of the world.** This can be done in a number of ways. The simplest and most common way is the traditional prestige approach: project a certain social status. The latest, somewhat more subtle and refined way that many truly modern prestige brands choose is: help me live up to my own principles and expectations, be they social, political or ecological. Help me mitigate feelings of guilt through over-shopping by donating to my favourite charity (an example is fraisr.com). Provide gravity in a world of upheaval through something handmade (etsy.com). Neutralize my bad eco-footprint through local sourcing and production (chipotle.com). Let me save the cows and protect our world from industrial farming by having a better yoghurt (stonyfield.com). Or make me feel sensible and substantial while spending US $50,000 on a watch through a tale of investment and posterity (patek.com).

Consequently, a recent study among consumers as well as marketing experts came to the conclusion: 'Some 73 per cent of consumers prefer brands that have a strong identity and a clear role in the world' (Wooldridge, June 2013). These days, credit card slips are not just proof of payment but are becoming more and more something akin to modern letters of indulgence. Or, to look at it in a less cynical way: we increasingly make our purchases voting cards for a better us and a brighter future.

Mission route 1: Noblesse Oblige, or the price of greatness

Winston Churchill once said 'The price of greatness is responsibility', and while he certainly wasn't talking about something as banal and crude as branding this quote could have made him something of a bellwether for today's number one route of mission-driven marketing. We call it 'Noblesse Oblige', after the old French dictum that the entitlements coming with status and leadership must be balanced with social responsibility and honourable behaviour. It would be hard to find a better mantra for what it means to be a prestige or Ueber-Brand these days.

Edelman, a global PR company, has been issuing its 'Good Purpose' study since 2007 and has shown a consistent rise in the importance of doing business with responsibility – social, political, ecological or all three. The number of people who claim 'social purpose as the most important factor when quality and price are the same' is now well over 50 per cent (Edelman.com, 2012). And when former P&G CMO Jim Stengel commissioned a study with Millward Brown in 2011, they found that the 50 most purpose-driven brands outperformed the US S&P by almost 400 per cent (Stengel and Garbe, 2011). All this, by the way, is irrespective of industry, because the 'Stengel 50' brands range from personal care (Dove) to digital services (Google), or from household cleaners (Method) to fruit juices (Innocent). What all these brands do share, however, is being esteemed as higher value, independent of whether they charge for it or not, and having the mission to be a force of good – beyond being good to themselves or their shareholders.

What's most surprising in this is that, according to various studies, emerging markets seem to be even more bullish in demanding that businesses are more considerate and responsible than Western societies. Now, one could argue that this is driven by those markets' recognized lack of transparency and integrity, and that Western consumers simply have already developed a higher degree of cynicism. But even if you do suppose this increased interest to be just the 'catching up' of less regulated economies to global standards of ethics, it does support the central point that the idea of a 'purpose-driven economy' or 'ideological branding' has become a global necessity for Ueber-Brands, whether they operate in the United States or Europe, Asia or Latin America, emerging or developed markets – or across all of them. **True greatness in prestige branding today can no longer be achieved without a larger sense of responsibility – independent of economic levels and categories.** Having an incomparable and irresistible mission – and sheltering your brand from price sensitivity – in contemporary terms cannot happen without having a cause. So much so, that some marketers already talk of purpose as the fifth 'P' – next to the four classic Ps of every marketing mix: product, place, price and promotion.

From fleece to flour

One of the best-known and most successful examples in this arena is Patagonia, a Californian brand of high-end outdoor clothing founded in 1972 and with sales of roughly US $600 million in 2013 (see also the case study at the end of this principle). Yvon Chouinard, the founder, always declared his goal was not just about outdoor apparel but 'rethinking production, consumption and the civil responsibilities associated with it'. These two priorities have almost swapped, relegating the business to a quasi-funding machine for his higher-order purpose to 'inspire and implement solutions to the environmental crisis' as per the company's website.

But by no means has this radical socio-eco focus compromised the brand's prestige or the quality of its products: it is actually the opposite. For instance, the company invented Synchilla™, a synthetic material recognized as superior to natural ones in terms of water resistance and durability, all while being ecologically sound. And when in 2011 the brand asked consumers not to buy its products (but rather fix their existing ones) it reported an annual growth of 30 per cent, way above the then-industry average of 4 per cent.

Another example that is similarly self-surmounting and a great case of becoming an Ueber-Brand fast by eschewing conventional marketing mechanics and pursuing an incomparable mission is Tesla. Perhaps not coincidentally, Tesla Motors Inc. is also California-based and equally about 'saving the earth', or, in the words of Elon Musk (PayPal billionaire and Tesla founder) 'helping expedite the move from a mine-and-burn hydrocarbon economy towards a solar electric economy' (Musk, 2006). According to the company's website this is to happen 'in three ways: by selling its own vehicles... components to other automakers and serving as a catalyst and positive example to other automakers'. Now that's a really unique mission if ever there was one: start a business to enable competition and make yourself superfluous in the long run. But their success seems to support this audacious approach. Tesla has moved from zero to third-most-sold luxury sedan in California (after BMW 5 and Mercedes E) and opened 35 stores across the United States, Europe and Asia in just a few years and garnered millions of followers and the positive attention of pretty much every motor journalist between Sacramento and Shanghai. Only the future can tell if this 'self-less' endeavour can really sustain itself or if the company will die of its own success as intended, but for now Tesla is the car Ueber-Brand of the moment, giving the BMWs and Mercedes a run for their money.

Tesla is building its Ueber-Brand through a tightly controlled network of its own showrooms, like this one in Berlin, all more akin to fashion boutiques than car dealerships

Photo: W Schaefer

A much less daring example from a completely different, more traditional terrain is Edeka, the more than 100-year-old German quality groceries corporation that has recently managed to reinvent itself and turn the tide in the largely price- and discount-driven food wars. With their mission and tag-line 'We love food' they've repositioned themselves as what they've always been – the local specialist in higher quality food – and have thus become the clear antidote to the all-pervasive and dominating discount chains such as Aldi or Lidl (market share over 40 per cent), even managing to win points against the ever-growing organic chains. They have re-humanized, re-emotionalized and thus re-elevated a service that was in danger of killing itself, through a single-minded focus on functional aspects. They have superseded the ruin-ous competition on the traditional 'Ps' (price, product, place and promotion) with a bigger P of purpose and thus lifted their brand, their 12,000 stores and 300,000 employees to a higher ground, where they can live much more comfortably and profitably.

While Edeka may not be an Ueber-Brand in all respects, they prove that successfully applying Ueber-Principles isn't something reserved for lofty 'do-gooders' with big socio-political or ecological agendas like Patagonia or Tesla. Like the US retailer Whole Foods before it, Edeka shows that this can also be achieved in an established and down-to-earth category with rather traditional values and purposes. 'All' it takes is a clear ideal that guides and ignites everything and everybody, first inside the company then outside. Because that's what happened with this traditional grocery chain: it was first and foremost their more than 4,000 independent store owners that became galvanized and who then in turn inspired their employees who ultimately won over the hearts of their customers, again and again. Of course, as we have said already, it didn't suffice here to just have an ideal. Edeka needed to follow through on a daily basis with new own-label products like Omega 3 sausages or healthy energy drinks, and a total dedication to quality prod-ucts, especially produce, meat and cheese, which are most directly linked to the retailer as they are largely bought non-pre-packed.

In addition, they required a pro-active and engaging way of communicat-ing through owned media around the 'love of eating and cooking'. One par-ticularly inspiring and inspired purpose activation in this was the campaign 'Nobody is Perfect', an initiative against food waste that Edeka started in 2013 and which allows people to buy slightly damaged goods for a little less (*The Local*, 2013). This is a great way to prove how they truly mean it when claiming to 'love food', while at the same time creating a very tan-gible and competitive advantage in a time of economic pressure and secur-ing a higher price point, even for their less-than-perfect quality goods. A masterclass in claiming and solidifying a truly noble position, prestigious and honorable, like a real Ueber-Brand. And one that inspired others, like France's Intermarché, to follow suit with their 'Inglorious Fruits' campaign (YouTube, Intermarché, accessed August 2014) or Jamie Oliver with his love for 'wonky veggies'.

Principle before profit

One other essential thing that Edeka's 'Nobody Is Perfect' initiative shows is that you must put your ethical mission at the core of the brand or better yet the entire company if you want to become a truly credible and revered Ueber-Brand. The days of social and/or ecological responsibility as an optional add-on are quickly coming to an end.

For one, there is always the suspicion of just trying to 'greenwash' yourself – to use some CSR programme as an alibi to cover up or balance otherwise non-sustainable behaviour. People have been disappointed far too often in the past. They no longer believe companies to be good simply by seeing them sponsor some good cause here and there. These days, we almost immediately suppose an ulterior motive and see a scandal in waiting when some company starts replanting the rainforest or financing a foster home. At best, we see it as smart 'reputation management'.

More importantly than the acquired mistrust and collective cynicism, however, is the fact that we seem to have reached a new (or old) level of consciousness when it comes to doing business. The Milton Friedman mantra that business should be single-mindedly about making money for its shareholders has run its course. There is a growing consensus among leading economists that profitability and pursuing a bigger purpose are not mutually exclusive. The British economist John Kay has even gone as far as saying that the sole pursuit of shareholder value can destroy the value of business. In 1996 ICI, for decades Britain's leading industrial company, transformed its mission statement from 'the responsible application of chemistry' to 'creating value for shareholders'. The company price peaked a few months later, to begin a remorseless decline that would lead to its disappearance as an independent company. Charles Hampden-Turner, a British management philosopher, came up with an interesting reasoning for this insufficiency of pure profit focus: 'Present profitability may be the consequence of several hundred decisions taken over the past decades...' (Curry and Stubbings, 2013). This means that profit is naturally rooted in the past whereas a company must look into the future in order to grow and adapt to changing realities. And in order to do this you need a clear vision of what should be versus what is. A mission that helps put the enterprise in its societal, cultural and economic context and sees which purpose it could sensibly and credibly fulfil today and tomorrow – to lead its category and us as a whole.

But there are also other, equally practical and economic reasons to make 'doing good' integral to doing business. A study by Harvard University and the London Business school compared a group of 'high sustainability' companies with a comparable group of 'low sustainability' ones over the course of 18 years and found that the former outperformed the latter throughout. As was expected, they were able to ride out bad publicity more easily, but they also attracted more long-term investors, which lowered their cost of capital, retained good talent far better and even commanded greater brand loyalty in the case of B2C businesses (Wheelan, 2011). This confirms what many HR people and business leaders told us: young people, in particular, no longer choose their career based on financial calculations alone. Making money still ranks highly, but it's no longer a sufficient condition on its own. The same holds true for consumers: today, value is being defined more broadly than it used to be, at least by those more affluent. Values do count as well these days, beyond price and quality.

That is why most Ueber-Brands, especially those with a younger target customer and higher ambitions, are really serious about their commitment and dedication to their mission. They live it (see principle 6) and go to quite some expense to make good on it. Take Lonely Planet for example: the travel guide company, despite various corporate takeovers, still continues to publish niche titles like *Micronations*, their guide to 'home-made' nations. They are not bestsellers, are hardly recognized and barely useful (who travels to micronations and how much danger is there of getting lost?), but they are a perfect example of the brand's passion for its purpose of discovering and guiding us into even the most remote or tiniest corners of the world. The same holds true for Ben & Jerry's and their commitment to very niche flavours, because for them peculiarity and idiosyncratic tastes are not a hurdle; they are their springboards to success and their fans' loyalty.

In the modern world of prestige it is no longer enough to think of your mission or social or ecological responsibility as an occasional act of kindness or a half-hearted CSR programme. If you want it to matter in building your Ueber-Brand you need to put it at its centre. Edelman, in their Good Purpose study of 2012, called this 'The New Imperative: rather than merely exercising their licence to operate, leading brands and corporations of the future must move beyond operational imperatives and social add-ons to establish their "licence to lead"' (Edelman.com, 2012). Our perspectives have become more holistic and multidimensional – as investors, employees, consumers... as people. We are becoming true Bobos – Bourgeois Bohemians. In other words, we are moving from being primarily focused on financial or functional rewards in business to a commerce that is more encompassing and integrated, that respects spiritual, social and ecological aspects as well. **We are evolving from decades of shareholder capitalism to a capitalism where it's about all stakeholders.** And if you want your brand or company to be accepted in this new world and to play a prestigious, leading role it doesn't suffice to be seen as doing some charity event, you must be recognized for having true convictions. You must put an all-encompassing purpose at your heart and act and radiate it with authenticity. You need to follow the guidance that Michael Bordt, Jesuit and professor of philosophy in Munich, gives to modern managers, not just on an individual but on a corporate level: 'Your behaviour must be reflective of your soul. Otherwise you have no chance of being healthy and stable and successful in the long run' (Finger, Jungbluth and Ruckert, 2014). Or, as Bill Bernbach, one of the founders of the large advertising agency DDB said a long time ago in a more business-minded way: 'A principle isn't a principle until it costs you money'.

Our shift to a Bobo culture

Apart from being a great example of mission-driven marketing in traditional, everyday categories, Edeka is also a great illustration of why the whole move towards purpose as the driving 'P' of today's marketing has happened. It shows how humanity and personality can triumph over or at least stand up against price and power – the standard criteria in the grocery wars.

Trust has been shifting from brands to companies and back to people. In a recent *New York Times* article on Airbnb, the website that in no time became the world leader in holiday accommodation, Thomas L. Friedman quoted Brian Chesky, its founder, as not being in the business of online rentals but of creating a network of trust:

It used to be that corporations had all the trust, but now a total stranger can be trusted like a company and provide the services of a company. There is a whole generation of people that don't want everything mass-produced. They want things that are unique and personal. (Friedman, July 2013)

This thought isn't glaringly new, but it has reached its 'tipping point' it seems – at least so much so that it can help a beleaguered German grocery cooperation stand up against the discount behemoths.

David Brooks announced in his 2000 book *Bobos in Paradise* that 'the world of ideas and the world of business have merged, and the much-longed-for reconciliation between the bourgeois and the bohemian has come to pass' (Brooks, 2000). Hence the term Bobos, short for Bourgeois Bohemians. 'The new elite prefers a different set of words, which exemplify a different temper and spirit: authentic natural, warm, simple, honest... sincere'. In 2015 this ideal is no longer restricted to the new elite, but holds true for an ever-increasing part of the population. Where Karl Marx once wrote that the bourgeois takes all that is sacred and makes it profane, Bobos take everything that is profane and make it sacred again. Disillusioned by a world dominated by marketing and endless scandals, and lost in a sea of spiritual and ethical options without any binding reference systems, we are looking to find truth and guidance wherever we can find it. We long to make our actions meaningful. That means we long to make shopping meaningful, because shopping is what all of us do a lot of the time. It's the easiest way for us to express ourselves, our concerns and our opinions and make a difference. It's faster and more direct than voting and certainly easier than actively engaging politically or socially. We are trying out something that could be called Enlightened Capitalism, where we overcome years of commerce taking over all other societal spheres. We are on a path to rebalance and reintegrate the commercial with the ethical, the social and the ecological. And that means we are expecting more from companies and brands than just doing business or making good products. They have to be doing good on top of it, because we want to be doing good – without sacrificing our creature-comfort capitalist lifestyles. We want to be both bourgeois and bohemian at the same time. We want to explore the world while protecting it, drive at 100 miles an hour and improve air quality simultaneously, eat our cake and celebrate it at the same time. And purpose-driven companies like Patagonia, Tesla, Burt's Bees, Moleskine and Edeka, to name a few, are allowing us to do just that.

Mission route 2: Reinvention, the little brother of responsibility

As Edeka showed, setting yourself apart and above through a mission is not reserved for high-minded ventures out to save the world. It works just as well in the everyday and mundane. The following examples will take this even further by showing that you can even build a 'missionary' Ueber-Brand and achieve strong modern prestige status when you don't have an ulterior – or rather superior – motive at all, when you are 'just' concerned with your core business, your category and its products.

One of the primary examples that springs to mind in this case is Starbucks, the little coffee shop from Seattle that revolutionized and up-traded an entire category and a whole generation, all through the simple idea of serving Italian roasted coffee in the United States and doing so in fantasy-Italian style and language. Of course, there was the often-reported idea of the 'third place' that Howard Schultz wanted to establish between home and work and which didn't really exist in the then-coffeehouse-free New World. But arguably, it was his 'basic' concept of reinventing and upgrading one of the oldest and most commoditized products, coffee, which did the trick. It took a hell of a lot of courage, of course, because as with most truly revolutionary ideas, it didn't look anything like a slam dunk (no pun intended) in the early days. Starbucks started in 1971 and stayed relatively small and local for a long time until the mid/late '80s when Howard Schultz took over and the specialty coffee trend took off. Yes, it was all built around specially roasted, high-quality coffee, but that alone didn't do the trick. Actually, it often seemed more problematic and limiting, as consumer tests showed again and again. The US public were enamoured with their bottomless cans of 'brown water' and the Starbucks roast was far too strong and bitter for the mainstream. A lot of critics argue to this day that Starbucks coffee is anything but superior. What was unarguably genius, however, and is broadly recognized as key ingredient for their success, was the shrewd (and sometimes also ruthless) marketing. They didn't just introduce a new, debatably premium product, they created a whole new world with its own language, standards and rituals. Grande Skinny Latte? Double Shot Venti Frappuchino®? White Chocolate Mocha? Just a couple of decades ago hardly anyone of us would have known what these meant. Now it's become a morning ritual for many of us, at least in more affluent, (sub-)urban areas: so much so that some sociologists already speak of the 'macchiato set'. We have been initiated and introduced to a different way of starting our days, taking breaks and hooking up with friends. And that's what turned Starbucks into a global prestige parvenu or Ueber-Brand.

The point: Starbucks never even so much as attempted to sell anything but overpriced coffee and its accoutrements. They offered no cleaner environment, healthier living or better society. They did jump on the fair trade and recycling bandwagons, but relatively late, and their sometimes questionable marketing practices or treatment of employees have usually been much more in the limelight. No, nobody goes to Starbucks to do good – other than to him- or herself. What really made this brand become the phenomenon it is and gave it Ueber-Brand status is that it dared to reinvent a well-known and well-loved product and thus the entire category. Different taste, different packaging, different names, different distribution – everything about Starbucks was unique and thus incomparable, at least outside of Italy. Not necessarily better, but distinct. **And that's the key of Mission Incomparable through reinvention: you don't need to improve everything to be seen as better. You must break some rules, not even all, but enough, to establish a new playing field and put yourself outside established standards.** That's what makes you incomparable, and that's what puts you above and beyond the rest – in perception as well as price. In a world over-saturated and bored by sameness it's standing out that's at a premium and thus the road to riches.

A similar example is Red Bull, the premier and premium-priced Thai–Austrian energy drink that created its own category and an almost 5 billion Euro business in the course of just two decades (see case study Principle 2). 'Syrupy', 'toxically sweet', 'medicinal', 'gross' are just some of the terms we heard being used to describe the taste – hardly what you dream of hearing about your product. Yet, it's exactly this polarizing taste that sits at the basis for Red Bull's success. Because it puts the brand outside of anything that had ever been seen or tasted in soda – thus creating curiosity, intrigue and exclusivity. It's at best what you'd call an acquired taste, just like Starbucks was, and thus it easily and very effectively separated those who are 'in' from those who are not – the core motivation to hit if you want to charge a premium and become a prestige brand.

Beyond this, the 'sickly' taste and the reddish colour also serve a functional purpose: they support the mythical power of Red Bull. Medicinal features = medicinal function, it's as easy as that. What looks and tastes like a drug is highly likely to actually work like one. Especially when you fuel PR around taurine, the key ingredient, keep rumours about it being made of ground bulls' testicles and the like alive through a smartly chosen logo and build a marketing world strongly rooted in high-energy sports and all-night raves. All focused to do one thing – set yourself way apart and ahead of all existing standards. Make yourself completely incomparable through a strong mission, materialized in a more-than-unique product and expressed and enriched through a never-ending stream of high-octane marketing events and courageous stunts.

Where imagination meets conviction

A category that has actually made reinvention its lifeblood and is thus a great way to get an insight into this approach is fashion. Fashion is by nature about the new, the next, the unseen. Even when you're recycling ideas from the past, fashion is always about the future. The interesting bit: it's not enough to come up with a great, innovative idea once, when you start your business. Fashion brands need to come up with a new collection at least twice a year. Yet, like any other brand, they also must create something like a signature look, and build recognition. Their solution: find a strong, courageous and visionary personality. Almost none of the big fashion houses would be where they are and survive without a strong designer – dead or alive or usually both. Coco Chanel and Karl Lagerfeld, Louis Vuitton and Marc Jacobs, Gucci and Tom Ford, Yves Saint Laurent and Hedi Slimane… the list is endless. They all are centred around the signature of a strong hand with a clear eye.

This tells us one thing very clearly: having a great, inventive idea may be the basis when you're in the process of building your name around reinvention, but it's nothing by itself. You still need a strong grounding. Just like the 'big brother' brands that are building themselves around responsibility you still need steadfastness. You must be a rebel, but a rebel with a cause. Or, as Aerin Lauder recently said on CNN, the most important thing she learned in guiding her grandmother's brand and launching her own was to say 'no': reject what may be right for the times but wrong for the brand (CNN, 2014).

To build an Ueber-Brand you always need both imagination and conviction – and a whole lot of courage. You must be on a mission to become known for having a Mission Incomparable. That's why most of the examples we analysed were all strongly reliant on an outstanding leader at the core. Because nothing is as perfect at constantly changing and yet basically staying the same recognizable self as us people. We can contradict and reinvent ourselves every five minutes and are usually, despite this – or because of it – true to ourselves. We follow the beat of our hearts and that's what lets our minds wander without ever completely losing course. We can keep our feet firmly on the ground and yet reach for the stars – which is what Mission Incomparable ultimately means.

One Ueber-Brand that most painfully learned this in the past through the loss, re-instatement and then again loss of its founder-hero-visionary Steve Jobs is Apple. Perhaps that is why they are now pursuing a quite unorthodox and, it seems, well-calibrated HR and mergers and acquisitions policy. In 2014 they hired in quick succession two fashion executives for top posts, Angela Ahrendts of Burberry fame and Paul Deneve, who used to run Yves Saint Laurent. They also brokered a deal with Beats Music, started by music impresarios Dr. Dre and Jimmy Iovine, which includes a personally curated music streaming service aimed at taking on the algorithmically driven streaming superstar Spotify. 'This whole idea of human curation we think is huge' said Apple CEO Timothy Cook in a recent *New York Times* article (Manjoo, 2014), 'It's something that a technology company alone wouldn't do'.

Of course, one could easily just look at these moves in terms of brand equity, seeing them as marketing-driven stunts to prop up the brand's point of difference, given that Apple has always tried to distinguish itself as the more human side of tech. Or you could even go as far as Ben Thompson, who writes the tech blog Stratechery (stratechery.com) and argue that Apple is perhaps trying to morph into a fashion house, making up for gradually losing its functional edge. But even though Ahrendts is hired mainly to oversee stores and the Apple watch, it nevertheless seems a smart strategy beyond this. It's probably the best way to ensure the brand – and all its actions and decisions, right or wrong – stays true to itself yet forward moving. Hiring and connecting yourself long term with cultural and economic leaders that have a clear affinity to the brand (which all four personalities have shown in the past) ensures not only that the brand keeps its 'human factor', it's also the most likely way to stay on track as iconic tastemaker and trendsetter.

And that's what modern prestige and Ueber-Brands must do: build and keep cultural resonance beyond individual relevance. Stay true to themselves and their convictions yet also evolve, keep things fresh and translate and re-insert their story into always surprising as well as reassuring experiences. Because while their mission may convince and pre-dispose us to liking them, it's the ways they bring it to life that make us fall in love with them, just as in any good and lasting relationship. After all, brands are also just people…

Quod licet Jovi, non licet bovi

Yvon Chouinard, the aforementioned founder of Patagonia, put it this way, not too long ago in *Fortune* magazine: 'If you're not pissing off 50 per cent of the people, you're not trying hard enough' (Mackenzie, 2013).

This is a perhaps somewhat drastic statement, but a very important point about what you need to be recognized as an Ueber-Brand with a Mission Incomparable.

Where most brands, especially mass brands, are concerned with never alienating anybody, modern prestige or Ueber-Brands must alienate to attract. It's hard to be seen as having a clear POV if everybody and their grandmother agrees with it. There are few things in the world that are broadly accepted but where you can still be seen as courageous for taking them on: fighting against the mafia comes to mind. In general however the rule stands: if everyone can agree with you, there's nothing special about you. If everybody can like you, you're vanilla. And if you're vanilla well… you're vanilla, not really worth paying a premium for or able to evoke any strong reaction. Positive or negative. Yet that's exactly what Ueber-Brands want and need: to evoke strong reactions, provoke loyalty way beyond reason and inspire a true fan base with exceptional commitment. This you can only achieve by being committed to yourself and your idiosyncratic, even polarizing stance.

That is why we like the old Latin phrase *Quod licet Jovi, non licet bovi*. Jupiter and a cow are not the same and they should never act the same. They are held to different standards – the divine can get away with things that the bovine cannot. More importantly though, they also need to live up to different expectations. If you want to set yourself apart and above, you must also behave that way. Take liberties to prove you can. Play up the entitlements that come with being a 'cut above'. Dare to go into uncharted and unsafe territory to show you have the will and the power to lead.

One brand that has embraced this point wholeheartedly for decades and doesn't show any sign of slowing down or mellowing out is certainly Harley Davidson (see also Principle 4). Their beliefs video has become legendary – and not just among fans and marketers. Their whole success is built on not fitting in, going against the grain and not being afraid of insulting or enraging many if not the majority. They have a mission and they live by it (Harley Davidson, 2008).

Equally Ben & Jerry's, the legendary ice cream brand, has always taken and voraciously supported controversial stands from 'anti-war' to 'pro-gay marriage' or given their iconic concoctions names like 'Hazed and Confused' or 'Yes Pecan' (to celebrate Barack Obama's election to the presidency). They are certainly polarizing and provocative for the notoriously light-treading US culture.

One company that does it perhaps in a bit more 'stylish' way is Sebastian (sebastian.com), the iconic and iconoclast hair styling brand now owned by P&G. Sebastian was founded in the '70s by a stylist couple in LA, and became quickly famous for its celebrity styles such as Barbra Streisand's crimped curls and groundbreaking products from Microweb Fiber to Molding Mud. The brand grew bigger and blander and ultimately lost its way in the late '80s and '90s – like a lot of us. But since its re-launch in 2007 it's done a commendable job of going back to its roots and re-embracing its fiercely and fearlessly forward-oriented attitude. Under the guiding thought of 'what's next?' they stopped at nothing and took a lot of risks to put the brand back where it once was and where it belongs: at the cutting edge of fashion and styling. They collaborated with visionaries in all kinds of creative areas from Hannah Marshall (fashion) to Charlotte Ronson (music) to Warren Du Preez and Nick Thornton Jones (film and video). They hired a leading creative team, Michael Polsinelli and Shay Dempsey, to drive their innovation and inspire the brand's and people's imaginations. They courageously streamlined and reorganized their portfolio and cut back on diversion, putting their money (or rather the resulting lack of revenue) where their mouth was. And they projected a provocatively, uncompromisingly creative attitude and artistry in all their communications and interactions. They were not afraid to step on many people's toes and that's exactly what made them regain the hearts of the ones they wanted: the fashion-forward stylists. They showed passion and conviction, and that is what inspired the same in their followers, winning the brand many accolades from WWD's Best Brand Re-launch in 2008 to numerous stylist and consumer choice awards.

Ben & Jerry's speaking its mind

Courtesy of Ben & Jerry's

Principle 1: The rules for a 'mission incomparable'

1 Think ahead
   To rise above and secure your brand an Ueber-position.

2 Be more than your competition
   And than your target can be without you.

3 Have a purpose
   Something you believe in and your followers can aspire to.

4 Take responsibility
   It's the noblest way to shine. And the one that today's consumers are most likely to reward – with loyalty and price elasticity.

5 Live up to your principles
   Put values above value if you want to make sure that price isn't the key point.

6 Re-invent
   And set your own standards. Originality often beats superiority.

7 Dare to differ
   Be distinct to offer distinction. Only if you're set apart can you seem special.

Ueber-Brands need to be on a mission. They must pursue a daring idea or, better yet, ideal, and follow their convictions without compromise. Only then can they be above and ahead of us and we can aspire to them. Because they're not just a 'brand as a friend', they are a 'brand as a guide'.

Ueber-Brand case study 1 Patagonia – the meaningful exploration of nature

Patagonia is a leading outdoor apparel and specialized gear brand known for colourful, high-tech (and high-priced) outfits with an 'eco twist'. It all started very humbly, however, with an 18-year-old Yvon Chouinard, an outdoor enthusiast selling climbing spikes out of his parents' backyard. Yvon was hanging out with like-minded climbers and surfers. They had little money and sometimes lived on squirrels and other poached critters. It was to supplement his budget and to share his superior designs that Chouinard started a little business in the early '60s making hand-forged climbing pitons from old car axles. By 1970, the company had become the biggest climbing gear seller in the United States. (Back then the company was called Chouinard Equipment: the Patagonia brand was created in 1976.) As his pitons became popular, Chouinard found more and more scarring signs of their use along climbing routes, defacing the previously pristine landscape he admired. So he took the decision to discontinue his best-selling product – representing 70 per cent of sales – and replace it with aluminum chocks to be wedged into existing cracks. He explained the decision and made a passionate appeal for 'clean climbing' in a 14-page essay in his company's catalogue. It was to be just the first of several rather dramatic business decisions Chouinard would make to 'do the right thing'.

Nevertheless, the annual growth rate of Patagonia sales has been well above industry-averages for most of the past 40 years. In 2014, the brand had over US $600 million in retail sales to its name.

On a mission to explore without exploiting

Stopping the sale of pitons is an iconic moment in the brand's history and one of the foundations for Patagonia's mission: 'Build the best product, cause no unnecessary harm, and use business to inspire and implement solutions to the environmental crisis' (Patagonia.com, accessed July 2014). And Patagonia has proven this mission is not just lip service. Having moved from equipment to clothes in the '80s, the company found its rugged cotton garments becoming very popular. But they also realized the negative eco footprint and potential health danger of industrial cotton. So they went on a laborious and expensive quest to 're-source', and made Patagonia the key user of and vocal advocate for pesticide-free cotton, creating the demand that triggered the birth of the now world-leading organic cotton industry in California (Chouinard and Brown, 2008).

It kicked off a journey towards being 'completely responsible', which they readily admit is never ending (Gerald Amos on Patagonia.com, accessed 14 June 2014). And while the majority of the brand's customers might ignore these tall ambitions, the brand knows about the missionary effect of bold moves. In 1973 it invited an environmental activist with the crazy dream of re-naturalizing an industrial canal to operate out of their offices. This was unheard of at the time, but it rallied employees and the community and is still cited today as one of the first examples of Social Corporate Responsibility. In 1985, Patagonia was also one of the first to institutionalize corporate 'tithing', committing 10 per cent of annual profits to grass-roots efforts in wilderness protection. A recent example is the 'DamNation' project, which unites employees and fans in their passion to un-build dams or make them compatible with fish migration. Chouinard produced the namesake documentary to spread the message and sells limited edition t-shirts to boost awareness.

In 2013, Patagonia upped the ante yet again, making headlines by tackling the 'white elephant in the room' – growth-based capitalism, itself. The company changed its corporate classification to that of a 'benefit corporation' and made itself publicly accountable to 'create a material positive impact on society and the environment; expand fiduciary duty to require consideration of non-financial interests' and to be audited – despite being a privately owned company (benefitcorp.net, 2014). To some this might sound like utopian dreaming. To Patagonia's target audience, setting yet a higher ethical bar is, however, what makes the brand aspirational, worth their loyal support.

Behold: How to un-sell – more

True to this mission, Patagonia products are simple, highly functional and durable to serve rugged exploration, and thought through to minimize negative impact on humans or the environment. The brand tells stories around these aspects to make them relatable and easy to pass on.

One of these stories is about Chouinard going berserk over a shirt losing a button and instructing product design to find an unfailing way to fix the fault – no matter the cost. Another talks about the principle of garments having as few pockets as possible because they can get caught in something while climbing, plus they require the use of unnecessary material. All this is authenticated by a group of about 80 'Ambassadors' appointed for their exceptional outdoor sportsmanship as well as by 'normal visitors' of the Patagonia website. The Ambassadors relate their adventures through a plethora of blog posts, essays and films of documentary quality. In the adjoining 'Worn Wear' section the larger community is encouraged to relate 'The Stories We Wear'. Amateurs tell of garments that have stood by them at important times and over long periods in their life adventures – not all of them Patagonia. In both, the stories come across as deeply authentic, never feeling like forced 'product placement' or staged 'torture tests'. The adventurer-activists are the heroes, but the brand becomes the inseparable helper in the journey.

There is also a very visible effort to lay bare the environmental DNA of key products, for example in their 'Footprint Chronicles'. A typical story will tell of how Patagonia suspected that some of their feathers might be sourced from foie-gras farms where geese are force-fed, and so carried out a long audit until it was finally able to certify its down as 100 per cent cruelty free in 2014. Until that point the brand recommended that those opposing such practices avoid these products; a kind of self-indictment that elevates Patagonia and its products into a higher league. In stores, you can pick up a copy of 'Truth to Materials', a free book containing essays and a glossary on the responsible sourcing, treating, recycling, reclaiming, reusing or composting of Patagonia's garments over 117 pages. The book is beautifully illustrated, inviting you to leave it on your coffee table.

A 2013 ad brings together all these elements of 'beholding' the product while 'un-selling' – literally. One of Patagonia's iconic fleece jackets is put in the spotlight to be admired, but in a way that does not feel like a sale – quite the contrary: fleece was a new, synthetic fabric that Patagonia stumbled across in the '80s and adopted for its coveted warming, wicking and water-repelling characteristics. It also turned out that the fleece could be made from recycled materials like toilet covers or empty soda bottles. Spin that yarn (no pun) into comfy, bright coloured garments (versus the earthy tones typical of the category) and you have a true icon of what Patagonia is all about. Snap-T sweaters or R2 jackets still sell briskly 30 years later and were thus a natural choice for a full-page ad in the *New York Times* on Black Friday, a key shopping day in the year. However, the oversized headline is shocking – 'Don't buy this Jacket'. Instead of just describing the product's durability and manufacturing from recycled materials, the body copy – which we encourage you to read – focuses on the unavoidable negative environmental impact of buying new garments before they are worn out, driving readers towards the 'Common Threads Partnership', an initiative to repair, resell or recycle Patagonia garments, rather than discarding them (scan QR code in Preface for a link to Common Threads).

DON'T BUY THIS JACKET

It's Black Friday, the day in the year retail turns from red to black and starts to make real money. But Black Friday, and the culture of consumption it reflects, puts the economy of natural systems that support all life firmly in the red. We're now using the resources of one-and-a-half planets on our one and only planet.

Because Patagonia wants to be in business for a good long time – and leave a world inhabitable for our kids – we want to do the opposite of every other business today. We ask you to buy less and to reflect before you spend a dime on this jacket or anything else.

Environmental bankruptcy, as with corporate bankruptcy, can happen very slowly, then all of a sudden. This is what we face unless we slow down, then reverse the damage. We're running short on fresh water, topsoil, fisheries, wetlands – all our planet's natural systems and resources that support business, and life, including our own.

The environmental cost of everything we make is astonishing. Consider the R2® Jacket shown, one of our best sellers. To make it required 135 liters of

COMMON THREADS INITIATIVE

REDUCE
WE make useful gear that lasts a long time
YOU don't buy what you don't need

REPAIR
WE help you repair your Patagonia gear
YOU pledge to fix what's broken

REUSE
WE help find a home for Patagonia gear you no longer need
YOU sell or pass it on*

RECYCLE
WE will take back your Patagonia gear that is worn out
YOU pledge to keep your stuff out of the landfill and incinerator

REIMAGINE
TOGETHER we reimagine a world where we take only what nature can replace

water, enough to meet the daily needs (three glasses a day) of 45 people. Its journey from its origin as 60% recycled polyester to our Reno warehouse generated nearly 20 pounds of carbon dioxide, 24 times the weight of the finished product. This jacket left behind, on its way to Reno, two-thirds its weight in waste.

And this is a 60% recycled polyester jacket, knit and sewn to a high standard; it is exceptionally durable, so you won't have to replace it as often. And when it comes to the end of its useful life we'll take it back to recycle into a product of equal value. But, as is true of all the things we can make and you can buy, this jacket comes with an environmental cost higher than its price.

There is much to be done and plenty for us all to do. Don't buy what you don't need. Think twice before you buy anything. Go to patagonia.com/CommonThreads or scan the QR code below. Take the Common Threads Initiative pledge, and join us in the fifth "R," to reimagine a world where we take only what nature can replace.

patagonia.com

TAKE THE PLEDGE

Once you have read the ad and followed the ensuing debates it triggered across the media, you recognize the ingenious way in which this act of 'un-selling' furthers the awareness and respect consumers have for this brand – particularly Patagonia's core target of rugged adventurers, who have a rather critical attitude towards commerce. Note also that, in the context of such ethical commitment, asking for the price of these garments seems almost frivolous.

The 'Dirtbag' myth – and a community longing to belong

The myth of Patagonia is that of a hedonist-explorer overcoming his natural reluctance to become an activist as he discovers the negative consequences of his adventures and our collective consumption. The brand logo hints at the connection to the great outdoors, showing the Andes skyline with Cerro Fitz Roy at the centre, one of the most challenging mountains in the world to climb. But for most the Patagonia name alone will do the job.

Those who dig deeper will find that Mount Fitz Roy is a monument to the brand myth. It was 1968 when Chouinard and a bunch of friends left Ventura California to go on an exhilarating journey to its top. The films and stories they brought back became part of the lore of the 'Dirtbags', a group that to outdoor enthusiasts has become legend: people who commit themselves to scaling the outdoors to the point of abandoning civilized life. While some might dismiss them as 'hippies', many city dwellers will find their choices courageous and liberating and will want to be part of that group – even if only through the faint association of wearing some of their outfits.

Chouinard and the brand constantly and consistently relate the Dirtbag myth, for example through reports that the millionaire founder still drives a beat-up car, doesn't own a cell phone or computer and would rather spend his time fly fishing or hammering away in his forge than going to the office (Stevenson, 2012). The brand website serves as a forum for the Dirtbag community to relate their thoughts and feats, abundant with pictures of people heating cans on a camp fire, dipping in mountain streams, climbing a sheer face or playing hacky sack on a ledge. All, however, with a distinct sense of calling and pride in the mission to 'save our earth'.

Naturally, it helps to strengthen a group when the 'outsiders' are also clearly identified. That's why fashion is an 'f-word' at Patagonia and there is a rather open contempt for those who follow it. Yet, the fact that more Snap-Ts are worn by hipsters than by fly fishermen with pictures of celebrities donning 'Patagucci' at chilly Sundance Film Festival après-parties has not been lost on the brand: 'We outgrew our loyal customer base... selling to yuppies, posers, and wannabes… These people don't need this shit to get in their Jeep Cherokees and drive to Connecticut for the weekend' (Swansburg, 2012). Such harsh words, by the founder, reassure the hardcore fans that the brand has not sold out and that they are the only 'real' Patagoniacs, without diminishing the appeal of the myth to the rest who keep the production lines humming.

A reluctant businessman, living the dream

The way the company organizes and acts, its offices, websites and stores, all bear witness to the Patagonia beliefs and tell the brand story. There is a shrine behind the headquarters in Ventura, which consists of a corrugated tin shed that served as the piton forge in the early days. Chouinard makes it a ritual to give interviews there in his worn-in clothes and apron while fiddling around on an improved camping knife or stove.

In *Let My People Go Surfing: The education of a reluctant businessman* (Chouinard, 2006) he summarizes his organization- and business-building experience. Patagonia is a self-selective organism where like-minded people thrive. The Patagonia campus is famous for being a place where employees play beach volleyball in the backyard, enjoy an organic food cafeteria and on-premise child care – and it has been like that decades before Google was around. The management 'board meetings' held in wetsuits are lore. Lunch break is known as 'surf time'. Product development takes the form of owner and employees going on excursions, to return – sometimes months later – with feedback on products, ideas for new ones and new recruits. There is an 'Environmental Internship Program' providing paid leave, which has led to the most diverse causes being initiated or supported by employees and shared via the blog 'The Cleanest Line'. The passion for surfing or fly fishing is shared via dedicated customer service lines that are toll-free (the product ordering line is not).

Patagonia's storytelling, values and rituals are naturally carried into the flagship stores, which have the look and feel of mountain lodges, just like the headquarters. Between the gear you will find pictures and artifacts that re-tell the Patagonia myth, ranging from historic images of that 1968 Mount Fitz Roy trip or the back of a beat-up VW van hung on the wall, to a gallery documenting the life cycle of a wool garment from the organic grasslands of Patagonia to a first life as a garment and then a second one via Patagonia's unique reclaiming process. There are 'Truth to Materials' collection items made of reclaimed wool, down and polyester stacked on a table next to the gallery. The store staff are encouraged to join environmental causes, and are empowered to do right by the customer.

There are stories about customers getting their shorts exchanged after a decade of use – before it became a corporate policy with the 'Common Threads' initiative. As a consequence, employee turnover is a low 25 per cent, compared to an average in apparel retail of well over 100 per cent (Henneman, 2011).

Patagonia's mission, myth and activist nature come to life in store (here Soho, NY). Note the appeal to vote – for the right cause

Photo by JP Kuehlwein

Such consistency and depth of dedication is not achieved overnight and requires a special type of ownership. Over the decades Chouinard has declined many offers to sell or to inject private equity money to fuel growth, going for an organic growth pace, instead. He thinks one of the biggest mistakes he ever made was to succumb to the immense popularity and growth Patagonia enjoyed in the free-spending '80s and bring in 'professionals' to help manage it. Their profit-maximization approach fundamentally clashed with Patagonia's organization values – despite the 'suits' being kept off-campus (Welles, 1992). And then, when the financial crisis hit, the fad disappeared and so did bank credits and the managers. Large piles of inventory had to be sold down and the company had to let go of 20 per cent of its workforce to save itself. At that tragic juncture, 'industry experts' judged that it was Patagonia's unconventional approach to business that would be the demise of the brand. Eddie Bauer President Wayne Badovinus commented in a 1992 interview with *Inc*. magazine: 'A lot of people assume that these tribal rituals make a business better. But in the final analysis, clear measures of your progress – sales and profits – help guide you a lot more' (Welles,1992). History proved him wrong. Eddie Bauer went bankrupt in 2009 and was picked up by private equity. Patagonia recovered standing by its values. The business has had a compound annual growth rate of 16 per cent over the past 35 years – despite trying to fight it…

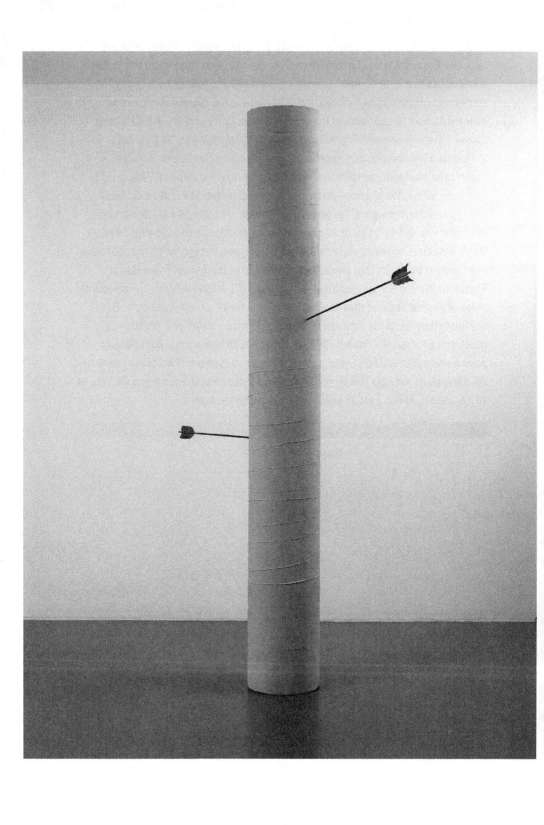

Principle 2
Longing versus belonging
The challenge is both

One of the key objectives in marketing is reach: reaching as many people as possible to win the biggest number of customers. Size and scale don't just matter, they are often *sine qua non* and prime motivation in one: they are the 'be-all and end-all', big time.

When it comes to prestige brands, however, it is not quite as simple as that. Of course, the ultimate goal remains maximizing sales, but in order to build and protect the brand's equity, one has to be much more careful and mindful. It takes a much more nuanced approach that is not afraid to be a bit less single-minded but more multi-considerate. It takes willingness and an ability to embrace the contradictory realities of our human psyche and soul. Why? Because where traditional mass marketing is mostly about serving needs, prestige brands are in the business of creating desire. Their job is to keep us wanting while we're having – way beyond what we need. Their products are usually not 'fast moving consumer goods' but products with a longer life span. Or, if they are so-called 'packaged goods' for quick consumption and regular replenishment, they try to charge much more than the average comparable product in their category does. They stand and shine above and beyond their competition, luring us to leave most reason behind to splurge and indulge. They don't just need to sell to us – they need to seduce us: and seduction is a mighty tricky business. It's not just emotional – it's completely irrational. It plays on the ultimate (and for the most part subconscious) human tensions of individuality versus collectivity, safety versus freedom, dominance versus acceptance. Many modern prestige brands have thus perfected the art of equally embracing these contradictions. **Where their predecessors were more singularly concerned with rarity and restraint, prestige brands nowadays stay slightly out of reach, while growing at the same rate, balancing inclusivity with exclusivity and giving us a sense of belonging while still keeping us longing. They keep on making us feel special despite our better knowledge or the obvious reality that we are not.**

Most do this by following two strategies, which in themselves already reflect a nice dichotomy and deal with the Ueber-challenge of balancing proximity and distance:

1 Reaching high to win up

2 Laying low to stay up

The first strategy we will look at concerns itself with a particular approach to targeting called top-down vs. bottom-up. Modern prestige or Ueber-Brands very carefully differentiate between their design and their strategic targets. Usually, they try to first foster relationships with a small base of tastemakers and trendsetters within their category. From this they grow gradually, leveraging their original fans, both as continuous proof of their superiority and desirability as well as missionaries to help them target and convert the broader market.

The second strategy we will discuss is less about the people and more about the products and services: creating a sense of rarity to build a feeling of exclusivity, and strategically controlling supply to foster demand. This is nothing new, but it is still important – as it always was and will be. There is a multitude of possibilities, from special or limited editions to seasonal collections to special access goods to highly controlled, obscure or fancy distribution tactics. Plus of course there's always the plain old way of simply pricing some consumers out to give the rest a feeling of being in. We will look at all of those ideas and provide ample examples. We will place a particular focus on how this works in naturally 'democratic' and mass categories, because while it's easy to apply a 'scarcity' approach within high-end durables or indulgences, it's much more challenging to do so when your product is one that needs a certain degree of ubiquity – as often happens to be the case in modern prestige.

The power of the velvet rope

Prestige brands don't have it easy. They don't just need to sell. Actually they shouldn't sell us too much at all (see the following principle). They must seduce. They must make us desire them, not just need them, because only then might we be willing to shell out the extra cash that they demand.

How do modern prestige or Ueber-Brands do this? How do they lure us in, often against our better judgement, and create that special appeal? To a large degree it's by making us 'long to belong': creating a sense that they can give us access to something we don't want to miss, something exciting that will enrich our lives, giving us an extra kick and a more fun, perhaps even a more meaningful experience. **In other words, they put up a 'velvet rope', not literally of course, but figuratively; a bit of a barrier which makes us want to look behind, get inside, try it out – which makes us feel as if the brand is a bit out of reach, even though it's just a couple of feet or a 'click' away.**

According to most accounts, the velvet rope was invented by George and Louise Boldt when they opened the first Waldorf hotel (later The Waldorf Astoria) on 33rd Street and 5th Avenue in New York City in 1894. The principle was later picked up and perfected by Ian Schrager and Steve Rubell, owners of another New York icon, the legendary Studio 54, which opened in 1977. Though the dance club only ran for four short years it has become the epitome of an ultra-selective door policy and the model for creating an Ueber-desirable brand. Night after night hordes of people would line up on 54th street in Manhattan for the off-chance the rope would be lifted and they'd be let in. Schrager and Rubell, had hit on a deep-seated human truth and taken it to the highest, most glamorous level, so much so that their approach is still applied by most (night) clubs around the world – as Christian Rhomberg, founder-chairman of the artist-elitist Kee Club in Hong Kong put it to us: 'what makes us desirable to our members is to make it past that velvet rope and belong to the Ueber-Tribe'. Brands, also like to style themselves accordingly. For instance, Abercrombie and Fitch literally apply a velvet rope in front of most stores, with beautiful, half-naked boys serving as bait as well as bouncers.

We people are torn by two conflicting needs: the need to congregate and the need to separate. On the one hand we are a very collective species. We need each other to survive. We must have emotional bonds, make connections, huddle and cuddle. On the other hand however, we have a sense of self, and that drives us to explore and experience our singularity – the fact that we are different or at least solitaires. As the saying goes: 'We are united in the need to feel unique'. But what makes this already contradictory set up truly paradoxical is the fact that we can only fulfil those needs with each other and against one another. We can only feel our individuality in the context of our collectivity. We need the others in order to feel ourselves. This drove Jean-Paul Sartre to write his famous, existentialist dictum 'L'enfer c'est les autres' – 'Hell is other people' (Sartre, 1947).

Studio 54, however, didn't 'just' make use of this basic human paradox, they took it even further, adding a particularly devilish twist: unpredictability. That's what made it so utterly irresistible, even to those who normally had no problem 'making the cut', like Liza Minnelli or Diana Ross. And, this is what turned it into the benchmark for successful modern 'prestige roping' – in clubland as well as in our brand world. You couldn't buy your way into Studio 54. Nor could you secure entrance by adhering to a certain dress code, as was the case with the original velvet rope at The Waldorf's garden court. And you certainly couldn't charm yourself in. You couldn't even be sure that you'd get in tomorrow because you'd gotten in today. It was all completely dependent on the subjective and ever-shifting moods of the 'doorman', Steve Rubell. He decided if you belonged – or were kept longing – every evening anew.

Ueber-Brands took this to heart, and then some. They don't just apply the 'velvet rope' principle in its traditional form as prestige brands always have and always will. Their exclusivity isn't one that you can necessarily 'buy' your way into or completely control in any other way. Their allure is built on the fact that they are, to some degree, beyond your control. Of course you are still the customer and as such 'king', but you don't control all the shots. Ueber-Brands don't make it so easy – and boring – for you. They don't put themselves out like a Walmart doormat with a cloyingly sweet smile. Rather, they keep you on your toes, never letting you be sure that, and how, you belong. They always stay true to their core, but they also surprise us, like designer fashion does so well, avoiding too much predictability by shifting alliances, redefining inner circles and moving the rope here or there so we consumers have no choice but to stay mesmerized and follow. They have perfected the balancing act between in and out. They have turned the velvet rope into a tightrope on which they walk magically and alluringly, pulling us along.

The new rule: Yes, but

The MINI brand is a perfect example of this balancing act (see case study, Principle 4). It's been managing to walk the fine line between longing and belonging for nearly six decades, but most admiringly since its re-launch in 2001, when the BMW group started to build it into the Ueber-Brand it is today, and a modern textbook case on how to market without over-marketing. They built desirability and equity while growing at double digit rates, all by strictly adhering to a rule of ambiguity: Yes, but.

One of the first and most obvious signs of this 'yes, but' approach was MINI's US launch in 2002, truly a going-to-market with the brakes on if ever there was one. Instead of going at full speed, they deliberately limited sales to 25,000 cars of the 200,000 that were then produced annually. Yes, they wanted to conquer a new market, heck, a new continent, but they wanted to build and protect their elusive-exclusive equity at the same time. A tightrope indeed, and quite a gamble, but it paid off. They were sold out before year's end, and achieved the same for the following three years in a row. More importantly however, the brand's awareness skyrocketed from 12 per cent in 2001 to 53 per cent at the end of 2002, a hike of almost 400 per cent in 12 months (just-auto.com, 2013). This was unheard of, especially considering that their media budget was US $20 million, a mere pittance compared to what the average car brand spends on advertising in the United States. And, taking into account that the price for the standard version was around US $20–25,000, which was certainly not a bargain compared to the competition. Yet, then again, that was part of the point: MINI was not comparable. It was launched with a mission to be incomparable (see Principle 1): to show the American Goliaths what a David can do. MINI was and still is 'the little car that could', and that's what it showed. Playing hard to get and yet, or rather because of it, making it all the way to the top.

In other words, MINI didn't push. What they applied was a masterclass in pull marketing. **They didn't attack, certainly not in full force: they tried to attract our attention, and our desire to be special**. It was the intrigue and curiosity of their target market and of us all, which they piqued and which lifted them to ever-new heights. They created a sense of scarcity and exclusivity, but not in the traditional way, in the new way. Like Studio 54, which 'exercised the same discretion people exercise when inviting others to their home' (Yuan, 2007), they 'chose' their clientele and thus created a strong sense of collectivity, if not family. Where it's not money that will guarantee access but where you have to qualify in less predictable and more complex ways to belong to the 'chosen few'– metaphorically speaking at least. Because unlike Ferrari, who really choose their customers like New York condo boards do, you could of course buy a MINI if you only waited a bit. Actually it was pretty much first-come first-served, working off a long list of pre-orders from the start. But the perception was that you had to belong to a certain aspirational elite of creative and cultured sophisticates in order to be allowed to make a MINI your own. Only if you shared the rebellious nature of the brand would you be considered and could you prove worthy of being part of the tribe and owning a MINI yourself. The brand became hot. And so did you, if you managed to get your hands on one.

In the meantime the brand has perfected this 'velvet rope' approach to marketing by creating all kinds of insider groups and clubs, establishing a true multi-levelled community of more or less like-minded insiders. They even launched real MINI lounges, lounges in Madrid or Budapest. And although they are without actual velvet ropes most of the time, it does bring the unique, urban and unconventional clique-ish spirit of the brand and its fans to life in the most literal sense.

MINI Bar in Budapest – the velvet rope idea of Ueber-Brand building taken literally

Photo by Tyukodi Laszlo, Courtesy of BMW Group

Yet the 'yes, but' rule of the velvet rope goes much further. In essence it requires modern prestige brands to embrace an ambiguous, somewhat unpredictable modus operandi in all customer interactions. Always playing on the tension between being accessible, and yet not, thus building up the allure, keeping their audience transfixed, always wondering if they'll pass the rope or not. **It's about balancing proximity and distance at every touch point, at every action, in every choice.** Being available, but never too easily. Being everywhere, but always special. Promoting your brand, but not necessarily your product – and certainly never your price.

From a targeting and marketing standpoint there are two simple 'musts' that make the whole principle quite tangible: 'reaching high' and 'laying low'. Let's first look at 'reaching high' in more detail.

Velvet roping 1: Reaching high to win up

The first and arguably most important aspect of making the velvet rope work for you and keep your targets longing to belong is the people. The whole concept is based on us being torn between collectivity and individuality. Naturally, those who are supposedly 'inside' are the ones who will decide about who is going to wait 'outside', defining the aspirational pull you can expect or exert.

This is why modern prestige or Ueber-Brands follow a different target approach than most others, one that could be called top-down vs. bottom-up. Just like any marketing textbook, they will define their strategic target, the group of consumers they ultimately want to and need to reach in order to be successful and profitable. But on top they clearly map out what's often called a 'design target', the idealized version of their clients, which we like to call the 'Ueber-Target'.

Ueber-Brands 'reach high to win up': they play with our curiosity and desire to get what seems out of reach, belong to where we don't quite belong and take a walk on the wilder or greener side of life by connecting with a social group that exudes a certain pull, 'promising' their customers the same sense of cool in the eyes of others that this group has for them. This 'Ueber-Target', the elite version of their true customers, is the benchmark for all their actions and they take great pains to always be associated with them. Because they know they only keep us dreaming – and spending the extra cash – as long as they can connect us with the dreams we have. And those are mostly dreams about ourselves – how and who we would like to be, and who we'd like to be seen with.

The Tesla top-down

A quite contemporary case for this is Tesla, the car brand of the moment and third most sold luxury sedan, at least in California. Quoted already for its clear and compelling mission, Tesla is equally smart and perhaps even more noticeable for its very coherent top-down strategy. Elon Musk, the CEO, very carefully and intentionally planned on using the vanity as well as the allure of the rich eco-tech freaks to help him build an ultimately democratic empire, with an e-vehicle in every garage. The whole company is founded on a very simple yet clear cascading model: first get the top of the market with the highest margins and then develop down, using the capital generated on the top to fund the expansion and successive democratization. Consequently, Tesla started by launching the Tesla Roadster, a highly charged super sports car, in 2008 and followed in 2012 with the Tesla Model S, a fully electric luxury sedan.

The roadster was priced above US $110,000 and the sedan runs somewhere around US $90,000 – anything but cheap, especially for a company without an established reputation. And yet it worked – by applying the velvet rope principle. Musk made it his mission to place the car in the context of Hollywood, and succeeded. From Ben Affleck and Jennifer Garner to Laurence Fishburne to Brad Pitt and Angelina Jolie, the fans of Tesla read almost like the guest list of an Academy Awards party. There's even a movie in the making about the 19th-century electrical engineer Nikola Tesla, after whom the brand is named. And although people at Tesla were quick to state that they don't care about such marketing tricks and that 'everybody driving a Tesla is a celebrity', they also conclude that 'there are other buyer segments where being "in" on Hollywood's A-list definitely helps stoke interest'.

What Tesla fans also recognize, however, is that the biggest star of them all is Elon Musk himself. He has managed to accrue so much wattage that he can outshine the entire industry, with more than a million followers on Twitter alone. And that certainly is not an unimportant factor, especially if you see him as a messiah of car making, which is what a lot of people do. He is Steve Jobs and Al Gore rolled into one, a 'creative-thinker-meets-power-player', combining cool and charisma with conviction. It is an almost irresistible pull, and not just to the eco-conscious elite. He is his own best Ueber-Target, projecting fame and fortune with a big dose of foresight, representing the guy we all would like to be. Crazy and courageous enough to think he could make the world a better place and cunning enough to make it happen.

Perhaps that's why it never really mattered that Musk pursues his top-down strategy to 'reach high and win up' in all openness. Everyone who wants to, can see that Tesla aims to eventually be anything but a prestige brand and mass-produce fully electric cars at a price affordable to the average consumer – and that Musk only uses the upper tiers to finance this goal. In August 2008 he blogged: 'So, in short, the master plan is: 1. Build sports cars, 2. Use that money to build an affordable car, 3. Use that money to build an even more affordable car, and 4. While doing above, also provide zero emission electric power generation options.' And to this day you can read the same in more detail on the website: 'The strategy of Tesla is to enter at the high end of the market, where customers are prepared to pay a premium, and then drive down market' (Teslamotors.com).

Elon Musk and Tesla never even tried to seduce us secretly. He always has and still does pull our strings in the most outspoken way – and yet we fall for it. Or actually, we don't really fall for it, we follow him willingly. We believe in his mission and are honoured and enchanted to help him along. The fact that we can be part of an eco-elite outshines any sense of feeling manipulated and lets us gladly become tools in the hands of the master, our eco-master.

Exclusivity through complicity

But perhaps it isn't just Musk's personality or his mission that lets Tesla get away with executing its strategy so unabashedly. Perhaps they aren't successful despite being so open about it, but because of it. Because they are playing something that is becoming more and more popular, something which could be called the next level of pursing a top-down strategy, or 'reaching high 2.0'.

Younger and better-educated consumers in particular have become so adept at marketing that the only way we can actually be tricked is through a certain sense of complicity. Eric Migicovsky used Kickstarter as a platform to create not one, but two communities of accomplices in his dream to create a wearable computer – the Pebble Smartwatch: On one end, passionate hardware and app developers and on the other a large crowd of individual investors. Pebble raised a record-shattering US $10 million in 2012 and has sold some 400,000 watches to date, for which countless apps can be downloaded. And even though the brand would have the cash today to develop and launch the latest model the 'classic' way, it chose crowdfunding again in 2015. Not only raising US $1 million in less than an hour but also keeping its communities vested in the brand – literally.

This illustrates how we like to see ourselves more as active participants than passive victims. We want to at least be in on the joke when we're being fooled. Because fooled we still are. We may think we see through the strategy of using a design target to lure us in, but we still can't help ourselves. We can't control our desires and our feelings. We still want to be a part of this dream group, as much as we may be aware that it's a dream that will be forever elusive and has only been set up to seduce us. It's like Daniel Kahneman, the Nobel Prize-winning psychologist and behavioural economist and his team discovered over and over again: our intuitive, instinctive side will always be gullible, no matter how educated and critical our rational, logical one is (Kahneman, 2011). We people will always act to some degree 'irrationally' and against our better judgement and will be prone to being manipulated by clever marketing, or anything else for that matter. But the new kind of top-down strategists are making it a bit easier for us, by mediating between our 'feeling' and our 'knowing' sides. They acknowledge our marketing smarts and placate our critical minds by giving us a sense of following willingly rather than having one pulled on us. In other words, they create a sense of exclusivity by being inclusive – by including us and both sides of our brains. They involve us as knowing agents and happily feeling followers at the same time.

Some, like Tesla, do this by stating their strategies outright and justifying them through their goals, or 'Mission Incomparable'. Another example in this vein is Lululemon, the sportswear brand that grew to a net worth of US $1.4 billion in just eight years. Lululemon started out being focused on practical yet attractive yoga gear for women, but in the meantime integrated men as well as running and other 'sweaty pursuits' as they call them, while still being environmentally driven – ecologically and socially. Throughout they haven't spent much on traditional marketing. Instead, they focused mostly on community building, pursuing a classic top-down strategy that employs their 'design targets' and most picture-perfect users as so-called 'luluheads' – knowingly and proudly. Instructors wear the clothing at in-store events like yoga or self-defence classes and goal-setting workshops, simultaneously building product awareness and forging ties with local communities. Through local Facebook pages Lululemon invites customers to share their experiences via Instagram and Twitter. On their website they encourage 'unique individuals... who embody the Lululemon lifestyle and live our culture' to become brand ambassadors. Once accepted, these individuals receive substantial store credits (US $1,000) and are featured on the Lululemon website with their picture, bio and all, allowing them to promote themselves and their pursuits as well as giving the brand a true club-like feel that it is absolutely cool to become a part of. Or, as former CEO Christine Day said: 'The number one goal is really building healthy communities. If I were to say Lululemon has a superpower, it's engagement. We're not afraid to have a good time, stand for something, create a conversation. Our clothing is a medium for people to live a life they love.' (Malcolm, 2013). This made Lululemon quickly become the Ueber-Brand that it is and a bellwether for modern prestige. Whether it will last remains to be seen (see also Principle 6).

A different way to build this 'inclusive' sense of exclusivity is a less serious one, applying irony and hyperbole. This is perfect for Non-Ueber-Brands that want to 'up' their prestige in a modern way, as Grey Poupon's Facebook initiative 'The Society of Good Taste' showed. Against the standard brand approach of trying to gather as many 'likes' as possible, Kraft Foods screened and limited the fans of their 'masstige' mustard. People had to first profess to be well read, like to cook and eat good food, etc. Only then could they apply to become 'accepted members'. It was a wonderful way to re-frame social media and elevate the brand to 'a notch above mass' with a wink.

No matter which approach you follow, if you 'reach high' in secret or in all openness, recruit your 'design target' through an incomparable mission or tongue-in-cheek, if the velvet rope is plush and relatively tight or quite checkered and permissive, the idea is always the same: **build a sense of 'in' vs. 'out' by connecting yourself with those who are tastemakers and trendsetters for the rest of your target to become fans and loyal followers.** Pl-- your brand ahead of the rest and put it at the centre of a social dy the same time. Make use of some of our most archaic and deep-root to pull us in and let us long to belong. And while the methods and tactics have changed in modern prestige, not the least because of digital possibilities, the basic principle is the same as it always was. It's about people needing people, and people defining and finding themselves through other people.

Designing an Ueber-Target

There are two ways in which strong design targets – or Ueber-Targets as we like to call them – typically emerge.

The first is through creator-founders who realize their own, ideal self in their brand. Many famous examples are found in fashion, beauty or 'lifestyle', for instance Tory Burch, who catapulted herself into the starry firmament of leading tastemakers in little time. She entered the Forbes list of fashion billionaires in 2013, only a decade after launching her eponymous brand, which mixes the luxurious elegance of the upper crust with the relaxed attitude and style of the hippies who roamed the world in the '70s. Nobody represents this lifestyle better than Burch herself, as followers of her prolific blog posts or the incessant media coverage will attest. Every interview or 'selfie' posted cements the guiding DNA of the brand. Fans feed on glimpses of Tory's meticulously curated mansion or gracious fêtes for celebrity friends.

If you are a guy and aspire to be part of that dapper intellectual elite with insights and opinions on the most esoteric subjects (does the Masuichi Kyakuden in Obuse serve the best breakfast?), then Tyler Brûlé – described by the *New York Times* as 'Mr Zeitgeist, [...] a globe-trotting connoisseur'– might be your idol. Brûlé first founded *Wallpaper* magazine, which became the bible of the urban creative class, in 1996, and then moved on to create the highly influential Monocle media empire in 2007. He spreads his cosmo-cool musings via his magazine, a column in the *Financial Times* or his internet radio channel, and true to his idiosyncratic style, shuns social media like Facebook or Twitter. Those who 'subscribe' to Monocle (in every sense of the word) will not only pay US $150 per year but will likely also buy into the Brûlé look by acquiring some of the retro-modern items in Brûlé's hand-picked Monocle X collection. To experience this one-man Ueber-Target, visit Monocle's zen-infused editorial offices-cum-shops-cum coffee bars in London, New York, Hong Kong or Tokyo. We even got invited to one of the get-togethers with the man himself.

The other route to developing an Ueber-Target requires being closely in touch with cultural undercurrents and tensions that motivate influential groups and create desires in broader segments of the population. Abercrombie and Fitch (A&F) is a great case to study. The brand has had two lives as a desirable lifestyle brand to date. The original A&F was founded in 1892 and catered to the 'genteel explorer', or those who aspired to A&F's celebrity customers like Teddy Roosevelt, Amelia Earhart and John Steinbeck. After the demise of these Ueber-Heroes and the decline of the brand, The Limited Inc (now known as L Brands Inc) bought it in 1988. Mike Jeffries was appointed CEO and went about transforming the brand behind the ultimate teenage Ueber-Target:

> We go after the cool kids... with a great attitude and a lot of friends. A lot of people don't belong, and they can't belong. Are we exclusionary? Absolutely. Those companies that are in trouble are trying to target everybody: young, old, fat, skinny... You don't alienate anybody, but you don't excite anybody, either (Denizet-Lewis, 2006).

And excite they certainly do. While some outdoor and heritage references persist, the emotional pull emanates mostly from a pure but powerful pan-eroticism that excites the young strategic target and meets them at all touch-points with the brand. From the shirtless youngsters who greet you at the door to the heavy cologne 'Fierce' that fills the air and the 'racy' photography on the walls by Bruce Weber, the company's famously provocative photographer. The fact that the American Decency Association or equal employment activists were upset at one point, tells the kids that Abercrombie is definitely cool and worth the US $100 for an otherwise run-of-the-mill sweater. Jeffries left the brand at the end of 2014 and so have quite a number of his Ueber-Target kids, especially in the US, making some predict the end of this success story. But we might see A&F regain its footing, yet again, if it succeeds in rekindling the love affair with those that made it big in the first place, the cool jocks.

For a company-groomed design target that's the opposite of a popular playboy, look no further than Harley Davidson. The quintessential Harley rider is a rocker, a rugged libertarian who plays with the boundaries of society and the law to a breaking point. Harley Davidson recognizes the fascination of men with groups like the Hells Angels as modern manifestations of the rebelliously independent and domineering American 'gunfighter'. As Douglas Holt shows in his book *How Brands Become Icons* (Holt, 2004), Harley skilfully made the outlaw myth its own and harnessed its most dedicated followers by penetrating Harley Owner Groups (HOGs), the modern day (and 'legalized') version of a cowboy posse. Their strategic target? Suburban 'weekend warriors' whose careers, family and comfort might keep them from living the outlaw dream every day, but who earn the money to buy a US $25,000-plus bike and 'feel' it on occasion.

Modern Ueber-Brands have 'Ueber-Targets' in the form of real or imaginary people who represent the brands and make us want to be with them... and not others. This might be jet-setting Tory or Tyler as opposed to the 'suburbans'. Or it might be the Harley rider proudly roaring out of his middle-class comforts, showing his fingerto all of them – at least on the weekend when he joins his HOG buddies.

Longing and belonging online

While being accessible to everyone every time, the internet can yet be a perfect place to put up 'velvet ropes', celebrating your Ueber-Targets in the most modern ways, fostering a sense of prestige that's only a click away, and yet so far...

Net-a-Porter (NAP), the luxury fashion e-tailer and lifestyle medium born in 2000, elevates its Ueber-Target – high-net-worth but time-deprived fashonistas – to 'EIPs' (Extremely Important Persons) and leverages them to build desirability. It delights these heavy shoppers (they spend 20 times more than the average) in very intimate, yet publicly visible ways, from a personalized look-book and free magazine to assigned personal shoppers, from pre-release exclusives and dedicated limited editions to same-day hand deliveries complete with bow-tied boxes and, on occasion, a little thank you surprise if they are in London, New York, Hong Kong or Shanghai. The average browser and 'normal' NAP shoppers – they still spend several thousand dollars a year – will know about this elite and their privileges from the site and from comments and blog posts in which EIPs rave about their beautiful outfits and the delightful service experiences. This broader target, however, has to stay outside, gawk, dream and wait for its turn to receive a 'what's new for you' e-mail, which will feature items that are still available. The 'velvet rope' principle played to modern, digital perfection.

Vogue quite officially leverages a hand-picked online 'Influencer Network' to increase its taste-making impact and reach a millennial target. Formed in 2011, the network is an exclusive club of about 1,000 bloggers deemed to have the passion, style, savvy and sway to influence followers in their fashion and beauty decisions. As Susan Plagemann, VP of publishing told us: 'There are a lot of self-appointed experts'. *Vogue* will only pick those with flair and a substantial influence'. There was an outcry by the blogger community about seemingly arbitrary selection criteria and about the fact that *Vogue* did not compensate network members for endorsements. But the reactions demonstrate the power of the Ueber-Brand and of such exclusive-inclusive social networks. 'Before it's in fashion it's in *Vogue*' applies here: bloggers want to be associated with *Vogue* and sing praises about 'being chosen'. Avid followers are reading the lips of the anointed ambassadors to guide them, and *Vogue* all the while multiplies its allure and advertising income.

MINI is a mighty Ueber-Brand (see case study, Principle 4) that leverages the web in multiple ways and community levels to create shared rituals, bonds and distinguish and elevate its fans. Enthusiasts can get on the 'configurator' to design their own MINI from a theoretical 10 million possibilities. Those who make the leap and become 'expecting MINI owners' will be admitted to the 'MINI Owners Lounge' to track the 'birth' of their custom car, and 'MINI Space' is 'where like-minded MINI fans meet to prove [...] they're the most colourful people on four wheels', we are told. But the brand also stays closely connected to its Design Target, from creating the global 'MINI Clubman Photo Awards' to distributing Ramadan Art car graffiti stickers to its most engaged MINI bloggers in the Emirates.

Moleskine, the brand that brought the notebook back to fame and practically 'owns' it today for all intents and purposes, is even more inventive. In a long interview, co-founder Maria Sebregondi explained in depth how the brand stays connected with their Ueber-Target of 'creative professionals and knowledge workers' and leverages their appeal to foster the brand's fan base allure. Apart from offline sponsorships and programmes they do an unparalleled amount of community building online, for instance through free apps and templates, which creative people can fill with thoughts and ideas and then share again with a wider audience – inspiring them as well as imbuing the brand with a sense of cultural cool (see moleskine.com/mymoleskine). Overall they are very much concerned with not just 'being human in the digital age' but bridging analogue and digital experiences, launching and supporting groundbreaking projects, for instance in partnership with Livescribe or Voyageur books. All this is mostly marketing expense for now since many of these projects and products are so forward-thinking that their economic value is still limited. But their power to connect with Ueber-Targets and keep them infatuated with the brand and thus create a cult you long to belong to is undeniable.

Perfect storytelling from analogue to digital and back again – Netbooking by Moleskine

Image courtesy of Moleskine, Zucker Kommunikation

All four examples show there are many different ways to turn the essentially democratic digital medium into one that celebrates exclusivity and discrimination in the most modern ways. Actually it can work better than any other: while the 'velvet rope' is often so discreet in the real world that only die-hards can see it, it's all out in the open in our virtual one. Letting us belong whilst at the same time being made to long, portraying the privilege of being 'in' as at our fingertips – yet a touch beyond.

Velvet roping 2: Laying low to stay up

The CEO of Porsche allegedly once said 'When I see two Porsches in the same street I begin to worry'. Now, in certain cities he would have more than anxiety attacks today, given the prevalence of this German icon of car making. But the quote says it all.

The second way to walk the fine line between 'longing and belonging' is less about the people and more about the products, or rather the perceived scarcity of them. It's still about the velvet rope, but one that separates 'in' and 'out' less through 'being' and more through 'having'. It's not so much about the aspiration of wanting to be part of a certain group, but about the desire stoked by dividing consumers into 'haves' and 'have-nots'. Creating exclusivity through rarity – and making all those who don't yet 'have' willing to go through hoops of cash to change that and 'upgrade' their status. Not a very new approach, but still as potent as ever.

The most obvious way to achieve this kind of social divide is simply to price certain consumer segments out. It's as old as any exchange of goods and it worked for aeons: lately it has even been neuro-scientifically proven. According to a 2008 study by the Stanford Graduate School of Business and the California Institute of Technology, 'if a person is told he or she is tasting two different wines –and that one costs US \$5 and the other US \$45 when they are, in fact, the same wine – the part of the brain that experiences pleasure will become more active' when the drinker thinks he or she is enjoying the more expensive vintage (Trei, 2008, accessed August 2014). But, price is neither as controlling nor as compelling as it once was. The more people can trade up and afford luxuries, even if just occasionally, and the more brands need to reach out and down in order to keep growing, the harder it is to use price as the ultimate gatekeeper. Large parts of the global population have reached the middle-class, with enough money to allow access to more and more luxuries, even if just in parts. In addition, there is hardly a prestige brand without a lower-priced, 'junior' or 'bridge' line – except for some stalwart French luxury houses like Hermès or Chanel. And even those have 'entry' products to expand their franchises, such as fragrances or accessories. The effect is that exclusivity is eroding, purchase by purchase. Luxury is losing its lustre (Thomas, 2007). Because if everybody can theoretically have it, its worth for social distinction is limited – or so the thinking, or rather feeling, goes.

However, it's not just growing wealth that undermines economically driven exclusivity. Again, it's also our growing knowledge of marketing and overall commercial experience that forces modern prestige brands to develop more subtle and less predictive ways to keep us longing. In the Experience Economy (Pine & Gilmore, 1999), buying your way in is not as rewarding as it once was. Even teenagers have felt for quite a while that 'everybody can do expensive', and while this may only be the reality of a limited socio-demographic crowd, the attitude is widespread – way beyond those who can actually 'do expensive' (Krueger and Schaefer, 1995). **Cash and other crude and obvious status dividers have lost their power. We are looking for more intricate and intelligent challenges, to pass more specific 'tests' to make 'the cut' meaningful, to make ourselves ultimately feel luxuriated and elevated.** In an environment where everything is more or less available, it's what money can't buy that's becoming truly valuable. And in the Information Age that's knowledge.

You know, or you don't

The Hermès Birkin bag is by pretty much all accounts the most famous handbag in the world. Why? Well, for one it's been iconic since its birth in 1984, not least because of the lovely story connecting it to the iconic French singer-actress Jane Birkin. Then of course it's very well crafted, made of the finest leather by superior artisans working on it for multiple days, like all things from the venerable French luxury house. And it's pretty pricey, starting at around US $10,000 for the 'basic' version, going easily up to US $100,000 for special ones, made from crocodile or ostrich skin. What really puts it at the top of desire, however, is its limited – and hushed – supply. The craftsmanship and materials are so exceptional there was always a waiting list, but that was abolished in April 2010. Now you can only commission special orders, as the ex-Directrice des Metiers at Hermès, Corinne Dauger, told us – which you need to know about. You can no longer put your name on a list and save until it's your turn. You can't work, wait and pay your way to bliss. Now it's pretty much beyond your control. It's up to lady luck and the discretion of the sales clerks to decide if you'll ever have the chance to strut your stuff. And we all know how unpredictable either of those can be. In other words, the Birkin bag, just like its smaller sister the Kelly bag by the way, have entered the realm of those rarefied possessions that the gods bestow upon you – or not. That's what makes them the epitome of modern prestige, despite having been around for decades – keeping them desirable beyond belief.

Hermès is actually so restrained (or ethical, depending on your perspective), that they barely make exceptions for celebrities, and certainly don't hand out freebies, as Dauger assured us. All that certain VIPs might get is preferred service. They still have to wait and pay like everybody else – and are happy to do so, as Victoria Beckham shows again and again. Because it not only confirms but qualifies their fame. It shows the world that they are respected or at least connected and valued enough to be part of the chosen few. Of course it still does happen that once in a while even one of those 'Real Housewives' is seen with a Birkin... there does exist a big secondary market after all (Jacobs, 2013). By and large, though, the Hermès bags are traded the way only very rare diamonds or blue chip art are – in backrooms, very discreetly and only among those in the know, or those who are known. The rest of us are left to admire them longingly from a distance.

There is an interesting side effect: as with all extraordinary feats, the 'acquisition drama' connected to a Birkin inspires a naturally self-perpetuating social dynamic. Those who 'succeed' will share their experience, adding a bit here or there, to celebrate their perseverance and social cunning, but also to neutralize a potential buyer's remorse.* With each account the mystique of the brand is heightened until it reaches mythical proportions, driving its desirability – but also the pride and protectiveness of its owners. Never mind the social currency of the celebrated objects.

But you don't have to be an haute-luxury purveyor or product to apply this idea of 'laying low'. A much less pricey and rarefied brand that's been seen using the same tactic and has given itself a bit of modern prestige is Panera Bread (panerabread.com), the eponymous café-bakery that's been taking North America by storm in the past few years. Go figure: sandwiches and salads as secrets only to be shared if you pass a social sense check, so to speak. But it seems to be working. Panera has established a 'hidden menu' of healthy, daily-changing items that's only available for those in the know. It's not listed in the store menu or on chalkboards with the other daily offerings, and not even volunteered by the waiters upon inquiry. Only if you're part of the 'Panera Club', have heard about it from your friends or found it hidden on the company website, will you be able to order and enjoy… giving you the feeling of being part of a community of culinary cool, insiders that are 'family' with special access and special service. This is not unlike what the chef's tables at Michelin-starred restaurants have done more and more in recent years – even though insider knowledge is not always required.

What makes Panera's 'Hidden Menu' or Hermès' handbags stand out in a very modern way, giving the brands an 'Ueber' flair is that you have to know about the brand, its inner workings and the ways to 'pass' into the sanctum of 'brother or sisterhood'. **It's a customer selection via insider knowledge, implying that only if you are as special as they are will you find out about them and gain access.** Or conversely, they make you as special as they seem to be if you do so. It's just like those cool clubs that are in hidden alleys, behind pawn shops or other obscure covers, without any door signage, so only those in the know will find them. They are so restrained and reserved that you very often don't even see the velvet rope. But you most certainly feel it as soon as you try to get close.

Catch me if you can

The other, more established, democratic and thus also mundane approach to 'laying low' and keeping us longing is to limit supply very openly – by season, by edition or by distribution. **Let the product be available only at very**

---

*Another indicator of desirability: There has been more than one book and blog written entirely about how to *Bring Home the Birkin* (title of a book by Michael Tonello, 2009).

defined times, places or quantities and thus make it much more desirable, presenting it as a true catch.

The premium confectionery from Ferrero called Mon Chérie that is very famous in Europe and somewhat of the grand dame of seasonally limited distribution. It's a cherry-filled chocolate that's only available during the winter months, because traditionally the summer heat made it logistically hard to secure stability. Nowadays logistics may still be somewhat of an issue, but for the most part it's just become a very successful marketing gig, taking the product off-shelf during the anyway slow summer months and ensuring a big re-entrance every year in autumn. Of course, the principle in itself is nothing new, having forever been practised by Mother Nature and her little helpers, be it in form of the Beaujolais Nouveau or the annual white asparagus craze in Germany. But it's interesting to see how many brands or small specialty shops are playing with it these days without any true need, simply to give themselves specialty status. And how we still buy into it, knowing full well that it's nothing but a scheme to build up desire and cash. Or, perhaps it's simply a nostalgic longing on our part, a yearning to step out of a 24/7 all-access-everywhere world and re-enter the days where we'd live by the rhythm that the Earth, Moon and Sun prescribed. It lets us feel part of something bigger, enjoy the ebb and flow of life and cherish the fact that not all is in our control – with the added hope that all this is also much more genuine, healthy and true.

In the same way as restricting your offer by season, limited editions have increased as a staple of building prestige. It's the easiest and still most profitable way to get people to buy something they already have or don't need and build the brand's equity at the same time.

Nothing will make us run for the shops like the feeling that something may no longer be there tomorrow. We all experience the effect at least once a year, when we're travelling. The fact alone that certain merchandise is locally specific (lo and behold in this globalized world!) and unavailable at home every day, loosens our purse strings considerably. Now imagine a product is limited per se. Not just because it's far away or expensive, but because there are only so many made. It automatically turns the opportunity to get one into a divine present, a lucky chance we would be foolish not to act upon, elevating brand and products into quasi-collectors' items, with a respective value increase and resale market. We can almost look at it as an investment, rather than an indulgence, and that helps both our rational justification as well as our emotional motivation.

MINI is playing on this brilliantly. Even as sales go into the hundreds of thousands these days, they are avoiding omnipresence by following a variant (ie horizontal) rather than a volume (ie depth of sale) proliferation. As at end 2014 MINI was on its 11th model in as many years after its re-introduction. Each model brings their interpretation of a distinct car class such as an SUV, a cabriolet, a sports car or a cross-over. This keeps the cars still feeling rare and more special than other mass-market cars and it plays to the brand's counter-cultural equity, as well as the buyers' desired individuality. The significantly above-average value retention is a nice bonus. But be careful: there is a fine balance between style and model proliferation, between limiting certain editions and changing your product every so often. The latter achieves the exact opposite of the former, and this has been a trap many carmakers have fallen into. Each time you issue a new, upgraded model, you automatically make the previous one less valuable. Step by step you're eroding your equity. That's why it's important to stick with the core of the product, but re-interpret it again and again: change the wrapping, but not the content. That way the product becomes perceived as timeless and beyond competitive pressure, and the re-interpretation of each edition is seen as a celebration of the product's iconic status rather than tinkering with or fixing something insufficient (see also Principle 5). You're building a positive spiral of compounding value that lets product and brand shine stronger and stronger with each version. Your customers bask in its glow and the security of knowing that what they bought has lasting value – if not forever, so at least for eternity.

Lastly, there's limiting your distribution: upgrading yourself by curtailing ubiquity. Redken, the semi-professional hair care brand, still likes to communicate that it's 'only available at professional salons' although everybody can find it stocked at every corner drugstore. This way they try to keep the allure – and the price point – of professional brands versus pure retail ones. Stihl, the German manufacturer of premium power tools, has for a long time run advertising proudly touting that they are 'not available at Lowes or Home Depot', the two dominant home improvement retailers in North America, arguing that only the service of smaller, specialty retailers are appropriate for their level of quality and their demanding customers.

The disproportionate growth of airport-shopping is also built on this idea. The Chinese alone make 25 per cent of all luxury purchases at airports (JingDaily, February 2013, accessed May 2014). This 'prestige purchase power' of airports is certainly not only rooted in their audiences being somewhat captive, enchanted that they made it past security. It's just as much because airports still provide a somewhat glamorous context of travel and leisure for many of us. They connect to the wide world, the idea of jet-setting to dreams, a cosmopolitan, sophisticated lifestyle. They are everywhere and we are often there, and yet they are special. And that's exactly the right balance that modern prestige or Ueber-Brands need in order to make themselves available yet anything but common.

All three ways of overtly limiting availability have been around forever, but they've been much more widely used in recent years, way beyond their traditional fields of fashion, gourmet food or accessories. Just like modern prestige has cast a much wider net – across borders and categories.

Principle 2: The rules of 'longing and belonging'

1 Reach high
> The best way to win up is to establish an aspirational design target.

2 Yes, but
> Carefully balance proximity and distance with the velvet rope. Let us be a part – but never completely.

3 Include to exclude
> Depending on your target, involve them openly in the game of building exclusivity. It tickles their marketing smarts.

4 Lay low
> Make sure to never be over-present but to always be seen as a present.

5 Let some know
> And others not. Knowledge is the most powerful divider these days.

6 Limit
> By season, edition or distribution. Less is always more. Now even – or again – in commodities.

To keep their targets longing while belonging, Ueber-Brands apply the 'Velvet Rope'. Connecting all their fans in one community, yet on different levels, with an inner sanctum for their Ueber-Target, those who epitomize their ideal.

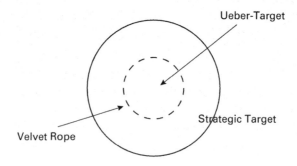

Ueber-Brand case study 2 Red Bull – longing to have wings

Red Bull (RB), the pick-me-up drink coveted by hyperactive teens, truck drivers and drowsy professionals alike, has built buzz about being an energy-giving potion since the late '80s. The concept has existed for a long time – Lucozade was commercialized as a 'recovery drink' in the '30s in the UK, for example – but nobody has ever achieved the kind of Ueber-Status of Red Bull. It all started when Austrian Dietrich Mateschitz discovered an oriental energy concoction called 'Krateng Dang' (Red Water Buffalo) while fighting jet-lag on a business trip to Asia. Thinking that it would have been a god-send during his cramming and partying student days, he was so intrigued that he decided to quit his marketing manager job and partnered with the Thai manufacturer of Krateng Dang. Then followed a five-year journey of adapting the formulation, pack, name and communication ('Red Bull Gives You Wings'), finding a bottler, miserably failing in taste tests and focus groups… but launching anyway, in 1987 in Austria. Many of the iconic sampling events later and having depleted all his life savings (an estimated US $2 million), Red Bull started to make money in 1990 with US $6 million in sales. From there, the brand expanded into Europe (1994) and the Americas (1997) – except where it was banned (more on that below). As of 2013, the brand is sold in over 140 countries with revenue exceeding well over $11 billion dollars – a compound annual growth rate of almost 40 per cent, far exceeding industry averages.

Longing to belong to the 'Dare Devils'

Red Bull's design target is people addicted to adrenaline rushes, be they x-sports athletes, stuntmen, race pilots of all types, rock stars or DJs. These people play a central role in the brand's events and in seducing the broader strategic target, because RB has mastered the art of the 'velvet rope' big or small. Let a few of the groupies and influencers 'in' on the heroes' challenge but always with plenty of others left to admire, desire and dream from the sidelines.

Take Frenchman Cedric Garcia, one of the pioneering winners of the Utah 'Red Bull Rampage' mountain biking competition in 2003. This event became so extreme that it had to be suspended for several years to figure out how to protect the lives of the riders. What made Cedric's victory a particular tease to fans in his home country was the fact that Red Bull and its stunts were banned there at the time. The victory stoked excitement and fed new members to an underground group of 'bootleg' Red Bull consumers. RB raised the stakes that year when it sent a man flying across the English Channel, dropping him from 33,000 feet to land 22 miles later in the forbidden territory – Felix Baumgartner's first collaboration with the brand.

National laws are rather large and symbolic 'velvet ropes' to jump over, but the brand shows a lot of finesse when it comes to managing the balance between 'longing and belonging'. Like most RB events, the Rampage is by invitation-only for the riders. Consequently there is a lot of pride involved in being part of the 'inner circle' and an entire trade exists around the exclusive gear that commemorates such events. The Red Bull Music Academy (RBMA) is another great example of managing the balance. Jeff Klingman of *The L Magazine* describes it as 'a highbrow combination of academic salon and experimental art fair… that teeters on an unpredictable line between transcendence and disaster' (Klingman, 2014). Artists submit their portfolios for chance to be selected for the month-long 'meeting of the minds', taking place each time in a different hip hot-spot. The festival around the RBMA is the only part where everybody else gets a chance to peek in and experience the vibe.

Red Bull has found all these events so effective in creating attention and desire that it is putting on hundreds of them every year from 'Collective Art Project' to 'Can You Make It' to 'BC One'… the list is endless. They are sometimes humorous, mostly physically demanding, often extreme and always exhilarating. They range from local soapbox derbies to NASA-like missions and never fail to impress for being unique and authentic expressions of the brand's daredevil spirit. Their mechanism is always the same: first, a select few are chosen to live out the Red Bull experience directly and tell about it, then a select crowd of influencers, supporters and spectators are admitted to bear testimony and fuel the hype. Finally, there is RB's Media House and Content Pool to ensure the amazing visuals and commentaries are dispersed to as wide an audience as possible – while keeping control and not over-commercializing it.

Fatal accidents have happened. In 2009, Swiss high-rise BASE jumper Ueli Gegenschatz and Canadian extreme skier Shane McConkey died infront of RB cameras rolling. While polarizing, the design target seems to experience these tragic incidents as further proof of the daring spirit of their heroes and their brand. From further out, the broader strategic target might be puzzled and scared, but they are certainly intrigued and looking at that can of Red Bull with a sense of respect that only dangerous and forbidden fruits provide.

Mission and myth: 'Giving Wings'

The headboard of the Red Bull website reads 'Giving Wings to People and Ideas' (energydrink-us.redbull.com). This mission is – literally – brought to life through the events enticing people to perform at the very edge of their physical and mental capacities. And it comes with an army of missionaries in the form of 'Wing Teams', driving around in MINIs with huge Red Bull cans strapped on their backs, spreading the gospel and handing out samples to ravers, taxi drivers, shift workers or anyone else in need of an energy jolt. The fact that the teams are often skimpily clad girls ensures a rather memorable uplift – at least for the male prospects.

The myth of Red Bull could be summed up like this: *'Red Bull provides super-human powers and hallucinatory experiences'.* A central part to this myth is the red, medicinal-tasting juice and its mysterious ingredient 'taurine'. Rumours re-emerge regularly that taurine is extracted from *bull's bile, urine or even their testicles.** Clubbers helped spin the myth from the get-go by mixing* RB with vodka, calling it 'liquid cocaine' or 'speed in a *can'*. Some claim it works like Viagra. The party island of Ibiza became a natural epicentre of consumption and a source of endless brand lore.

No wonder Red Bull has been treated with suspicion by regulatory bodies and parents alike. But bans such as the one in France or Down Under tend to only make the 'forbidden tin' more irresistible to youngsters. The brand recognized the appeal behind the polarizing myth early on: 'In the beginning, the high-school teachers who were against the product were at least as important as the students who were for it', Mateschitz told *Businessweek* in 2011 (McDonald, 2011). And RB language tries to keep the myth growing: 'Red Bull Supernatural' is a snowboarding competition. Their break dance championship is described as an 'epic break dance battle, [and] superhuman showcase of physical strength' (redbullbcone.com, accessed July 2014). In the end, though, who needs words when you see Red Bull contestants surf a ferocious tidal surge up an Amazon estuary for over half an hour, trying to avoid debris, logs, piranhas and other lethal obstacles!?

---

* In case you wanted to know, taurine is a sulfonic acid that is found in many bodily systems including humans. It was first isolated in the bile of an ox in 1827 hence the name derived from the Latin 'Taurus'. The taurine used in energy drinks is synthetically made and labelled as 2-aminoethanesulfonic acid.

The adrenaline-infused world of Red Bull from a break-dance jump to Garcia jumping off a cliff and Baumgartner jumping into the stratosphere. The Wing Team girls are never far, to feed fans with the magic potion (in this case in Bangkok)

Images Courtesy of Red Bull Media House. Photos: John Gibson, Jay Nemeth, Dean Treml

Behold: The Bull!

The Red Bull can is right up there in iconic package heaven with the Coke bottle – except that people pay about 3–4 times more per ounce for it. The brand has not touched the design of the compact 250ml silver and blue can with its thick aluminium walls (as if to contain high-energy content better) since its introduction in 1987, at least not to the layperson. They have, however, found impactful ways to imprint it onto our subconscious – in the form of an oversized icebox strapped on top of those MINIs or the backs of the Wing Teams, or morphed into fuel pumps as convenience store displays. The key elements – logo, charging bulls, and colours – appear repeatedly on the gear of the Red Bull contestants and their playing fields.

Clearly, events and sampling is where the Red Bull action and investment is and where it seems unbeatable. The making and filling of the drink, on the other hand, has always been outsourced and the R&D department must be small compared to other FMCG companies, given their low number of 'new' or 'improved' type of initiatives otherwise so common to the industry. Red Bull tried to enter the variant game late in 2003 with no-sugar, fruit flavours, cola, shots and limited editions but they never had much success. Its 'holy grail' clearly lies away from the supermarket floors and their perennial pricing battles. For example in bars, where Red Bull becomes part of a ritual and generates about a third of its sales at a significant premium over other 'soft drinks' – Red Bull Jaeger bomb, anyone?

Live it, don't sell it

Raymond Dulieu, owner of Freecaster.tv and Kjerag, agencies that have developed many events with Red Bull, explained to us how they bring the brand to life: 'The events are in total alignment with the brand's equity: you stimulate the mind to create the flying machine, and you stimulate the body in taking part in this large fun festival. It is of course not spelled out that way, but that is the message that is unconsciously anchored in the consumer's mind'. Red Bull and extreme sports are so intertwined that the editors of *Outside* magazine think that without the brand 'it's unlikely the extreme-sports boom would have happened at all' (*Outside* magazine, 2011).

What started because Mateschitz did not have the funds for major sponsorships turned out to be a blessing in disguise, leading the brand to a symbiotic relationship with its design target. Extreme sports had a very small circle of fans in the early days, but they were passionate ambassadors and brought in more and more – athletes and fans. To this day the brand supports talent like Baumgartner or Sebastian Vettel, and has done so from early in their careers. Vettel was nurtured and financed from the tender age of eleven. Rather than slapping their logo on his and other cars, Red Bull helped him build it, as they did his first go-cart before that. The Stratos space jump was conceived, planned, and executed by Red Bull and was seven years in the making. This is how to explain over a billion dollars in marketing expenditure but only a small share spent on the classic mass-marketing tools like adverting or in-store promotions (Döhle, 2012).

The fact that Red Bull is privately owned of course helps them to go these unorthodox and seemingly long and winding ways: Mateschitz can afford to be patient for payout. But, eventually, that payout comes, in the form of unique content such as a ninety-minute exclusive chat with Vettel just after winning his first F1 Championship title, which was streamed over Red Bull's Servus TV channel and website. The Stratos mission, conservatively estimated, generated media exposure worth US $170 million, with more than eight million people viewing it online and creating a social media firework (Hearne, 2012).

Such exclusive access and complete content control, ahead of anyone else, makes Red Bull a formidable extreme sports and lifestyle media powerhouse in its own right. This new media company is rather secretive though. Rumour has it that Mateschitz reviews all requests for interviews and that he still on-boards most new hires personally – no small feat when you have over 9,500 people operating in 160 countries. The little you can find out about the company and organization fits the bill of 'living the brand'. The offices are futuristic buildings shaped like volcanoes ready to burst, pierced by giant waves or featuring spirals that recall the trace patterns left by skaters, snowboarders or stunt planes. There are slides and skateboard ramps as alternatives to the stairs. The corporate culture leans on the experience of its founder, all about the underdog who achieves epic feats despite the predictions. The hiring of key employees and partners can be its own endurance test. Joseph Roberts, who was to become distributor for Australia-New Zealand, found all his inquiry e-mails were being ignored. So he flew over to Austria, camped outside the HQ in the snow until they let him in. The guerilla marketing plan he presented got him the distributorship. Nobody minded that he was a total novice in the beverage business (Cooney, 2006).

Red Bull is obsessive about owning or tightly controlling all core ingredients of its 'buzz creation' via a wide network of closely associated companies or long-time suppliers. 'Red Bull Creative' is the internal Agency, 'Red Bull Media House' and 'RB Content Pool' control content and there are film production companies, Red Bull TV stations, a *Red Bulletin* magazine, etc. Red Bull event managers and their teams are kings of their specific projects, which are formed into semi-independent divisions like Red Bull AirRace or RB Crashed (downhill skating obstacle race). Red Bull owns and operates not only dozens of sports teams (eg soccer and ice hockey across Germany, Austria, Brazil and the United States) but also purpose-built Red Bull Arenas (eg for the soccer team the New York Red Bulls in New Jersey). Red Bull Racing and Scuderia Rosso also own Red Bull Technology to develop proprietary equipment. There is even a Red Bull Diagnostics and Training Center for associated athletes to evaluate and heighten their performance, and a spectacular fleet of promotional airplanes, helicopters, ships – including a submarine.

Growth without end – from energy to experiences

Red Bull's expansion has been always internally funded, creating 'organic' growth. Awareness and desire came before broad availability. There was neither money nor interest, and sometimes not even legal opportunity, to distribute ahead of demand and drive sales through discounts and promotion. And it makes sense that way, as the product clearly is not about winning taste tests but about myth building. Thus, 'growing upwards and within' takes the form of ever more creative and challenging stunts and experiences. Driving the dedication of the design target while increasing awareness and force of association. There is some horizontal extension into accessories and event auxiliaries – think of the Red Bull Crashed Ice beanie – but the biggest income potential can be found within the ever-growing brand-owned media and event assets and their loyal following. Red Bull's over 600 athletes feed endless content into its YouTube channel of over 3.5 million followers (as of July 2014), compared to half a million for Coke or Monster Energy or 1.5 million for ESPN – and that is not even their focus channel. It won't be surprising to see Red Bull increase the monetization of their channels and events. The brand has already started selling advertising and sponsorships, and divisions like Red Bull Media House or the Red Bull Signature Series franchise are reported to have switched from marketing expenditures to being profit contributors (Jessop, 2012). Looking ahead, the business might naturally migrate from 'can' to 'can join', sourcing revenue no longer primarily from drinks sold at the bull fight but from the tickets sold to enter the arena – premium priced tickets, that is. Turning the energy soda more and more into an energy experience – as befits a strong and no-limits Ueber-Brand.

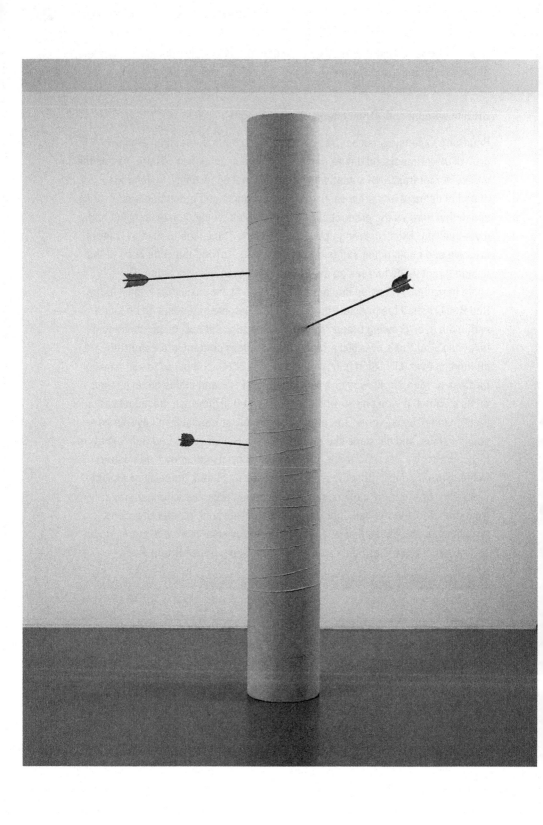

Principle 3
Un-selling
The superiority of seduction

The the previous principle explained in detail how modern prestige or Ueber-Brands navigate the fine line between proximity and distance, making themselves available, but never too much, so that we keep on aspiring or 'longing to belong' to the 'chosen few' – the 'Velvet Rope Principle'. This restrained and calibrated approach in their stakeholder – and particularly consumer – relationships doesn't however only apply to the targeting or distribution strategies of Ueber-Brands. It's actually most important and becomes most visible in their interactions that we are all privy to, even if we are not their customers and never will be: their communication.

Ueber-Brands must seduce more than they sell. They need to present themselves very differently from mass brands. Their biggest challenge is to create an image and an aura that attracts us, rather than attack us with big-mouthed sales pitches and low-priced super-offers. They have to pull our heart strings but should never be seen as pushing too hard. And in order to do that they turn the traditional rules of marketing communication and advertising on their head to a large degree. They Un-sell – mainly in four ways:

The first aspect, 'Of pride and provocation' is the most direct and obvious translation of balancing proximity and distance in communication. Ueber-Brands don't try to please us. They want to impress us. They go through great pains to make it very obvious that they aren't 'bossed' around by anybody, including their consumers. It's the brand that is boss here. They talk to us with a clear sense of self and confidence, often bordering on arrogance. They are proud, with a strong penchant for being provocative – if for no other reason than to show they can.

The second, 'Avert the overt' is, alas, more subtle and intricate. Here it's not about showing strength or clarifying mutual positions but about creating a certain intrigue and mystique. Evoking more than you are actually saying. Building a sense of mystery and leaving room for discovery, all with the goal of stoking desirability.

'It's an Art', the third aspect, is about the traditionally close relationship between prestige brands and art, which has lately been growing closer and closer, to the point that some are already afraid they could strangle or suffocate each other. While the first is clearly commercial and the latter ideally not so much, they both usually strive for something 'higher'. In that sense they can very much help and complement each other, one supporting the other through deeper pockets, the other validating the first through its respectability. Consequently it's a vast and very popular terrain for Ueber-Brands, but not without its dangers as we shall see.

The last point is the most recently developed one, but one which has rapidly grown to become key in 'Un-selling' Ueber-Brands: 'Walk the talk'. As 'Un-selling' is all about finding ways to communicate and connect with your target without appearing too eager or gauche, this makes perfect sense, because here it's practically not about selling anymore at all. Instead of 'paid' media or communication, Ueber-Brands make more and more use of 'earned' and nowadays also 'owned' media. Instead of 'talking' about themselves or their products they start 'walking' right away. Their communication often doesn't look or feel like advertising anymore. They rather present themselves as media, community centres, consultants… providing content, information, entertainment, services or simply access to a 'superior' way of being or a better, more interesting world in general – their world. Their products often literally almost seem like an afterthought, or at least are very cleverly wrapped. The purchase can easily start feeling more like a donation – for privileges already enjoyed. All this is made possible to a large degree through the digital revolution, which allows brands, and particularly modern prestige, to develop new and exciting ways in what was until now often simply called PR, restricted to standard press junkets or buttering up editors.

Of pride and provocation

Every one of us has noticed it a million times: you browse through *Vogue* and most models in the ads look like they're about to kill themselves, staring at us with utter disdain or at least massive ennui. You look at *InStyle* (a popular US beauty magazine) and suddenly they all grin and beam without a worry in the world. This is the most obvious way of the 'velvet rope' idea in communication, 'Un-selling' in action.

There is an old saying in beauty and fashion: 'With every millimeter the mouth opens (towards a smile), the price point goes down a notch'. And, whether we like it or not, there's a lot of truth to it. Low-priced mass brands can be all smiles and approachable in their ads, they even have to be, because their job is to make as many of us as possible like them. Ueber-Brands, however, have a different goal. Even when playing in more accessible tiers and territories they must create an image of superiority and distinction to justify their price point, and that requires their communication to be projecting a different attitude, namely one of confidence and entitlement. Just look at a campaign for Nivea lip gloss, for instance, on Facebook. It's headlined 'Live Life with a Smile' or 'Come Closer', and that's exactly what it does: it lets you break into a smile and makes you want to come closer. All these happy, friendly people and radiant energy instantly create a warm, positive feeling for the brand and the product – as they're supposed to do. Now compare that with Dior Addict for example, the French fashion house's famous and high-priced lipstick/gloss. You see Kate Moss looking at you from above, challenging to the point of being condescending, or Daphne Groeneveld, giving herself a 'head shot' of beauty or looking right through you. The tagline: 'Be Iconic'. Granted, lately Dior has done a commercial and print ad showing Daphne and her 'addiction' in a somewhat more lighthearted manner, stylizing her like a 21st-century Brigitte Bardot. But the basic premise remains. Dior Addict makes you 'iconic', and that's no laughing matter. That is serious work.

The point is that there is no right or wrong, just different ways to communicate if you are a mass brand or want to become an Ueber-Brand. **Mass brands approach you at eye level, in a friendly way, to make a connection. Prestige brands, even if of the modern kind, talk to you from a more privileged and controlling position, to instil a sense of aspiration.** This is most evident in beauty and fashion, which is why a lot of the following examples are from this area. The fact that we often weren't granted permission to reproduce visuals by these brands only supports our case.

A promise of confidence

It's the ultimate prerequisite for any prestige brand to promise you a sense of social elevation. The most immediate and thus also most traditional way of doing this is by showing it outright in the imagery you associate with your brand – hence the phalanx of tight-lipped models in ads or on catwalks. In the modern world this has become a bit more relaxed, and sometimes you even see something like self-irony shimmer through (just think of Lagerfeld's Chanel show in spring 2014 with Cara Delevingne and Rihanna in shopping carts). But it works much easier and faster to make the girls – or guys – look stern and brooding, because we humans have learned over thousands of years to interpret this intuitively as strength: 'This person doesn't need to create an atmosphere of harmony, he or she is not afraid to confront us, because he/she is confident in his or her power.' In transactional terms one would call this an imbalanced relationship. The normal and healthy approach of 'I am OK and you are OK' is replaced by 'I am OK and you are not OK' (Berne, 1964). The message being sent is one of reserve if not derision. But it works, for the most part, like a charm. Of course we won't consciously accept ourselves as being inferior (why would we!?) and some people even react with outright resentment, but most of us involuntarily attribute our opposite with notions of superiority. And in the case of brands this means we instinctively assign them the power to lift us 'up' – where we belong or want to be.

The fun part: this little 'game', as Berne would call it, can work just as well if we are facing people that in reality are weaker than or equal to us. That's why you can look at a meek 18-year-old boy in a Brioni ad for example and can't help but see an air of privilege and entitlement, a promise of strength and confidence. Of course it doesn't hurt that he's leaning against a roman sculpture in an assumingly massive private park and is himself of exceptional beauty. Beauty is always awe-inspiring, and so are grandiose settings, but it's his expression and poise that do the trick, so to speak. His attitude is so severe and sharp that you automatically transfer that to Brioni's tailoring – as well as the brand's position and its resulting badge value.

By the way, Brioni's tagline 'To Be One of a Kind' is in this sense rather old-school and distractive, something that may have worked in yesterday's prestige world, but less so in the modern one. Its clear statement of intent breaks the beautiful spell cast by the visual. It's an overt piece of salesmanship in an otherwise subconsciously seductive piece of communication. And that activates our cognitive system, which immediately starts questioning what we were so close to intuitively gobbling up.

A singular attitude

The other way to project a feeling of strength and superiority is to have the guts to go against the grain: provocation. It's less expected and thus more modern, but it's also more dangerous. Yet that's the point. **When a brand shows the courage to take a clear stance it endears itself to those who want to do the same. It polarizes and that makes it perfect for those who think of themselves as discriminating.** It projects a singular attitude and implies it would be able to imbue you with the same or at least match the one you already have.

What will come to mind here for many are probably the infamous, highly publicized marketing stunts, usually one-offs, that get immediately banned and become thus even more popular: Benetton billboards featuring an AIDS patient; Tom Ford's iconic yet racy 2004 ad where the model Carmen Kass gets a Gucci 'G' shaved into her pubic hair. Or the 1990s' Calvin Klein fashion commercials allegedly bordering on child pornography. Yet, those are one-offs, calculated gimmicks, created for outrage and attention. They are usually in line with the brand's general equity and personality, but taken to an extreme and not their regular way of communication.

A better example, in this case a small upstart of a brand that truly builds itself around a singular, daring attitude is Betones, a Japanese underwear brand for men created in 2009 that's gone global by going against anything you're used to or perhaps want. No sculpted torsos, no European or Brazilian soccer players shot in black and white like Greek gods, no oiled and toned sex appeal whatsoever. Instead they go for the opposite of sex-appeal: quirky, colourful designs often shown on hairy and at least not stereotypically pretty blokes. Yet Betones has managed to become quite a fad, selling their one-size-fits-all product for a whopping US $25 per piece. And that's certainly not only because they present themselves as a 'pioneer of seamless print underwear'. Their functional advantage is negligible, as recent all-out self-tests have proven.

No, it's mostly in the package, so to speak: the attitude they project. Fun underwear is nothing new, but laughs don't get you to this price point. Here you need humour with a punch, which is why Betones takes care to be witty rather than funny, daring not charming. They apply humour, but use it to go against clichés of attractiveness and masculinity. They push further, and are iconoclast more than merely being irreverent. And it's this strength that makes them still feel sexy – although they look anything but.

Betones underwear – no Ueber-Brand, yet, but building modern prestige with a punch, favouring iconoclastic rather than iconic imagery

Image courtesy of Betones

Another example of 'playing the opposite' is 42Below – the premium vodka from down under, New Zealand to be precise, that took the world by storm and was recently taken over by spirits giant Bacardi Limited. Just read the story which the founder Geoff Ross turned into a book (Ross, 2011). You will instantly understand what 'a singular attitude' can accomplish in brand building – and beyond. 42Below's success is almost entirely built on an audacious spirit (no pun intended). The world certainly didn't need another high-end vodka when Ross started in around 2000, some four years after Grey Goose (also owned by Bacardi) and a bevy of others. And all the product awards won by 42Below may be heartfelt, but it's more than dubious that the majority of their fans would be able to taste a difference in a blind test. Actually, Geoff Ross would probably be the first to admit as much. He has said numerous times that what made the brand so successful was not only the high quality of the product (yes, that too) but the way in which it took to the stage. Starting from the first print ads that caused a scandal because they offended a lot of politically correct sensibilities, all the way to the self-mocking tone in which they keep building their legend (see 42below.com) and promote their brand today. How about this one?: 'American celebrities are adopting our vodka like it was a third-world child'. In this way it is exactly the opposite of Grey Goose – the 'big brother' brand that arguably started the trading up of clear liquors and originally inspired Ross – not just in provenance but also in strategy. Where Grey Goose transferred the language of refined French wines and brown liquors onto a product category that didn't know them yet, 42Below turned 'refined' on its head – quite literally actually with its upside-down kiwi logo. They eschewed anything remotely 'cultured' in the conventional sense and went for outright counter-culture, starting their own tradition. Product quality was the only thing where they seemingly adhered to strict standards: everything else was up for grabs. And it seems that Bacardi Limited is smart enough to keep it that way, building a diverse portfolio where they service the sophisticated vodka connoisseur as much as the iconoclast one.

The perfect balance

The last example we want to discuss could in some way be considered one of those 'extreme' cases we initially mentioned, the ones that are more about shock value than true brand building. Yet we found it intriguing as it wonderfully unites both, being proud and a bit stand-offish while simultaneously pushing the envelope. It nicely straddles the line between traditional and non-traditional, where an established high-end brand with tons of pedigree chooses to step out of its corset and jump into the ring. If this too will be just a 'one-off' stunt for publicity or if the brand will truly continue on this balanced path between pride and provocation remains to be seen. In any case it is truly modern in the way it communicates its prestige.

Right around the time of the 2014 Cannes film festival Chaumet, the French haute joaillerie house dating back to the 18th century, launched a new campaign for their Liens jewellery that rattled a few feathers (scan

QR code in Preface to see the campaign). The star: Marine Vacth, new model-turned-actress it-girl who had just released her feature film in Cannes about a high-end teenage prostitute. The subject: a mysterious 'double take' picture that tells a story somewhere between narcissism and lesbianism, both subjects that aren't necessarily consensus building. The effect: from famous to infamous, from nice to must-have, from stodgy to trendy in a cultural nano-second. The trick: dare to go where others around you hardly do, but do so in style. Juxtapose heritage and high-end class with edge and controversy.

Of course Chaumet will not radicalize their image instantly, and neither should they. But they went against expectations and infused the brand with an energy that shows the world that it's still 'with it' even though it's been around for quite a while. They take their heritage and launch it into new frontiers, showing pride with a provocative twist. Ultra-stylish. Super-sexy. Ueber-Brand.

And this is the ideal way of Un-selling in the modern age: mixing pride and provocation. Sell yourself without bowing to your audience too obse-quiously but rather pull their strings. **Show that you are rightfully on the pedestal and that you have the power and the courage to take your audi-ence and our culture forward as only a true leader can and will.** Establish the codes, disrupt them and then put them back together in a new way as befits only an Ueber-Brand. Don't provoke for provocation's sake; that's too obvious and cheap. Neither be blatantly arrogant; that's boring and creates resentment, at least among those accustomed to these tactics. Blend both and oscillate. And should you go too far at one point, stumble or fall, do so gra-ciously. Get up and move on. Because kings – or queens – never say 'sorry'.

How Ueber-Brands turn celebrity endorsements on their head

Celebrities are extremely popular as endorsers. Take David Beckham, the ex-soccer player for instance, who has managed to be 'the face' of Adidas, Breitling, Burger King, Disneyland, Emporio Armani, Gillette, Motorola, Milk (got it?), Pepsi, Sainsbury's, Samsung, Sky TV, just to name a few. All that in addition to seeing products launched under his own name, like a perfume by Coty or underpants by H&M. You could call Mr. Beckham an endorsement mercenary.

While also 'employing' celebrities, Ueber-Brands shy away from those promiscuous endorsers and certainly from the common ways of using them – which usually involve somehow getting the product next to their broad smile. Brands so desperately in need of star-wattage obviously consider themselves less worthy: and that does not work for Ueber-Brands. They might want the uplift – but certainly do not want to be up-staged. Thus they usually turn the relationship between brand and endorser on its head, elevating the brand by showing the celebrity as humble user or as the one paying tribute to the brand. For before God, the king and the Ueber-Brand, we are all equal.

Maggie Cheung as a fan for Mandarin Hotels: celebrity endorsement in an Ueber-Brand way, shared values rather than paid endorsement

She's a fan.

MANDARIN ORIENTAL
THE HOTEL GROUP

To find out why Maggie Cheung is a fan visit mandarinoriental.com · ATLANTA · BANGKOK · BARCELONA · BODRUM · BOSTON · GENEVA · GUANGZHOU · HONG KONG · JAKARTA · KUALA LUMPUR
LAS VEGAS · LONDON · MACAU · MIAMI · MUNICH · NEW YORK · PARIS · PRAGUE · SAN FRANCISCO · SANYA · SHANGHAI · SINGAPORE · TAIPEI · TOKYO · WASHINGTON D.C.

Image courtesy of Mandarin Oriental Hotel Group, photo by Mary McCartney

The Mandarin Hotel has translated the idea of celebrity as fan literally into an iconic campaign. Since 2000 over two dozen famous faces from actors Morgan Freeman or Sophie Marceau to author Frederick Forsyth or architect I.M. Pei have been pictured as 'fans' (the fan also being the logo of the hotel). Their names, professions and the reasons why can be found in the fine print below, together with the note that the hotel is 'donating $10,000 to a charity of the individual's choice in appreciation of their support'. The modest donation suggests that the celebrity volunteered rather than being paid for his or her services – and many are reported to have done so in earned media.

Red Bull might spend hundreds of millions on its events but the extreme athletes performing in them never strike us as hired endorsers. From soap box racers to F1 champion Sebastian Vettel, the focus is on how Red Bull grooms and supports them in their endeavours, not whether they drink Red Bull. Testimony to this organic partnership is the fact that despite hundreds of sponsorships, hardly any formal contracts exist – at least, that's what's being reported.

Nespresso tells us that it was their Club Members who elected George Clooney as brand ambassador. He was 'admitted to the club', in a sense (see also case study, Principle 5). Consequently, the ads play with the idea of Nespresso being more important. 'George Who?' headlines one of them. Similarly, Jeremy Irons, in his ads for Berluti, the prestige shoemaker, is quoted to have been 'initiated by Peter Sellers'.

Some really seminal campaigns take this idea of mutual or reverse endorsement to the top, stylizing themselves as a privilege for the 'celebrity'. Think of the now famous 'J'Adore' commercial where Charlize Theron arrives backstage to model for Dior and is put into an array of timeless icons like Marlene Dietrich, Marilyn Monroe and Grace Kelly. This seriously begs the question: who endorses whom? Charlize, Dior or vice versa?

Avert the overt

The late, great artist Keith Haring, who certainly knew a thing or two about culture, commerce and communication in modern times once said: 'If there's no mystery there's only propaganda'. You could hardly find a better way to summarize this section.

Ueber-Brands prefer their communication to be less than overt, working with allusions to create an illusion, playing 'hide and seek' more often than doing a 'show and tell'. They try to craft a beautiful parallel universe in which the product may be the star but is never put out for sale. Where mass brands make sure their branding and their messages are always loud and clear, prestige brands and particularly modern ones tend to stay more veiled, creating an aura without over-promoting themselves front and centre. Very rarely will you find them touting any ingredients, facts or functional benefits of their products the way you see it during your regular commercial breaks or in mass publications. Yes, even Mercedes or Audi for instance will eventually talk about their miles per gallon, their seat comfort or latest technology. However, they usually wrap them in an enticing narrative (see Principle 5) and/or they reserve this kind of detail for more intimate forms of communication, when you're already lured into the franchise – be it on their websites or in brochures, catalogues etc. In public, they more often than not prefer to tell a story that celebrates the brand and adds another jewel to its crown, like the 2014 Mercedes Benz Super Bowl spot, which launched a new line of cars, but celebrated for the most part all their iconic models of decades past (superbowl-commercials.org).

There are various reasons why Ueber-Brands prefer to 'Avert the Overt' and choose the twilight over the limelight – apart from the fact that the former makes for prettier pictures. For one, overt selling is still considered gauche in certain circles – human or brand. Also, it would undermine any sense of dignity or pride (see previous section).

The main reason for avoiding outright promotion, however, is the air of mystery that Keith Haring talked about, an enigmatic depth, an aura of infinite power and quality.

From mystery to mirage

Prestige or Ueber-Brands need to stir our imagination, because it's our imagination that's much better at creating aspiration than anything else. They want to get our right brain engaged and make sure our left brain stays out of it as much as possible. Critical analysis and questioning would only get in the way of luring us into this beautiful dream they're just creating. They must make us believe that what we're getting is much more than what we're buying, because otherwise the price point could hardly be justified in most instances. In that sense they are the opposite of WYSIWYG (What You See Is What You Get). They are masters of building icebergs, turning us all into 'little princes' who like to see 'a boa constrictor digesting an elephant' where in fact the drawing only shows an old hat to most adult eyes (de Saint Exupery, 1995).

A good example here is the long-standing campaign for Patek Philippe (patek.com), the venerable Swiss watch brand. Under the selling line 'You never actually own a Patek Philippe. You merely look after it for the next generation', they have transformed themselves from a high-priced mechanical watch to a family heirloom. Which makes shelling out over US $10,000 suddenly feel much more like investing in your legacy than indulging yourself, especially once you behold the beautifully crafted timepieces and are educated about all the precious materials and labour that went into them. These are definitely not only made for taking time but for transcending it.

Of course it is much harder – but also much more important – to create this sense of mystery when you don't have a beautiful, substantial and distinctive product such as a fine Swiss watch, when there is 'not much there there', to use Gertrude Stein's famous pronouncement about her childhood home Oakland. Yet this also does happen with modern prestige or Ueber-Brands. They must sometimes not just create mystery, but true mirages. In this they follow the famous thought of Roland Barthes, French philosopher and cultural critic, about the difference between pornographic and erotic photography: the latter 'takes the spectator outside its frame, and it is there that I animate this photograph and it animates me' (Barthes, 1981). It's true for all good pictures, and it certainly should be true for all Ueber-Brand imagery, but in cases where the brand's reputation far outshines its reality it is indispensable. A good example of this is the aforementioned teenage fashion brand Abercrombie and Fitch. They hardly show any product in their ads, for good reason. They let you ogle half-naked lads instead (speaking of eroticism), and how they look without their A&F garb. And if you enter their stores they are lit like a bar or dance club, so that you can hardly see the merchandise, let alone any details. Yet you imagine all that happens 'outside of the frame', before and after you buy the sweater, and this helps you 'animate' the product to the point that it becomes worth the extra money.

For a fresher version of this take Evian, the French spring water and its famous 'Babies' campaign. Not to say that Evian is not a great water from a legendary spring in a pretty little spa town at Lake Geneva, but apparently that story felt too stodgy, or most likely wasn't really compelling enough. After all, there are lots of great spring waters from legendary springs in pretty little spa towns… Whatever the reason, in 1998 the brand decided to move away from advertising anything remotely specific about their product to something completely made up – CGI-crafted to be precise. Telling us to 'Live Young' they started showing computer-generated babies as synchronized swimmers, break-dancing reflections of their adult selves or, most recently, Spiderbaby, the little counterpart to Spiderman. And where the first spot still had at least a connection to water, the last ones don't even bother anymore. All they imply is that Evian rejuvenates. That's hardly an original proposition for water, any water, but least so for a premium one. Yet the originality of the creative idea lets us forget about all that and allowed Evian to take the category high ground. They 'own' water and its generic benefit of 'rejuvenation', which secures their position as the modern prestige bottled water and allows them to charge a nice premium. A true man-made or better yet machine-made mirage that skirts any overt claim yet helps create a stellar Ueber-Brand.

Between in and out

Naturally, sometimes a big chunk of the audience will not completely understand what is being communicated when you are not 100 per cent clear. People might like the Evian babies, but have no idea what they have to do with the product. Or they see the Patek Philippe ads and wonder if they are actually looking at a lease proposal rather than one for purchasing. But this is a price Ueber-Brands gladly pay, especially the ones on the upper end of the spectrum. After all, they don't want everyone to 'get' them – physically as well as intellectually. They are about distinction and separation, and that means intentionally keeping some folks 'out' in order to make the others feel like true 'insiders' – something that insider knowledge is best at today.

When Ueber-Brands do get the 'rubber on the road', so to speak, and share facts and details for the final push, they do this slightly differently as well, for the same reason. They stylize their sales materials much more like education than information. **Rather than looking at the purchase process as a negotiation Ueber-Brands like to make it feel like an initiation where they teach you about the heritage of the brand, the product and how it was made and the care you have to provide in order to be worthy of it.** Look at the little leaflets the next time you buy a box of Godiva chocolates or your Moleskine notebook, the coffee table book accompanying your new Mercedes or the hangtags on a Brunello Cucinelli cashmere cardigan for example. All designed and written to welcome you into a rarefied world of connoisseurs, confirm that this was indeed the right purchase and assuage any buyer's remorse or guilt you might feel: in marketing parlance, 'cognitive dissonance'.

Ueber-Brands are in the business of creating desirability, and they do this by surrounding themselves with an air of mystery. Because mystery inspires discovery, which is what Ueber-Brands need. They want you to be intrigued to discover, to be sucked in rather than feeling sold to. They know that the more you put into something the more you feel you are getting out of it, and the more you're willing to pay. It may feel like magic, but in truth its pure logic.

It's an art

Prestige brands have always aspired in some way to be art. Their products are creatively inspired and meticulously crafted, their packaging is beautifully designed and their prices are set for limited access. Of course their boutiques look and feel more like galleries than shops.

However, this link has in recent years become much stronger, with art having descended to become a more and more widespread status symbol and Ueber-Brands having ascended and broken into the traditionally very restricted museum world. Remember the outrage around the Guggenheim museum in New York launching the show about 'The Art of the Motorcycle' in 1998? Or, shortly thereafter, its Giorgio Armani retrospective? Ten years on nobody so much as blinked anymore when the Metropolitan Museum of New York put up 'Savage Beauty', an exhibit celebrating the designs of the late fashion star Alexander McQueen. Actually, it was the opposite: what was once considered the 'selling-out' of noble-minded cultural institutions is nowadays often hailed as innovative and ends up becoming a big blockbuster, as the McQueen show certainly did. And we are not talking about third-tier provincial museums here, which 'need the money'. And it is a global phenomenon as the show 'Culture Chanel', about the French fashion house, at Beijing's National Art Museum of China demonstrates.

Today, culture and commerce love to help each other – one with money and broad appeal, the other with cachet and legitimacy. Ueber-Brands can gain respect and recognition, cultural institutions or poor artists can afford things they otherwise couldn't and reach audiences they usually might not. As with any relationship, though, the two need to be careful not to lose each other in their embrace. They can easily cut each other's noses despite their beautiful and mutually adoring faces, as a recent article in the *Wall Street Journal* discussed again in conjunction with a Bulgari exhibition at the Houston Museum of Natural Science, which opened right in time for the unveiling of the brand's local flagship store (Gamerman, 2014).

Elevation by association

The oldest and most common way in which the two hook up is called sponsoring, where the rich bondsman (sponsor) pledges to support his loving bride (sponsa). This form of patronage is at least as old as the early renaissance, where the Medici family in Florence not only paid artists for personal commissions but funded public art projects and institutions to build their reputation.

Today there's hardly a major prestige or Ueber-Brand without a sponsoring programme or a foundation to their name. Kering, the world's third-largest luxury group (Gucci, YSL, Bottega Veneta, Chateau Latour *et al*) and its founder Francois Pinault have two museums in Venice alone; Punta della Dogana and Palazzo Grassi. The Fondazione Prada adds a third with its Ca' Corner della Regina and is currently in the process of rebuilding its headquarters south of Milan with star architect Rem Koolhaas. Paris has the Fondation Cartier as well as the Fondation Louis Vuitton, to name just two. And of course pretty much every big art event, show, tour or other cultural activity has their commercial partners posting their names left, right and centre to garner attention and recognition, to the point that they actually sometimes even jump from supporter to headliner, as for example in Chanel's Zaha Hadid-designed mobile art container, which toured the world a couple of years ago, starting in Hong Kong. Some Ueber-Brands, like Red Bull, focus their marketing activities almost entirely on such activities. Though in the case of Red Bull, they don't only sponsor but actually initiate and run a lot of these by themselves, most of them around music (see case study, Principle 2).

Some of the most popular meeting points and melting pots for this eternal yet super-hot romance between art and Ueber-Brands are of course the mushrooming art fairs, particularly the Art Basel franchise now crossing the globe from Basel to Miami to Hong Kong. Frieze, another such art fair franchise, originally from London, has already been dubbed 'the fifth fashion week' (Judah, 2013). Commerce and culture are so intertwined here that it's often impossible to separate the one from the other. Because here, there's not only a shared interest in mutual elevation, there is even a naturally shared target. An aesthetically sensible audience spending a couple of million on a work of art is of course pre-destined to also spend some tens of thousands on a new handbag to go with it. No surprise then that Dior Homme picked Miami Beach to shoot their 2014 Spring/Summer campaign. And not with Miami beach bums – they wouldn't have fit into Dior's notoriously slim tailoring anyway – but with languid aesthetes seemingly just sauntering over from a cool vernissage.

Inspiration through collaboration

The other, more recent phenomenon in the coupling of art and prestige is an even tighter one than the classic sponsorship approach: collaboration. One of the first Ueber-Brands to push this to the forefront of popular culture was certainly Absolut Vodka, introduced globally in 1979. Pretty much from the get-go, the Swedish company centred their marketing around their uniquely shaped, minimalist bottle. Yet this didn't mean they focused on the product or its ingredients, except for the very first ad titled 'Absolut Perfection'. For the most part the campaign took up – and still takes up – all kinds of cultural topics, preferably provocative (see 'Of pride and provocation' on page 86), and visualizes them by styling the bottle and adding captions such as 'Absolut Time', 'Absolut Miami', 'Absolut Out', 'Absolut Impotence' and 'Absolut Fantasy'. There have been more than 1,500 such ads, some of course also product themed, usually around a new flavour like 'Absolut Citron' or usage occasions like 'Absolut Mary'. The most remarkable, however, have always been artist collaborations, starting in 1986 with the king of pop art himself, Andy Warhol, who created a painting of the bottle titled 'Absolut Warhol'. He was quickly followed by Keith Haring, Ed Ruscha, Rosemarie Trockel, Damien Hirst... (absolutartcollection.com). The artworks themselves are now being displayed in the Spirit Museum in Stockholm. Absolut has since moved on to collaborate with lesser-known, up-and-coming artists. Now that their place as a cultural icon is cemented, they need to make sure to stay on the cutting edge...

Many impulses for creative collaborations between commerce and art have come in the past years from the fashion world. Marc Jacobs kicked this off in 2002 by having the iconic Louis Vuitton bags 're-interpreted' by graffiti artist Stephen Sprouse. The collection was instantly sold out. Since then he has done this kind of thing with many others like Takashi Murakami or Yayoi Kusama, shot his campaigns with artists' friends Juergen Teller or Sofia Coppola and collaborated with the likes of Olafur Eliasson for LV's store designs. Many have followed suit, with Saint Laurent and Dior taking the trend to the top in some ways. They almost simultaneously hired Hedi Slimane and Raf Simons respectively as chief designers, both known for their closeness to the arts in general and not their perfect fashion training. The task of Ueber-Brands is to anchor themselves in the culture at large rather than just their category. They must think beyond their products and see themselves as arbiters of style in general. And one of the best ways to become this constant source of inspiration is through collaboration. Creative minds unite.

PS: as said before, it's completely irrelevant that the majority of their consumers probably have no idea who Olafur Eliasson is, or that they won't recognize the light sculpture in LV's 5th Avenue store as one of his or even as an art object at all. All that matters is that the cultural elite sees it, because this is their Ueber-Target, these are the people they need to stay close with and respected by in order for the rest of us to value them as well (see previous principle).

Exception via execution

It almost goes without saying that prestige or Ueber-Brands need to also make sure that their communication is executed and produced in an ueber-normal way. If you want to be exceptional you first and foremost have to look it, and not only in your product and packaging but at every point of contact. That's why many Ueber-Brands, especially those in aesthetically driven categories, invest handsomely in the production values of their campaigns, working mostly with top talents in their respective fields, often celebrities.

Consequently, their ads often feel highly artistic themselves; beautifully staged pictures that communicate on lots of different layers as true art does. Many of their photographers regularly cross over between high-end commercial work and true art photography – like Philip-Lorca diCorcia, David LaChapelle, Irving Penn, Guido Mocafico and many others.

One of the classics in this regard is the long-running American Express campaign shot by Annie Leibovitz, one of the world's best-known photographers by now. They are artful portraits of celebrities like Ellen DeGeneres or Conan O'Brien that can absolutely stand up to, if not surpass, portraits shot for purely artistic reasons. Another, completely different case is the famous Chanel No 5 commercial from 2004, which is still regarded as the most expensive spot ever made. No wonder, at US $42 million, of which US $12 million went to Nicole Kidman alone, the main protagonist (Chanel No 5 – The Film). Creatively, the film's merits are debatable, but from a production value it is still impressive, even a decade later. Shot by director Baz Luhrmann, then fresh of 'Moulin Rouge' fame, the spot's aesthetic was very similar to that blockbuster, mixing camp, cinematographic grandezza and furious editing with the storyline a CliffsNotes version of its 'bigger sister'. Actually, it was indeed considered more of a short film than a traditional commercial because of its length (180 seconds), costs as well as style. It has been largely credited with starting the whole shift towards branded content, which we will talk about in the next section. No wonder Chanel tried to re-stage a similar coup in 2014, again with Luhrmann, but this time starring Giselle Buendchen as a flirtatious celebrity 'working mom'. And it worked – it received five million views in no time, and business went up concurrently by 30 per cent, not only for the fragrance, as we were told by insiders.

What was and still is most notable in all these cases of 'Ueber-Art' is the perfect coming together of various 'geniuses' on equal footing. The brand becomes part of an artistic collaboration, fully integrated and in synch with the celebrity talent, the creative director and the artistic narrative. Some-times with more and sometimes with less mystery, but always way above the fray. In this sense it's not important if you spend millions and millions as Chanel did and does, or if you choose to work with little-known and much less expensive up-and-coming designers, architects or artists. Actu-ally, depending on your mission and the idea you want to project, the latter can be much more beneficial, as the Japanese avant-garde fashion brand Comme des Garçons has shown again and again, or as Aēsop, the Austral-ian brainy beauty brand does with their standard-setting interior designs (see case study at the end of this principle).

What does matter is that you continue to set cultural impulses. Because while it is almost 'verboten' for Ueber-Brands to sell themselves they cer-tainly must make sure to remain part of the conversation – and cultural cool.

Walk the talk

This last section on 'Un-selling' is about one of the most recent develop-ments in marketing, because it is very connected to the digital revolution: Ueber-Brands creating their own content and turning themselves into a medium. Which is why, nowadays, marketing talks a lot about the move away from paid media towards owned and earned media. 'Paid media' is traditional advertising, where a brand inserts itself into independent pro-gramming and pays for it. 'Owned media' is the brand itself creating content that it 'owns' and either shares through its own outlets like websites and Facebook pages or other social media platforms like YouTube or Twitter. Lastly, earned media is what's traditionally called PR – where the brand does not pay for the communication, at least not directly, but gets talked about by others. And while this might not sound new, it actually includes some of the most inspiring and intriguing new forms of marketing. There's a whole new generation of ideas and activities that are not just making others talk about you, they do the talking themselves – as they walk. We call them ideas that do.

It's easy to see how all these new opportunities and shifts from paid to owned and earned media are very important in the context of Un-selling. **Ueber-Brands that don't want to be seen as over-promoting themselves but still need to communicate with their constituencies have suddenly many more options to create and control the world they want to inhabit and share with their followers.** They can go into much more depth than a 20-second commercial or a double-page spread ever allowed. They can create more meaningful, nuanced and experiential interactions with their customers, and they can do this generally in ways that are much more cost-effective.

One of the most recent watershed moments in all of this has been *The LEGO® Movie* released in early 2014. The *New York Times*, a paper not necessarily known for hyperbole, headlined an in-depth article: 'The brilliant, unnerving meta-marketing of *The LEGO Movie*' (Havrilesky, 2014). The *LA Times* was equally ecstatic. And, most importantly, the movie got across-the-board splendid reviews from critics and consumers alike (96 per cent on Rotten Tomatoes) and blessed the company with its best financial year, yet. Personally, we weren't so impressed by the dramatic and narrative strength of the movie. We were a bit bored. But we do agree with Havrilesky when she summarizes: 'The brilliance of *The LEGO Movie* lies in providing every piece to the modern branding puzzle, including the surface-level subversion.'

It would have been astounding enough that a film written and produced by a brand about itself wasn't immediately dismissed as self-indulgent merchandizing. But to be hailed as a new, welcome form of marketing, that's a feat! It shows how things have changed. We – including intellectually more demanding if not snobby *New York Times* editors apparently – have come to accept that the borders between commerce and culture are fluent. And that this isn't necessarily something to lament about but to shape. We can appreciate a brand not playing this cross-genre heavy handedly, but with enough aplomb and self-irony so we can indulge without feeling duped. We can start embracing it for what it truly is: the big new frontier in marketing, or 'the modern branding puzzle' as Havrilesky calls it. Especially for Ueber-Brands trying to 'Un-sell'.

Another similar example, but from a totally different field, is the Prada short film *A Therapy* (scan QR code in Preface to get to the video) which premiered at the 2012 Cannes Film Festival. Where *The LEGO Movie* is 100 minutes of all animated characters (except for Will Ferrell at the very end), this one is only four minutes long, but star-studded with Ben Kingsley and Helena Bonham-Carter and directed by Roman Polanski. What both films share is their ingenious way of celebrating the brand and its products in a highly equity-specific narrative while at the same time mocking themselves – though just to the point where it doesn't undermine the message but only makes it more palatable.

Prada's short was more entertaining to us, but that may simply be due to our higher target affinity. Both cases are undoubtedly 'Un-selling' at its best. They sell you without ever overselling. They seduce you and break down your guard, but in a way you don't mind because their meta-level creates a sense of complicity. They celebrate themselves and their products while simultaneously not taking themselves overly seriously. They talk to you from a position of strength and confidence, but they are never over-bearing. They are true works of art yet always very clear and open about their partiality and intent. And best of all they let you right then and there experience the world they want you to buy into. They truly 'walk the talk' and take it to the next level – of marketing in general and modern prestige in particular. An Ueber-Brand level.

Brand as medium

One of the most committed to embracing the fact that brands are media themselves is the world's leading luxury conglomerate LVMH. Their flag-ship brand Louis Vuitton has been providing travel literature forever and recently evolved their campaign to travel storytelling at its finest. When you enter their Hennessy website you read about 'wild rabbits' (their term for passion) and watch lots of videos before you come across a bottle of their cognac. And their luxury shoe brand Berluti has created a whole world of refined living, making their homepage feel more like a magazine than a brand site.

Their biggest venture in this regard was and is however Nowness, the 'editorially independent website... for the culturally curious' (lvmh.com) launched in 2010. It's a cross-company endeavour beyond brands, seem-ingly truly beyond corporate interests, 'showcasing the best of fashion, art, gastronomy, entertainment, and travel in a highly creative and technologi-cally advanced approach', as they boast about themselves (nowness.com). And the platform is indeed open to anyone who wants to submit articles, videos, ideas, projects, creative work... anything that 'culturally curious' people could find interesting or enchanting. Of course there's an editorial team scanning and evaluating your submissions, but there are no standing restrictions in terms of provenance or content. Nowness is, at least theoreti-cally, as open to competitive brands and talents or completely unaffiliated ones as it is to LVMH's own. Those who don't know would actually have a hard time even detecting signs of LVMH's ownership.

It wouldn't be surprising if LVMH were to start monetizing Nowness and tie it closer to its commercial heart – they did launch 'shoppable' videos in early 2014 where you can click on items to get directed to an e-shop for purchasing. But they've achieved one thing for sure: huge goodwill within the creative community, especially those involved in fashion and high art. And thus premier access to the world's brightest and most creative talents to source from.

Two other brands who have made content their premier marketing vehi-cle and styled their brands as media outlets and community magnets rather than mere product venues are Red Bull and Net-a-Porter. The first we have already discussed and included a whole case study on. So suffice it to say that they've actually developed an entire media emporium. Red Bull Media House (redbullmediahouse.com) offers anything from games to apps to TV to print, largely sourced from all the creative collaborations and sponsorships Red Bull is undertaking anyway, thus providing a great opportunity for secondary usage and income stream – in addition to brand and community building. Their aptly named *Red Bulletin*, for example, started as a sports newsletter distributed freely at events and through other newspapers but evolved into a globally sold magazine (magazines.com).

Net-a-Porter is 'the world's premier online luxury fashion destination' according to its own selling line (net-a-porter.com). It was certainly the first of its kind. Founded by Natalie Massenet in 2000 it was bought in 2010 by the world's third largest luxury holding, Kering, for over US $500 million. Massenet has meanwhile turned into a cultural figurehead like Elon Musk from Tesla, but she started out as an editor for all the big fashion and beauty magazines. And that's what shaped her idea. Net-a-Porter was from the beginning not just an online shopping site but much more a magazine based around fashion and luxury that also allows you to buy things. It's exactly what the media companies should have done: luring people in with great editorial content and then allowing them to shop, if they come across something they like. Culture and commerce, content and convenience all fused in perfect symbiosis. It is only fitting, then, that in 2014 NAP began publishing 'Porter', a global glossy magazine bridging the off- and online.

Ideas that do

The other, even more visionary aspect of 'Walk the Talk' and in our minds the emerging holy grail of 'Un-selling' Ueber-Brands are 'Ideas that Do'. **This is about taking PR and event marketing to a whole new realm by morphing the two into marketing activities that don't just communicate the brand and its benefits but allow people to interactively experience them right on the spot. Marketing ideas and programmes that prove as they promote and already add value to people's lives as they convince them about the value of the brands they present. Hence 'Ideas that Do'.**

The LEGO Movie or Prada's *A Therapy* are examples of how this can play out in film or moving content. There have been lots of others like Dior's *Secret Garden*, Ferragamo's truly interactive *Walking Stories* or Infiniti's creepy and arresting *Déjà View* (all on Vimeo or YouTube). But the truly interesting cases are those that move beyond the traditional formats and create new experiences and benefits in their own right. Like Burberry did with their *Art of the Trench* or *Burberry Kisses*, live streaming of fashion shows or the weekly upload and promotion of music bands.

Tate Tracks (tate.org.uk) is another example, coincidentally also from London, where the British temple of modern art managed to engage with younger targets not through traditional marketing but through a project that ultimately added a whole new product or dimension to their services and experiences. They asked hip bands like The Chemical Brothers and New Young Pony Club to get inspired by a Tate artwork of their choice and translate it into a soundtrack. Initially you could only listen to those tracks through audio set-ups in front of their respective artwork, literally attracting a lot of young fans to the museum and getting them engaged with modern 'high' art – which was exactly the point. In the meantime they released the music on a CD and for streaming services, spreading the word – and the joy – even further.

Both directions, evolving your brand to become the medium that it truly is or letting it shine with 'Ideas that do', are great new possibilities to address the issue of selling yourself without doing it too forcefully. They allow new people to get in touch with the brand, experience it and develop a feel for it without seeming too eager or too pushy. They perfectly straddle the 'velvet rope' and strike the balance between 'in' and 'out' by giving you a glimpse without letting you in all the way or making you commit to a purchase. On top they give highly targeted but globally active brands wide reach for relatively little (extra) cost while at the same time enabling them to control the brand experience they are creating. No wonder they are the big future of 'Un-selling' and that you hardly find a modern prestige or Ueber-Brand not toying with them.

Principle 3: The rules of 'un-selling'

1 Be proud
And keep the distance. To promise strength and confidence.

2 Go bold
Provoke and polarize with a singular attitude. Not everybody should 'get' you.

3 Avert the overt
Create an aura of mystery for a sense of discovery. Aspiration thrives on imagination.

4 Inspire and be inspired
Think of yourself as a work of art. And present yourself accordingly.

5 Don't skimp
Every executional detail counts. You have an image to build – and uphold.

6 Be the medium that you are
A magnet for a loyal community rather than just a vessel for products.

7 Do more than you talk
Prestige is a quiet thing. And while its modern brother may be a bit louder, it still is better experienced than promoted or explained.

Ueber-Brands reverse the traditional marketing rule: they are boss, not their consumer. They put themselves 'above', creating an image and an aura of distance and superiority for us to aspire to. They don't sell, they seduce.

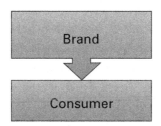

Ueber-Brand case study 3 Aēsop – un-selling beauty

Aēsop, an Australian beauty brand in the process of conquering the world, was created by Dennis Paphitis in 1987. The son of a family of barbers who had emigrated from Greece, he followed in the tradition. His Melbourne salon quickly gained a reputation for high craft and service and for using essential oils that made it a pleasantly fragrant place, rather than one smelling of ammonia. Passionate about the idea of nurturing beauty as naturally but efficaciously as possible, Paphitis and his business partner Suzanne Santos stepped out of the salon business in 1996. They went on to create a 'cerebral beauty brand' that seeks to appeal as much to the intellect as to the desire to live and look healthy. The brand opened its first store by building-out a parking garage ramp in a Melbourne hotel in 2002 and went international in 2006, starting in Paris. By 2012 some 60 stores around the world were generating most of their estimated AUS $64 million in sales. This is when Brazilian beauty company Natura bought a majority stake in Aēsop, promising to support its global expansion but also protect the brand's independence.

Fabulist un-selling

'Spectacular Performance, Minus The Drama' is written on a card featuring a stunning black and white photo by Ruven Afanador showing two fierce-looking flamenco dancers entangled by their hair. On the back of the card Aēsop's hair care line is introduced in a matter-of-fact way. This artistic yet determined piece of communication is representative of the ways in which Aēsop breaks with beauty marketing conventions. There are no pseudo-scientific product demonstrations or celebrity endorsements, no mass-media ads or (e-)mail blasts. And despite its heavy use of natural ingredients, the oft-claimed 'organic' is missing. There is no serial-launching of 'new and improved' products, either. Rather, social media like Pinterest show the beautiful store interior and quote Paphitis on there being 'an obscene amount of choice and variety for the sheer sake of it […] Luxury is less but better, substantial over fleeting, meaningful over mindless' (Farrow, 2013).

So where and how does the brand approach consumers and spread the gospel? It meets them where they go and looks to become one of their places of congregation. If you are part of the sophisticated jet set, chances are you will find Aēsop's soap and moisturizer set placed in the bathroom of 'in' spots you have on your bucket list, for instance Kapok boutique in Wan Chai, Hong Kong, Claska gallery and hotel in Tokyo or Die Brücke restaurant in Hamburg. This halos the equity as much as it reaches the target.

It might also have been the beautiful interior of an Aēsop shop that caught your eye while strolling through that hip neighbourhood. The seductive product will be dispensed outside, but not as sales pitch, more as silent benefit offer and invitation to come in. Inside, the staff are guided to talk about factors like the climate, pollutants, the diet as well as their personality to aid correct product selection. As Matteo Martignoni, General Manager Marketing told us:

> From the beginning this brand decided that nobody should be 'sold-to', which means pushing products to customers and promising them those products will do whatever they wish. That is disingenuous.

So why not talk about a book, play or museum that might further your spiritual beauty as well? The objective is to engage intellectually. Being introduced to the products via this personal and holistic approach is so important to the brand, that the Aēsop website recommends a visit to a store rather than a first order online.

Aēsop is very selective in its digital strategy anyway. It uses the web to project its Ueber-Serious core: 'The Fabulist' is a brainy 'monthly literary digest' through which Aēsop publishes original essays and interviews that would seamlessly fit *The New Yorker*. The brand also tweets 'since we love writing, and synthesizing important thoughts in two lines represents an exciting intellectual challenge' Martignoni tells us. But these tweets are rather 'heavy stuff' compared to the usually light-hearted chatter by beauty brands and see few re-tweets. Pinterest posts highlighting Aēsop's stunning aesthetics, on the other hand, radiate the allure further than the stores alone could … and are more easily digested.

Why this rather restrained, one-way use of the internet? Why no Facebook page with fan-fed stories or syndicated content on the website? As an intellectual Ueber-Brand, Aēsop wants to contribute original thought rather than simply borrowing attention. As CEO Michael O'Keeffe put it to Jo Bowman at *CNBC* magazine: 'We see ourselves as leaders rather than followers. We're not reading the latest Wallpaper* looking for the next cool cafe to partner with' (Bowman, 2010). And that's why Aēsop is respected by the global avant-garde and gets their help in 'Un-selling'.

Mission and myth of a sage

Aēsop strives to be an 'honest and thoughtful beauty brand that acknowledges your intelligence and sophistication' says Martignoni. Promising eternal youth or to change the world are anathema. Instead, there is a quiet confidence to own the moral high-ground and to win over consumers with a humble but efficacious offering. Beyond the product, the mission is to inspire and be inspired by intelligent people. Their website declares:

> Aēsop values all human endeavors undertaken with intellectual rigor, vision and a nod to the whimsical. We advocate the use of our products as part of a balanced life that includes a healthy diet, sensible exercise, a moderate intake of red wine and a regular dose of stimulating literature. (Aēsop.com)

And there are, indeed, Aēsop chocolates and wine in the stores. Not to be sold but rather to be consumed there, fuelling conversation and passing on the word to like-minded friends: 'Don't compromise yourself; you're all you've got' reads a Janis Joplin quote on an Aēsop sample.

The myth of this brand starts with its name (Nomen est omen!). It is not entirely clear why Aesop, the Greek slave turned teller of fables, was chosen as a brand name. Some attribute it to Paphitis' Greek background while others relate it to the fact that he is a bookworm and avid student of philosophy. Martignoni says that the deep moral lessons conveyed by Aesop provided a moral compass for what was to be a commercial entity. As one follows the brand's history, a myth emerges of a sage (Paphitis) trapped in the body of an entrepreneur who despises the shallowness and mendacity of the industry he finds himself in and sets out to create a brand that attracts the people of thought and sophistication he admires. 'I guess the reason I started my own beauty company was that I wasn't patient enough to be a philosopher, nor tolerant enough to be an architect', the founder told Bethan Cole of the *Independent* newspaper (Cole, 2008).

But one does not need to study the founder's interviews. Just look at the hand wash, which comes with a quote by Carl Jung: 'Often hands will solve a mystery that the intellect has struggled with in vain'. Doesn't that say all about beautiful minds and faces? And don't such high-reaching hands deserve to be pampered with a potion of 'Resurrection Aromatique' – at US $30?

Intelligent beauty to behold!... and long for

If many high-end beauty brands feel like shiny temples then Aēsop is a monastic library. Aēsop's aesthetic follows a strict, unassuming, functional code on the

Monastic magnificence: Aēsop stores and headquarters (at top right and bottom)

'Whether zeal or moderation be the point we aim at, let us keep fire out of the or

Images courtesy of Aēsop

outside but reveals rich, elegant detail once you take a closer look, step inside or open the bottle.

The circa 100 different Aēsop products are packed into quasi-identical brown bottles or squeezable beige metal tubes, to be mindful and focused. Identical containers and dyes are economical, printing all product information on the container makes cartons or leaflets unnecessary, the brown tint or metal protect the content against UV damage and help to minimize the use of preservatives. Also 'the cream and brown label' is meant to blend into the bathroom. 'We do not want to stick out' says Martignoni. 'More with less' par excellence.

The same goes for the actual products. It is hard to believe that an 'anti-oxidant mix of parsley and blackcurrant seed oil, enhanced by orange or violet petal' would be guided strictly by what is efficacious only. It just sounds and smells far too beautiful. Yet that's what seems to be the case.

But, then there are also the subtle, philosophic rather than functional details. The 'macron' set over the 'e' adding an elegant, capricious note to the logo and a little mystery around the pronunciation. Long rows of identical bottles in uneven numbers giving beautiful rhythm and symmetry. The simple brown paper bags (plastic is a waste and too glossy) with cultural tips printed on them. And the stores having water basins where customers are encouraged to try the indulgent products – which of course doesn't just make for great ritual but also infuses the room with incense-like aromas.

The branding expert Mark Tungate would probably call these stores 'big dog whistles' as they might go unnoticed by many shoppers but are 'compelling to those on the right wavelength' (Tungate, 2011). And indeed, to be treated to that Aēsop wine and chocolate mentioned earlier can be experienced as a form of ritualized ascendance to a 'beauty poet society', the inner circle of intellectual sophisticates who associate with the brand. At least it felt that way at a party in their Sheung Wan store, Hong Kong. The talk was of slow food, urban cycling or low-fi electronics. Most people were visibly enjoying each other's company yet business was brisk, one buyer explaining that he was stocking up 'to help the store succeed… happy to have one in his neighbourhood'.

Aēsop prides itself on these close relationships with their neighbourhoods – physical and spiritual. Bonding with a worthwhile customer segment, a modern, moneyed, intellectual 'cultural cohort', as Douglas Holt would describe them, seeking sophisticated yet unpretentious products to distinguish themselves from the nouveau riche with their showy brands. To them, Aēsop is cult and they are willing disciples of what Paphitis calls 'a small movement that's best described as the Muji-Hermès paradigm' (Flaherty, 2012). Especially since, typical of an Ueber-Brand with a myth that 'reaches beyond' to a higher, more educated and spiritual level, the meticulously staged brand and its idiosyncratic world can be quite intimidating to the uninitiated. Who of the hoi-polloi would appreciate a surreal beauty meditation film with a Salvador Pániker quote: 'Better than a face-lift, to stay young we need to be permanently in a state of intellectual curiosity'? Which is exactly the kind of thing you can find at any Aēsop store at any moment.

Living the dream and moving with gravitas

Obviously, the brand has chosen to make the stores its principal manifestation. 'The first one was some six years in the making, but it was so well thought through, we still execute them in the same spirit' according to Martignoni. Unassuming from afar and just marked by the simple logo, they become stunning experiences in modernist design on the inside. Tellingly, a search for 'Aēsop brand' on Google yields mostly pictures of the sculptural interiors created in collaboration with cutting-edge architects like Ciguë, Torafu or Weiss-heiten. One can admire 7,560 amber glass bottles used as a ceiling of the Adelaide store or thousands of reclaimed copies of the *New York Times* stacked up to serve as product pedestals at New York's Grand Central Station, and other artistry-cum-ideology statements. Regularly, Aēsop will transform their spaces into culture centres where products are replaced by works of authors (Gabriel García Márquez) or designers (Jo Meesters), installation artists (Frida Escobedo, Hiroko Shiratori) or ceramic sculptors (Ray Chan). Or Aēsop moves right in with the artists as it has done at the Invisible Dog Art Center in Brooklyn, New York.

Apart from carefully selecting its customer, this exacting, high-brow attitude also attracts a special type of employee – art students, freelance writers and designers. 'It keeps the noise down, lets us talk intelligently and do the right things, just like at the headquarters' says Martignoni. Those headquarters are ruled by a triumvirate of Paphitis the Artist, Santos the Alchemist and O'Keeffe the Operator. Fastidious perfectionism and a tight control of all elements of branding are evident in the organization and operations. Rumours that all Aēsop researchers wear the same apothecary coats, use the same type of black BIC pen, that charts are coloured in Aēsop cream and that even the toilet paper is chosen by the boss are not being denied. There are the obligatory quotes, stark wooden desks and identical black books lining the room and walls. Martignoni confirms that eating at the desk is not allowed. Instead, employees are encouraged to cook together and visit the library for breaks. On birthdays the company gifts books from the favourite list.

All this might appear a bit *1984* and the brand has its detractors, but the resulting 'intellectual energy' (from an Aēsop job posting) gives the brand a spirit and level of authenticity which makes it hard for others to copy: 'Great spirits have always encountered violent opposition from mediocre minds' (Albert Einstein) – a quote on walls of Aēsop headquarters in Melbourne, Australia.

When it comes to business expansion, Aēsop is also the perfect Ueber-Brand, following its namesake fabulist who lets the tortoise win over the hare. In the hotbed market of Asia, for example, Aēsop refuses to join everyone else in launching a whitening product because it sees the 'negative cultural and personal ramifications'. And, as of mid 2015, the brand has not set foot on China's mainland because the state requires testing on animals, as O'Keeffe told Kathy Chu of WSJ Live (Chu, 2013). Even in sampling the brand follows its own rules: Aēsop amenities would be in high demand by boutique hotels all over the world, if the brand was willing to have them contract-made at a much cheaper cost, like everyone else.

Of course, part of this comparatively slow speed of expansion is the fact all stores are hand-picked and designed by the small management team – with a store on Paris's Rive Gauche appropriately bourgeois in design and its sibling in the Marais reflecting the bohemian flair of that neighbourhood. Consequently, there are about 25 Body Shop stores for any one of Aēsop's and even choosy Kiehl's has more than twice as many (see Principle 6). In the end, though, it's not logistical limitations, it's strategic intent and cunning that let the brand grow 'organically', at its own pace and in synch with its neighbourhoods and clientele. This way the expansion – even within a same city – is never experienced as inflation and the brand's Ueber-Power is kept up.

The challenge will of course be to maintain this restraint after the acquisition by Natura. But Martignoni seems confident: the investor was chosen 'based on matching philosophies. Not the money'.

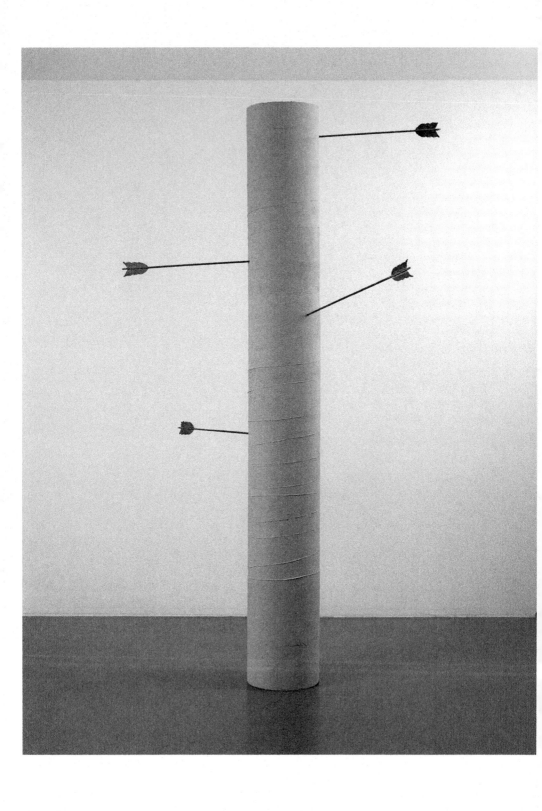

Principle 4
From myth to meaning
The best way up is to go deep

Principle 4 sits at the centre of the seven secrets or principles. This is not by chance, but because this principle constitutes the foundation in constructing Ueber-Brands. It's the core without which all the other principles run empty. Because if all your external interactions, the ways you present yourself, aren't leading to a clear brand legend, they will not add up to much indeed. Equally, if all your internal behaviours have no clear narrative that inspires and unites them, you'll be hard-pressed to ensure all your various stakeholders stay 'on script' and all your actions feel in synch and coherent.

Ultimately, you could say that Ueber-Brand building is thus an exercise in building your brand myth. Because a myth gives your brand meaning. Or better yet, it translates your brand's meaning into an emotionally compelling and memorable script. In other words, the best way up is to go deep – deep into your history, deep into your mission (see Principle 1), and deep into the human psyche. There's nothing that inspires and intrigues us like a good story – internally as a brand's employees or externally as its consumers – and that's why all you do or don't do should build this story, enrich it, embellish it and elevate it until it reaches mythical proportions.

Consequently the first part of this principle will be all about storytelling and why and how it's so crucial to us people. How stories sit at the base of our cognitive needs (stories are human), how they drive and structure our thinking, our memorizing and our decision-making. It's also about how storytelling has become even more important in re-connecting us with a world, its brands and its products that we feel more and more disconnected with (stories provide background). And why and how stories are the best and most fun way to bypass rational filters and make us believe rather than question (stories make us believe).

But, of course, Ueber-Brands wouldn't be Ueber-Brands if they didn't go beyond what other brands do. That's why in this chapter we're not just talking about brand storytelling but brand mythmaking.

What's the difference between a story and a myth? Isn't a myth just a 'false story'? Yes and no. Yes, myths often involve elements that are beyond the factual, to put it nicely, but no, they aren't just false stories; they are much more than that. They are Ueber-Stories. They talk about that which words alone cannot express, about something bigger and more meaningful than the stories themselves. They explain the world and the way we like to see it. They are our way of making sense when science and reason can't make sense anymore. They 'reach beyond', which is what we have called the first sub-header of this chapter ('Reaching beyond through myths'), and is one of the Ueber-Brand mythmaking ways we will analyse in detail. We will look at some quite famous brand examples and how they elevated themselves and their products way beyond reality to a level of supremacy and adoration that put them at a very nicely cushioned position on the top of their categories. All by connecting to a higher truth.

But myths aren't just helping us to reach or grasp beyond, going 'meta' on the physics. They also provide some very 'down-to-earth' guidance. By 'teaching' us lessons they present mores and rules through which they form, confirm, reject or transform codes of conduct and help us decide and navigate through life. This is almost more important when it comes to Ueber-Brands and thus their second strategem ('Guiding with myths'). If your brand manages to translate its mission (see Principle 1) and its history into a myth, it's on its best way to reach the ultimate status, becoming a true cultural icon beyond any price considerations. Chanel is a great example here as we will see, having managed to mythologize its history through relentless retelling and turn itself into the icon of modern, emancipated elegance.

Finally, in the last section of this principle, 'Making myths: what to respect', we will get deeper into the 'how'. Based on our experience and the cases we analysed we will outline some of the practical 'musts' to turn your history into a strong story and ultimately into a culturally relevant and guiding myth: the need to listen, the guiding quality of a name, the importance of elements of struggle, the seven steps and last, but certainly not least, the big question regarding truth. Because, as we said earlier, myths may contain elements that are not completely verifiable. If they are all fake, however, they can never do what they are supposed to, which is connect us with a higher truth. The brands that try to go down that path are burned quicker than Icarus.

The power of storytelling

Since the advent of internet and all the talk about content creation there has been a big renaissance in storytelling. Today you can hardly speak to an advertising agency without getting a pitch on brand narratives. There is an annual high-profile congress on 'The Future of Storytelling' (futureof storytelling.org). Retailers, traditionally not the most innovative and imaginative among marketers, have turned raconteurs: 'We're not just about buying certain products, but curating and storytelling,' Andrew Keith, President of Lane Crawford, China's premier luxury retailer told us. Some brands even base their whole concept on storytelling, like H&M's upmarket offspring, &Other Stories: 'Our collections are built around inspiring fashion stories... offering women a wide range... to create their personal style, or story' (stories.com, accessed July 2014).

Of course there are good reasons for this new-found popularity of one of the oldest 'tools' of mankind. Some are eternal, based on the way we're wired, but recently re-confirmed through the latest forays into neuroscience. Others are more contemporary, driven by the evolution of our marketing world and our digital technologies, as we already outlined in Part 1.

Stories are human – now more than ever

There are many extraordinary insights in Daniel Kahneman's enlightening bestseller *Thinking, Fast and Slow*. For the purpose of marketing and myth-making there are two of particular interest: 'The confidence that individuals have in their beliefs depends mostly on the quality of the story they can tell about what they see – even if they see little', and 'Memory composes stories and keeps them for future reference' (Kahneman, 2011).

We are 'sense-making machines'. We cannot help but 'connect the dots' and create narratives out of the stimuli that are being picked up by our senses – often even against our better judgement. What's truly mindboggling is that we don't worry so much about missing links or the hunch that the pieces we put together are flawed. All we care about is the picture (aka story) we can create. Because the more perfect that picture is, the more perfect the judgement – so we think-feel. We trick ourselves into being confident in our decisions through the stories we construct ourselves. Just imagine how much of a sucker that makes us for stories that come ready-made – for instance by marketing folks.

The other 'problem': this preference for good stories continues from deciphering information all the way through storing and retrieving it. In other words, our memories are also hooked on stories, and so are our remembering and decision-making selves. And somewhere in the process of filing and re-collecting the stories we construe, we make them even better – while not necessarily truer. We add drama and suspense, for instance, by focusing on the high points and the end, just like a good Hollywood director. This makes for golden memories, but is not necessarily a reliable base for future reference. Yet it is perfect for building brand preferences, because it means that if you tell your customers great stories with lots of suspense they'll memorize your brands forever and in the best way. Hopefully you will create nice little positive biases for the next time they go shopping and make a 'conscious' purchase decision.

Someone who has truly built their business on our human need for memorizing and writing stories is Moleskine, the Milan-based brand of notebooks. Or, as ex-CEO Arrigo Berni put it when going public, Moleskine is about being human in the digital age (CNBC, 2013). And the brand truly practises what it sells – perfectly. Every Moleskine you buy contains a leaflet outlining their story from origins to re-invention in epic length, as does their website. They talk about the notebooks Van Gogh, Hemingway and other artists used for 'invaluable sketches, notes, stories, and ideas that would one day become famous paintings or the pages of beloved books' (moleskine, accessed July 2014). And of course they talk about Bruce Chatwin, the great peripatetic American writer who dedicated an entire section of his book *The Songlines* to his notebook entries (Chatwin, 1987), and how Moleskine sees it as their mission to bring this 'legendary but lost partner for the creative and imaginative class' back to life, providing 'a family of nomadic objects' (moleskine (a), accessed August 2014).

But, Moleskine wouldn't have become the Ueber-Brand they are without also doing a phenomenal job in bringing their story to life, continuously building on their myth. For instance, they released a notebook with unpublished Chatwin letters and an interview with his wife in conjunction with the Premio Chatwin, a Genoa festival, in 2010 (moleskine (b), accessed August 2014). They've also created a large number of free templates and apps inviting young or accomplished creatives to promote the brand and its products by capturing and publishing their thoughts. Co-founder Maria Sebregondi is intimately involved with the global 'cognoscenti', sponsoring many projects and initiating very innovative directions: 'We don't think in terms of products but our people's needs', or rather desires and interests, we might add. Sebregondi is constantly part of workshops, think tanks and other labs 'writing' the future of communication. Moleskine supports three to four schools per year from Tongji University in Shanghai to Politecnico in the brand's hometown Milan. They commissioned the big 'Detour' project about collective creativity with 250 notebooks by artists, writers, directors, sculptors, which were sent on a museum tour, crossing the globe since 2006. And together with non-profit organization lettera27 they are currently stewarding the eighth book of *Ecriture Infinie*, a project to capture the story and power of human handwriting for future generations. Truly, a never-ending story.

All these projects go way beyond traditional CSR. They aren't 'doing good', they are actually 'doing right' – the right and essential things in pursuing the brand's mission and building and expanding its myth. Giving it depth and breadth and meaning and cultural relevance way beyond the actual products.

Consequently, Moleskine has been used by everyone from Francis Ford Coppola to young Peruvian architecture students (My Architectural Moleskine, accessed August 2014). The brand has also appeared in an endless number of blockbuster movies from *The Talented Mr. Ripley* to *The Devil Wears Prada*, again and again linking Moleskine with seminal moments in culture, the telling and retelling of the collective stories that connect us.

This gets us to the other, more contemporary aspect of why storytelling is so human and has become such a hyped part of modern marketing and brand building. Thanks to the digital revolution, today's communication culture is, once again, about passing things on, creating buzz and word of mouth. It's no longer about what we as marketers say or do, but what people do with what we do. Mass monologuing is over. Multiple dialoguing is in, and stories are the best conduit for this, especially if you create them in an open, accessible and inspiring way. They travel across all media and touch points, ignite passion or rejection, allow everybody to spin them further to their own delight and ultimately motivate action and participation. And they increase knowledge – which is the way to set yourself ahead and apart in the information age (see also Principle 2). In an article in *The Atlantic*, ethnographic researcher Min Lieskowsky from ReD Associates was quoted on a tequila research project: 'Stories are a way to let people show humour, or to declare that they are, for instance, the kind of Austin lesbians who, upon finding exotic elixirs in far-off lands, are brave enough to try them' (Wood, 2013).

No wonder that brands and particularly Ueber-Brands have become such avid storytellers. Because stories not only let us create perfect brand pictures and memories, they also let us talk – about those brands as well as ourselves. They inspire us to connect and share, just like the old troubadours and story-tellers of yore used to. They allow us to create our own 'story', our identity as knowledge leaders, insiders and sophisticates, something no Ueber-Brand can do without.

Stories provide background – which we miss so dearly

The other strength of stories is that they provide background, and this is increasingly important in a world overflowing with brands and products of dubious provenance. Konrad Paul Liessman, philosophy professor at the University of Vienna put it this way: 'Things have lost their materiality, their dignity' (Liessman, 2010). For the most part we don't know where and how anything is made anymore. Products just pop up on our shelves without us having any connection to them being produced. In previous times we at least knew they were made in a factory on the other side of town: we sometimes saw, smelled or heard signs of their production and most of us still had at least some memory about how things were created before the machines took over – what it takes to make a shoe and why it needs different skills and training than making a saddle or a handbag for example. Nowadays, most of what we consume is produced completely out of our sight, probably in China. This is why a lot of things have become just stuff for us – meaningless, soulless, immaterial material. It is why, now, a lot of people are re-embracing locally sourced and crafted goods, starting with groceries and slowly expanding to all sorts of things. These products have a face attached to them, and you can see their roots, sometimes literally, always metaphorically. They feel whole and thus more wholesome, and they have an integrity that we can connect with. They are truly goods and not just stuff.

However, what if you can't build personal connections between your brand and its customers because you're a prestige brand with a far-flung distribution? Then the second best way is to simulate this by storytelling. Reconnect consumers with the products and the brand by letting them in on the production, the values, the company's history, the process of production, the hardship, the landscape and mindset that created them, the spirit in which they were invented. Tell your story in the most detailed, evocative and personal way to create a sense of immediacy and integrity and to give things back their dignity and their soul – or their materiality, as Prof. Liessmann would say.

Many big prestige brands have tried this lately, especially the ones previously connected with excess or a vacuous lifestyle. The ones that are doing it best, though, are often small brands like French coutellerie Laguiole for example. Laguiole's brochure accompanying every Sommelier corkscrew or set of steak knives covers over 20 pages, all in colour, showcasing the brand's heritage, with little anecdotes throughout as well as a detailed guide to their craftsmanship. See the depth in which they talk about their village of origin alone… 'Laguiole village is located in Aveyron Department, in Aubrac Region which covers three departments: Aveyron, Cantal and Lozère. The junction of these three departments is named the Three Bishops Cross…' (Laguiole, accessed November 2013). On and on it goes, telling you about every street and building in the village and why things developed the way they did, which family bought what and who feuded with who and what it all meant for the Laguiole forge and the knife industry in general.

You could easily read this elaborate report on irrelevant details and get annoyed, dismissing it as completely self-indulgent. And yet you don't, because it is written in such a charming and almost unprofessional manner. It comes across as honest and heartfelt, just like parents too proud of their children, never stopping blowing their horns. It completely over-markets every little aspect, and yet it appears under-marketed and real, with a true human soul. You feel like you are personally in the village and have caught the forger himself on a good day, where all his passion comes out and you don't just purchase a utilitarian product but a little work of art – and love.

Stories make us believe – and believe we still want, after all

Earlier we discussed how our mind creates stories whether we want it to or not and how this influences our memory and our decision-making. Let's go a step further and look at what happens when we 'lose' ourselves in a narrative created by someone else, especially one that's not only verbal but comes with all the audio-visual bells and whistles, as most 'moving cc brands does these days.

German-Austrian lawyer Georg Jellinek established the idea ⟨ mative power of the factual'. In the case of storytelling we like to ⟨ normative power of the fictional'. Kahneman says 'A compelling ......ative fosters an illusion of inevitability' (Kahneman, 2011). We all have experienced this numerous times. We read a great novel or watch a captivating movie and we question the flow of events as little as we argue with the outcome. It all makes perfect sense and makes us very happy. Conversely, however, if a story is not well crafted, the exact opposite happens: we bicker about inconsistencies or improbabilities, lighting and make-up and quickly dismiss the whole plot as stupid. How come? Why are we so not critical in the first and overly critical in the latter case? Because we suspend reason when a story is good, and we bring it back full force if we feel deprived of this sweet abandon. Theatre thus talks about the imaginary 'fourth wall', the one that protects the fictional space as well as our fantasy. Or, which can destroy the make-believe and wake us from our 'spell' if broken. Psychologists call it 'narrative transportation' (Van Laer *et al*, 2014).

We love to get lulled into a narrative and we react like an addict gone cold turkey if someone or something takes that away from us. Stories are like a drug, they shut our brains off for a while or at least they calm them down. They let us escape the non-stop thinking and flickering of our minds and allow us to go with the flow – quite literally by the way. Recent fMRI (functional magnetic resonance imaging) test have shown how totally we become engaged and transformed by stories: 'the brain doesn't look like a spectator, it looks more like a participant in action' (Gottschall, 2014). And that feels so good, so much so that a multi-billion dollar entertainment industry thrives on it and marketing pushes more and more to get in on the fun as well.

Take the Chanel video *Once Upon a Time...* for example, a film by Karl Lagerfeld on the very early days of Coco Chanel's store in Deauville (Lagerfeld, 2013). It simply tells a bit of Chanel history, but by turning it into an engaging little story and shooting it in black and white with Keira Knightley as protagonist it quickly breaks down all our filters and puts us in spectator – or even better yet – participator mode. And that means we stop thinking and start experiencing. The fourth wall is well up and we are part of the game, outside of reality and 'inside' the play. We re-live Gabrielle Chanel's first attempts, the rejection she faced and the courage she showed and how this made her 'break through' and succeed. It subtly yet very forcefully lures us into her world and makes her appear like a heroine, proving to us beyond a doubt that she was ahead of her times and most likely still is, revolutionizing female fashion and with it the feminine ideal as a whole. It reaffirms that the brand is quite naturally an Ueber-Brand, the leader in fashion that it is, residing at the epitome of luxury and style, beyond question.

Apart from all that, this personal portrait of course also humanizes what has by now become a commercial behemoth, imbuing the brand with much-needed warmth and empathy, but without making it too approachable; rather adding to its pedestal and cementing Chanel as the queen of fashion. Just a bit more nice than ice-queen.

An arguably less successful example of putting us under a spell and 'making us believe' is *La Legende de Shalimar* by Guerlain (Guerlain, 2013), though many of the comments are quite approving. The production is certainly grandiose, much more so than the Chanel video, which by comparison feels almost like a chamber play. The casting, however, is so questionable and the acting so poor in our opinion that in combination with some other details like location choices the film doesn't really fascinate. The 'fourth wall' is wide open and the effort falls flat.

No matter how you personally feel about the success of either film – and we would strongly encourage you to watch them both and decide for yourself – what they show is the power of a story, or the lack thereof. Stories can make us embrace a construct wholeheartedly by quite literally engaging us, but they can also provoke disproportionate rejection if we feel let down.

If well done, stories, especially the ones executed with all the effects of a good movie, take us on a journey and captivate us so immensely that we are 'spellbound', transfixed in all senses of the word. This transportation-transformation-fixation makes us convinced things had to happen the way they did and that the outcome or moral is beyond discussion. Of course, we 'know' that any story is as partial or subjective as any other form of argument, but their stringent, emotionally charged narrative makes it appear less so. We feel like we 'lived through it', and although this 'experience' was a vicarious one, it makes the conclusion a 'verified' lesson learned and not a debatable opinion. **We like to believe, and stories can make us believe because they let us suspend reason and follow our hearts.**

Stories pay – or rather make us pay, significantly

Of course, by now it should be very clear that our preference for stories has strong commercial and financial implications. We decide much more and much more often as 'homo narrativus' than 'homo economicus', putting our dollars where the stories pull us rather than where sense should guide us. We know this, Hollywood knows this and marketing is re-learning it quickly, with Ueber-Brands leading the way.

But if you need more proof of the monetary value of stories, there is a quite entertaining experiment recently made and published by two editors, Rob Walker and Joshua Glenn (Glenn and Walker, 2012). Glenn and Walker and some friends collected 100 trinkets and then turned them into treasures – merely by inventing (!) a story around each of them. They bought totally mundane things, some would call them junk, for US $1.25 apiece at garage sales. Then they put them up on eBay, but only after embellishing each item with a little story as descriptor. To be transparent they clearly stated that the stories were fictitious. And yet, all these 'insignificant' objects became suddenly 'significant', at least judging by the prices they reached. As Glenn and Walker report: 'The exchange value of these unwanted and sometimes un-lovely objects was increased by more than 2,700 per cent', many selling for US $50 and some even for US $100.

What's more, these newly 'charismatized' things often started a narrative chain reaction. Once imbued with a story and thus with meaning, these inanimate things 'sprang' with emotional energy, becoming characters in novels or inspiring others to invent further stories and so on – showing that narratives don't just elevate through emotion but inspire our imagination.

In short, the power of storytelling is infinite because stories are by nature never-ending. To be continued…

Myths as Ueber-Stories

Even more powerful than merely recounting your brand's history or translating it into a story, is elevating it into a myth. Myths live high above 'normal' stories; they are meta-narratives, existing beyond time and space, illuminating our realities from afar with their magical magnetism and radiant power. We like to call them Ueber-Stories.

Brand myth manifested. Aēsop store in North Melbourne.

Image courtesy of Aēsop

According to the *Oxford Dictionary* a myth is defined as 'a traditional story, especially one... explaining a natural or social phenomenon, and typically involving supernatural beings or events' (*Oxford Dictionaries*, accessed May 2013). Of course, there is also the secondary meaning of 'a widely held but false belief or idea', which is how the term is often popularly used, or more positively 'an exaggerated or idealized conception of a person or thing', which already gets closer to what we mean by myth. But the best, simplest and most eye-opening definition comes from Joseph Campbell, the great mythologist of the 20th century and patron saint of comparative mythology. He calls a myth 'a public dream' (Campbell, 1988). It's what collectively drives us, what we all aspire to. And this is what makes myths, or mythical stories so interesting and important for marketing and Ueber-Brand building. **By 'mythologizing' the brand story you will take the idea of writing a compelling narrative to the ultimate level. If you do it well, you craft a story around your brand, which lifts it to 'supernatural' iconic status while at the same time giving it depth and meaning, providing a script for all followers to believe in and for the rest of us something to admire or aspire to.**

Four functions, two Ueber-Ways

So, what makes a story a myth? Of course, ultimately it's your audience – or all of us. If we don't 'hold the belief', embrace the narrative as meaningful and enlightening and your audience doesn't view it as aspirational, something relating to their dreams, you'll never reach mythical power, no matter how beautifully you craft and spin your story. But there are certain things you can do to increase your chances, because according to Campbell a myth becomes a myth when it serves at least some of the following four functions (Campbell, 1988):

1 **The Metaphysical Function**
   This is about a sense of 'awe' and wonder. Myths talk about that which words cannot reach, let alone express. Mythical metaphors and allegories have the ability to awaken and connect us with that which transcends reality, the overall mystery of life. They always point outside themselves to something bigger, more meaningful, something omnipresent and eternal. By 'reliving' them we can feel this ultimate mystery.

2 **The Cosmological Function**
   Myths help us make sense of the world, especially those parts that are beyond our control and understanding. In pre-modern times myths were used to 'explain' nature and its seasons, the cosmos and the stars, birth and death and everything in between – basically all phenomena people were 'dealt' and which they couldn't grasp. Just think of the Greek gods and their vast mythology and you get the idea.

3 **The Sociological Function**
   This is all about societal order – and the breaking with it.
   Myths have the ability to guide us by presenting certain rules and
   decisions as almost divine or at least natural. They help confirm
   social norms and make us conform. But they can also do the opposite
   by inciting us to take on a battle, stand up and fight. In the end,
   though, right usually does win over wrong, and right is ultimately
   what integrates us.

4 **The Pedagogical Function**
   Lastly, there is the same guiding function on a personal level. Myths
   can help people navigate through life and master challenges by
   setting examples, providing 'blueprints' for certain situations. A
   good example is *The Catcher in the Rye*, J.D. Salinger's mythical
   coming-of-age story, the ultimate reflection on adolescent angst that
   helped millions of teenagers cross the difficult bridge from youth to
   adulthood (Salinger, 1951).

Translating these categorizations into prestige or Ueber-Brand building
and analysing all the brands that we have, we definitely saw a lot of cases
that mix the functions. Just as 'real' myths do. Take the battle of Troy for
instance: Achilles 'teaches' how to deal with anger and pride, his fight with
Agamemnon 'confirms' the social need to stick together, all the divine med-
dling 'explains' fate, and his relationship with Patroclus 'transcends' to the
eternal power of love. Myths, like anything else, are not clear cut and like to
grow in between and beyond systems.

Yet, if you look closely at prestige and/or Ueber-Brands, most do
exhibit a clear tendency for one of two approaches: they either follow the
'metaphysical-cosmological' route, which we call 'reaching beyond with
myths', or they pursue the 'sociological-pedagogical' path, which we termed
'guiding with myths'. They are either more 'mystical-spiritual' in that they
give us a sense of connecting with a higher power or truth. Or, they are a bit
more 'down to earth', providing guidance or support in the here and now.
Beauty brand Aveda, with their zen-eco philosophy, could be an example of
the former, Apple and their different thinking and acting of the latter.

One last thing to note: all the following is most of the time not dealt with
consciously – either on the consumer, or the marketer's side. Brand makers
or managers let mythical dimensions develop intuitively rather than crafting
them deliberately, driven by category drifts, their brand's personalities or
individual hunches. Look at Aēsop for instance. Its myth is definitely about
'reaching beyond', which makes sense when you hear Dennis Paphitis, the
founder: 'The thing with us is, we like to go deep rather than wide'. However, he said this in the context of his expansion plans (Fairs, 2012), never
about an intent of mythologizing his brand. But: no matter how consciously
or not these mythical dimensions are dealt with, they are there, and they
are mighty powerful. They shape the brand and its customer relations quite
dramatically, so it's important to shed some light on them.

The first Ueber-Way: reaching beyond through myths

Napoleon once said: 'Glory is fleeting, but obscurity is forever.' In a way this could be the mantra for 'reaching beyond through myths'. Of course not literally, as no brand, including these Ueber-Brands, can afford to stay really obscure. After all, they have products to sell. But most brands that follow this route build their glory – and myth – through staying more veiled, interacting in more subtle, sometimes even cerebral tones – without limiting the strength of their proposition. The opposite is true: they draw us in exactly because they give us a sense of connecting with something sublime. And that's hardly ever a shouting match.

Cirque du Soleil is a perfect mix of 'reaching beyond' while still pleasing in the here and now

Image courtesy of Cirque du Soleil, costumes by Dominique Lemieux

Florent Bayle-Labouré, Senior Director of Brand Management and Strategy for Cirque du Soleil told us:

> For our true fans, going to the Cirque is a spiritual, transformative experience. For others it's just stimulation, beauty and fun and that's ok too. There are no spoken words in the Cirque, so everyone can understand it their way. You choose your degree of engagement. This comes from the 'fête foraine' (street fair) roots. We want to be accessible... but we take it to the mythical.

Another case in point is La Mer, the prestige beauty brand from Estée Lauder, which was one of the first to take a beauty product to a sublime level and turn itself into an Ueber-Icon of mythical branding by consistently telling their story, but never spelling it all out. In short, their narrative goes like this: Dr. Max Huber, a physicist, suffered burns in a lab test. Nothing could heal his scarred skin until he discovered the regenerative powers of the sea, specifically sea kelp. He concocted his 'miracle broth' and the wonder of La Mer was born, transforming skin ever since by way of the ultimate source of all life: the sea. Just check out the video on their website (La Mer, accessed August 2014). It's very simple, but with all the trappings of a strong myth – establishing a hero (Dr. Huber, aerospace physicist), linking yourself with an eternal power (the sea), overcoming adversity (the burns, the many trials) and culminating in a miracle (the broth). Yet, you never really learn many details. A picture of Dr. Huber? Hardly. Biographical details? Nothing. A bit more on the ingredients? Never. An explanation of the miracle broth? God forbid. The whole story is very rudimentary and most remains unsaid, yet that's exactly what makes it so compelling. You have to believe, and believing is the opposite of knowing. Besides, Ueber-Brands love a bit of hide-and-seek anyway (see Principle 3, Avert the Overt).

What La Mer does to bring its myth to life and make it tangible, though, is provide a ritual that makes the miracle come true, an insiders' trick to activate the powers of the sea: you must rub the cream between your fingers until the warmth softens it and releases the unspeakably powerful ingredients. A truly spiritual ritual: Do. Believe. Hope.

The male counterpart to La Mer in a lot of ways is Cool Water, the classic man's fragrance from Davidoff that is still among the top 10 in most markets, more than 25 years after its launch. Like La Mer, Cool Water also connects itself with the power of the ocean, only this time less re-generating and more re-energizing. Equally, Cool Water sports a hero, though naturally more physical than physicist, and one that's being updated more regularly, lately including Laird Hamilton, Paul Walker and Scott Eastwood. Cool Water is as religious about sticking to its script as La Mer, only it doesn't verbalize its myth but visualizes it – again and again: shirtless, muscular guy jumps into ocean, tumbles with the waves and jets out again full of vitality and virility. It's a very simple and archaic story, as much as the one for La Mer. But that's where the power of both these Ueber-Brands resides – they each occupy a primal motif, and that reaches way deep into our souls, and our pockets.

Cool Water is much more 'glorious' and much less 'subtle' than La Mer – in everything from its name to its packaging to its communication. That's mostly due to its target – men do tend to prefer strength over subtlety – and to its premise – it is physical as much as it is metaphysical. But, in their respective contexts they both do clearly play on the quieter side, exuding a sense of iconic gravitas befitting an Ueber-Brand, 'reaching beyond' rather than an imperative clarity, which would be more 'guiding'.

Lastly, a very different example, and one that at first glance might feel neither very 'prestige' nor very 'mythical' or 'reaching beyond'. Yet, Method does check all three. Method is a cleaning supply company founded in 2001 by two California roommates, Adam Lowry and Eric Ryan, with today's sales somewhere 'north of US $100 million' (Eng, 2013). Not gigantic yet, but growing steadily. Anyway, what matters more here is the thought leadership they've shown, how they managed to revolutionize a very staid category and establish themselves as the Ueber-Brand in it.

Again, their mythical story is powerful in its simplicity, and it's told with exuberant charm and wit, on their website and in their book (Ryan and Lowry, 2011). Eric and Adam literally present themselves not as heroes, but 'SUPER' heroes, 'set out to save the world and create... home care products... more powerful than a bottle of sodium hypochlorite. Gentler than a thousand puppy licks. Able to detox tall homes in a single afternoon' (Method (a), accessed August 2014). The myth they occupy: our deep-seated human need to turn chaos into order and wrong into right. Their narrative: young and fun Davids fight old and overpowering Goliaths. Their approach: change dirty and commodity into beauty and humanity – through smart thinking and daring design. Their mantra: 'People against Dirty'.

The last part, their tagline, is almost one of their strongest assets, apart from the guys themselves, their culture, the products, the design... 'People against Dirty' works on all levels. Mythical: a call for purity and clarity. Ecological: a rejection of bad or toxic substances. Practical: a promise of clean, livable environments. And last but not least, spiritual: a spirit of positivity and growth. No wonder they have become the beacon and Ueber-Brand they are. There certainly is 'method' to all their playful 'madness'.

As different as these three examples are, they all share two things: they definitely are modern prestige or Ueber-Brands. And they've reached this status not least by very rigidly building their story into a myth, just like Moleskine, which we discussed earlier, or LEGO® and their famous movie. They all gave their brand depth and meaning by reaching beyond, or, as Joseph Campbell put it, by turning the brand into 'a mask of God – a metaphor for what lies behind the visible world' (Campbell, 1988) be it the 'Source of Life' (La Mer or Cool Water), 'Purity beyond Dirty' (Method) or 'Creativity and Imagination' (Moleskine and LEGO). **Every one of these brands allows its targets to feel like they're connecting with a higher truth or power, and that's how their customers in turn allow these brands to elevate themselves beyond most of their competitors.**

Lastly we should say that you can of course also 'reach beyond' in more high-energy and high-pitched ways, as Red Bull and its promise of 'giving you wings' has shown successfully for almost 30 years. But that's the exception to the rule – as true superheroes always are. In general, mythical reaching for the eternal and the sublime is a more subdued thing, something where mystery is of the essence. Because that is where the eternal resides – beyond the earthly here and now.

The second Ueber-Way: guiding with myths

'When a person (or a brand) becomes a model for other people's lives, he has moved into the sphere of being mythologized' (Campbell, 1988). That's the thought behind Ueber-Brands which 'guide with their myths', the second Ueber-Way to achieve mythical status.

One of the best examples here is certainly Chanel, which we already talked about earlier. It's impressive how this Ueber-Brand has over the past years re-strengthened and expanded its myth, guided by Karl Lagerfeld, but probably also in preparation for the time after his exit.

Obviously, at the core of this myth is Coco Chanel, her personal as well as her professional story, since both were so intricately interwoven. There have been two full feature movies, *Coco before Chanel*, with Audrey Tautou and *Coco Chanel & Igor Stravinsky*, both released in 2009, the latter with the brand's explicit support. In 2008, there was also a made-for-TV movie starring Shirley MacLaine. And there has been a whole slew of mini-films made by the brand for online release, including the already mentioned *Once Upon a Time...* but also others, even more overtly building the myth, like the 'Inside Chanel' series.

Although the topics of these works differ, they more or less all play into the single, overarching narrative: Gabrielle Chanel, born to a single mother, raised in a convent, fiercely independent by nature or fate, revolutionized fashion and liberated the modern woman – from corsets all the way to romantic or social conformity. Consequently, there is hardly a classic Chanel item that avid or even just casual users of the brand cannot connect to a piece of 'CoCo lore', constantly rehashing and building the brand's Ueber-Status. How she chose the name for her most famous and lucrative creation, Chanel No 5, as a statement of stark modernity, or why the chain strap of the Chanel bag and the little black dress are reminiscent of her convent days, and how the tweed costume broke with all conventions, appropriated masculine materials and became an icon of female liberation as much as of a modern, paired-down aesthetic. It's amazing how streamlined and consistent the myth is, despite or because of all the little kinks and swirls. Gabrielle Chanel, and by extension her brand and all its products, have become the icon of modern femininity and emancipated elegance. Not a role model in the traditional sense, but certainly a 'guiding light', even for today's women and absolutely for the industry. An Ueber-Brand guiding with its myth – and being guided by it.

According to Campbell, there are basically two ways in which myths can guide us – along the 'Right Hand Path' or the 'Left Hand Path'. Logically, the first is teaching us the 'right' thing to do, the socially accepted norms. The latter is more revolutionary in spirit, demanding from the individual a surpassing of social norms, liberating him/herself and thus all of us. Great examples for either are children's books. The educational ones, especially from the late 19th century like *Der Struwwelpeter* (Shockheaded Peter) are clearly 'right-handed', heavily driven by 'dos' and 'don'ts'. The more adventurous ones, like *Tom Sawyer* or most famously *Pippi Longstocking* are more 'left-handed', giving kids room to test their powers, stand against authority and grow-up, so to speak.

Where would you put the early myth of Chanel? Probably more 'left-handed', no? However in the end, and certainly by now, Chanel turned pro-establishment, 'right-handed' so to say, but without ever quite losing its non-conformist undercurrent, thus giving the brand and its myth a nice intriguing tension.

A brand that is very un-ambiguously 'left-handed' is definitely Harley Davidson. We already mentioned their famous mission video *The Harley Experience. Living by It.* Just to give you a taste of its voiceover:

> We believe in bucking the system that's built to smash individuals as bugs on a windshield... We believe in flames and skulls. We believe life is what you make it, and we make it one hell of a ride... We don't care what everyone else believes – Amen.
>
> (Harley Davidson, 2008)

Now that's clearly 'guiding with myth'; some might even say it's 'inciting with myth' – the myth of roads, freedom and endless, unbridled individuality. Albeit a mostly masculine individuality, empowering a sense of archaic confidence and broad-legged swagger in an age where many men feel confined and confused. They speak to the 'rebel outcast' while selling mostly to the white-collar weekend warrior, actually female to a large degree. **That's the guiding power of myth: it projects an archetype that inspires and that we can aspire to, no matter what our reality looks like.**

To finish, let's look at the opposite, a brand or product whose success is clearly built on a more conformist, 'right-handed' form of heroism: 'Invictus by Paco Rabanne'. The man's fragrance, launched in 2013, shot into the top three in many markets within less than a year. The reason why is pretty clear to Marc Puig, CEO of the parent company: 'When you have a good story, it's like a self-fulfilling prophecy because then you show your partners, you show to retailers and everybody gets excited and wants to give you the most possibilities and opportunities to succeed' (Weil, 2014). Apart from that, it allows for a very clear and consistent development of the brand and its myth. In the case of Invictus this means all is fashioned towards the idea of 'winner takes it all': it is in the name, the trophy-shaped bottle, the victory wings on the pack, the POS (point of sale) displays and not the least the communication. The spot is a mix of reality and mythology, using Australian rugby star Nick Youngquest entering a stadium and ending in the locker room, victoriously surrounded by gorgeous groupies, but only after having beaten a bunch of 'statuesque' heroes and impressed more than one 'Greek' goddess.

It's not yet clear if Invictus will indeed grow into an Ueber-Brand like Cool Water has, for instance, and you do wonder sometimes, 'how can someone take this seriously? Isn't this so over the top, so clichéd that it doesn't fit our modern, ironic sensibilities? But that's the power – and the privilege – of myths. **Myths are by nature clichés; that's what makes them work. They're easy, we get them instantly and their message shoots straight to our heart – whether we want it to or not. That's how they capture us and how they can guide us. Besides, iconic always beats ironic, at least, when it comes to building Ueber-Brands.**

Making myths: what to respect

Given that 'mythmaking' sits at the core of this book and our principles for building modern prestige or Ueber-Brands, we think it's worthwhile to share some very practical insights on how to evolve a history into a clear brand story and ultimately into a compelling brand myth. Clearly, this topic is endless, and there are lots of very good books as well as seminars out there (info@ueberbrands.com), so here we will just alert you to the four most important aspects based on our learnings, each of which would definitely warrant a deep dive on its own.

1. The need to listen

The first important point: only if you're a good listener will you ever be a good storyteller or mythmaker. Sometimes this is called the Harun-al-Rashid principle: 'You'll only hear the unheard of when you take yourself back – and listen' (Frenzel, Mueller and Sottong, 2004). According to myth, Harun-al-Rashid, fabled caliph of Baghdad in the 8th century and key protagonist if not author of *The Book of One Thousand and One Nights*, would regularly venture out at night, in disguise. The reason: he wanted to understand how to lead his people, and he knew that he could only find out what really motivated or concerned them if he listened to their stories. So he did. And so should any marketer, trying to understand and build his brand's story and develop its myth. Angela Ahrendts and Christopher Bailey did it at Burberry (Ahrendts, 2013), where one of their first acts was to hire a cultural anthropologist to talk to employees to help them understand and record the brand story, of which they would then jointly write the next chapter or better chapters – as well as marketing and mythical Ueber-Brand history.

2. The name as a title

Nomen est Omen – it's all in the name. Or better, it should be. The more evocative your brand's name, the more connected to its myth, the better.

Your name is your header. Just think back to Invictus. Not only will almost everyone, even non-Latin speakers, understand 'invincible' and connote 'victorious', but because of the use of Latin you're also immediately transported to the world of ancient Rome, gladiators and larger-than-life heroes. Mythical indeed. The same goes for Napapijri, a European active and casual wear brand building its myth around polar expeditions and adventurous explorations. You'll be hard pressed to find anyone able to trace the name back to the Finnish term for polar circle. But it definitely sounds exotic – somewhere between Native American, Sami, Inuit or Japanese – as well as the fact that it links to 'knapsack' and phonetically mimics a journey from the familiar (nap) to the unknown (pijri). Not so bad for a brand that wants you to feel venturesome and connected with the myths of the poles. 'Mykita' on the other hand, the hot-as-hell optics brand from Berlin, goes a completely different route. The name literally means 'my Kita', with 'Kita' being short for the German 'Kindertagestaette', the place where the brand resides as well as the origin of its mythical rise, an abandoned kindergarten. No matter which way you go, connotative (Invictus), associative (Napapijri) or denotative (Mykita) the more the name sparks people's imagination the better. In that sense shooting for all three certainly doesn't hurt. By the way, a semiotic analysis of your brand and your name is never a bad idea, especially when building a myth.

3. The importance of struggle

'As a storyteller you want to position the problems in the foreground and then show how you've overcome them', says Robert McKee, one of the world's best-known screenwriting lecturers from LA (Fryer, 2003). Painting a rosy, streamlined picture is the farthest thing from a myth. It's boring and banal. Stories, and especially myths, have to connect with life if they want to help us 'reach beyond' or 'guide us'. Life is messy, a continuous struggle. That's why strong myths always have a great deal of adversaries for the protagonist to overcome. Only then do they ring true, can we believe in them. Plus, it is of course so much more suspenseful, attention grabbing and memorable, which is the cardinal point for any Ueber-Brand.

4. The question of truth

At last, the key question: must a myth be true? Yes and no. The core and everything that's material to the claim you're making must be. But you can embellish. Actually you must dramatize, because otherwise you are just recounting history. You want to stylize and elevate your brand to a position beyond time and place, and that means you have to move beyond, where reality meets mythology. A pretty good example in this respect is

Bacardi. Their 'Untameable' campaign does chronicle the brand's true history, but it also takes it to a higher, mythical level by using it to present themselves as a force of irrepressible passion. The question remains though if that fits with their product, rum, which is usually connected with a more fluid, relaxed energy. A negative example is definitely the much-hyped Himalaya salt. The whole idea of it being purer, healthier and tastier turned out to be more than dubious, and its customers suddenly felt much more ashamed than advanced. The same is true for The Body Shop, which had to live through allegations of foul play on pretty much every level after its founder, Anita Roddick, died in 2007. Consequently the brand could never regain the mythic Ueber-Brand status it once had and has been languishing ever since.

Seven steps to heaven

In Joseph Campbell's 'Mono Myth Model' (Campbell, 1978) there are 17 steps. We find this a bit much for our fast-paced age – though taking time is certainly a prerequisite for building and appreciating brand myths. Hence we developed a streamlined version of just seven steps. It kind of goes with the widespread theory that there are only seven basic plots in all of the stories we tell. And you know how we are partial to the magic of seven anyway.

Every mythical story starts with a 'Calling', a challenge in need of a hero. That sets your brand's original mission and purpose. The 'Calling' is answered by the 'Inspiration', your product or service idea. Then come the 'Challenges' until you get it right, financed or whatever; the struggle to make your idea come real. This is a very important part in giving your myth drama and credibility. This shapes your 'Belief', the philosophy you develop based on your original vision and all that you learned to get to the actual solution. The 'Apotheosis' is the seminal moment when your brand proves itself and you're being acknowledged as the hero you set out to be, the winning of the World Championship so to speak. Out of that you develop a mantra, your 'Principles', setting the order for the new age and the credo for all your disciples to live by. At last you're back where you started, but with the world a better place, or so the myth goes. It's the 'Future' you envisioned in the beginning and which has become reality – and the base for your next 'Calling'.

Separation, return and initiation

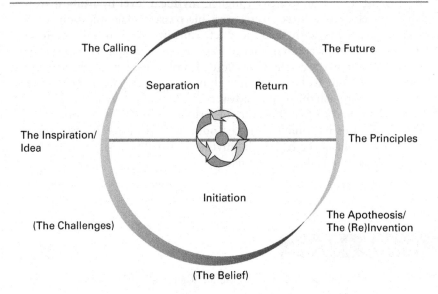

Principle 4: The rules of 'from myth to meaning'

1 Listen, deep!
      To your employees, your best customers, your long-time partners.
      That's where you'll find the core of your myth. Every detail counts.

2 Turn your history into a story
      Being truthful but also creative. And don't forget the struggle, you
      need it for your credibility and 'narrative transportation'

3 Share
      With all our stakeholders and let them spin it further. Spike their
      imagination. It will help feed your myth.

4 Write on
      Keep on building your narrative. A good story isn't written
      overnight. And a great myth takes even longer.

5 Move to a higher level
      Reach beyond, that's where reality turns mythical. Or guide and
      fashion your brand into an iconic hero that inspires.

6 Stick with it
      Myths are eternal, for better or worse. You can course correct but
      never reverse. That's why it's important to be clear where you're
      going from the get-go.

We call it the inverted iceberg: Ueber-Brands need to reach deep to
go up. They must translate their mission into narratives that build
them into a myth, connected to a deep-seated truth, where 80 per cent
is beneath the surface, but the 20 per cent visible is so alluring they
pull us in without end.

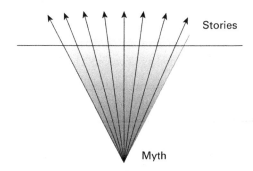

Ueber-Brand case study 4   MINI – myth revisited – from underdog challenger to fun provocateur

The original Mini was designed to answer to the need for an affordable and economical car. This was Britain in 1959, just after the Suez Canal crisis, when a growing middle class saw gas prices go up significantly. Initially priced at £497, the car became immensely popular. It was produced for over four decades, sold over five million times and its designer – Mr. Alec Issigonis – was knighted for the achievement. Eventually, though, the Mini star fell behind in innovation and interest. In 2000 the German BMW group picked up the brand and re-launched the classic as the 'New MINI' (they insist on writing this one in all-caps).

The New MINI was an instant hit in Britain and around the world. In fact, MINI in the United States quickly outsold all other markets despite very low in-going brand recognition. There are more MINIs sold in the United States – over 65,000 in 2012 – than all models of Volvo combined. Globally MINI sold over 300,000 cars in 2013 at a price ranging from US $20,000 to well over US $40,000 for a customized model. The upper end of that range is in line with the price of a roomy and plush Mercedes C-Class sedan or BMW X1 SUV. The equally retro 'New Beetle' or Chrysler 'PT Cruiser' were launched earlier (1997 and 2000) but have not seen the same success. The Cruiser was discontinued in 2011.

So, where does the appeal of the new MINI come from? Clearly, it is not practicality or price and it must be more than a quirky-retro look.

The myth of the underdog challenger

The myth of Mini is an example of a 'left-handed', guiding one. It developed in two distinct phases. In a first, organic phase, the little car created for the average person turned into a fashion statement and an underdog hero. As the myth began to fade, BMW revisited and evolved it to a more global Ueber-story of the 'fun provocateur', a small, colorful bundle of wit and speed which wins over the bulky and boring – at least in spirit.

As a British legend of the '60s, the name 'Mini' was telling of the minimalist design strategy chosen to make the car affordable. But its legend always loomed large. First, the frugality aspect was taken to stand for an anti-establishment statement – or rather a quintessentially British under-statement. The more 'junior' royals could be seen climbing out of diminutive

Minis rather than limousines, and this included pop royals like the Beatles. George Harrison had his 'psychedelic' one, and owning an intricately customized Mini became a mark of belonging to the elite of the 'swinging sixties'. There were Minis with Rolls-Royce grilles. Steve McQueen sported a turbo-charged version in wood and chrome. Elton John, Peter Sellers and Brigitte Bardot all had their own. Consequently, Mini assumed the role of counter-cultural status symbol, the stubborn little bulldog challenging the big dogs. The Mini Cooper, in particular, became an underdog icon – at least if you were British. A collaboration with F1 racing legend and car builder John Cooper, the namesake model won many rallies. Drama surrounds the – almost – four consecutive wins in Monte Carlo (1964–67) which infuriated the French. In a highly controversial decision, French judges disqualified the Minis placed first through fourth in 1966 and declared a Citroën the winner. As with all martyrs, the hero car garnered enormous sympathy and went on to win the next year to great fanfare. Even Enzo Ferrari was impressed and bought one. The 1969 film *The Italian Job*, starring Michael Caine and three Minis, marked the zenith of the first incarnation of Mini and cemented its underdog challenger myth: likeable British gangsters outsmart the Italian Mafia and the police by escaping congested Turin with their gold booty in three Minis – a red, a white and a blue one.

BMW extracts the myth, modernizes and globalizes it: three decades later BMW picked up where *The Italian Job* left off, but the brand did not stop at reviving the past. It updated and upgraded the idea of self-expression through custom designs and friendly provocation as guiding principles, while toning down the Britishness to a style element. *It focused on mythologizing 'the little car that can' against dull standardization and 'bigger is better', allowing the brand to drop affordable design and go premium and global.* Enough of the original DNA was retained for the classic fans and their clubs to stay loyal, while the modernized elements attracted new types of members and markets and made the brand globally relevant.

In the United States, for example, most consumers ignore the car's history but experience it as antidote to their family vans, pick-up trucks or SUVs. 'Fun provocateur' even translates in China. There, Mini's 50-year anniversary was celebrated with billboards exalting 'Adhering to the MINI policy firmly for 50 years', gently mocking Communist Party slogans. Some local governments forbade the MINI antics, but consumers swiftly picked up on them on social media.

It is interesting to contrast this successful re-launch of MINI with the failure of the New Beetle. The difference does not lie in the brand's original popularity, being first to re-launch, or in performance. History and VW dealers tell us that the Beetle wins on all of these measures (PrestigeVolkswagen.com, accessed August 2014). The difference lies in VW failing to pick up on the deeper meaning of the Beetle. In the '60s, it was the hippie's anti-statement to the gas-guzzling, large, ship-cars of their parents. Round and small like a baby, colourful with a distinctive sound. When VW re-launched they did offer a physical reinterpretation of the car and alluded to the 'flower-power' past by adding a little vase with a plastic daisy to the dashboard. But they neglected entirely to connect with any modern-day anti-establishment sentiment. The brand's legend was alluded to, but its mythical power remained locked. Now the brand is lost in fighting a 'cute' image via re-designs. Ueber-Potential lost.

Mythical MINI: memorabilia, McQueen and a fanatical fan (with tattoo)

Photos by Tyukodi Laszlo, Courtesy BMW Group

Longing to belong to those with a 'mission to motor on'

MINI is the small car that can, with a 'shit-disturber' personality, according to its Canadian Agency. It raises the spirits by applying a strategy called 'the FLIP' – Fun, Legacy, Individuality, Performance (Cassies.ca, 2006). The success of the approach has created a new class of car – the 'personality' car – and made the MINI its uncontested leader. People buy the car as much to express a non-conformist attitude as they do to get from points A to B. In fact, that last part seems often secondary. If Tesla is our 'eco-master' (see Principle 2), then MINI is our 'fun master', designed with an inspirational target in mind that is brought to life through a language, communities and events that make us long to belong.

MINI makes sure the design target stays aspirational. The long line of luminaries of yesteryear is continued with contemporaries from Will Smith to Paul Smith and Emma Stone to Britney Spears. Some are simply 'sighted' with the car, others use them in films or co-create designs. Sponsorship of racing drivers, club leaders, customizers and brand historians ensures the legend is being fed and spread. In the world of the clubs, the owners of 'original' or custom designed Minis are considered top of the crop. The racers come in to represent the rebel spirit and the brand's 'MINI adventure' films do so on screen, showing dudes out-manoeuvring a charging SUV, crawling back off the ledge of a bridge after an emergency stop or screaming their lungs out while drift-racing through the streets.

MINI's broader strategic target craves this spirit. They are part of the affluent middle class who seek to escape the idea of being conformist. In China an estimated 80 per cent of MINI owners are women, but the Shanghai showroom features pool tables and the owner's club organizes rallies across the Tibetan plateau or the Gobi Desert. These women do not want to be part of the 'kawaii* Hello Kitty' doll crowd dominating Asia (*Japanese for cute). Across the ocean, in the Bay Area, every 8 in 100 cars is a MINI, mixing tech types who want to stay young with 'soccer moms' looking to escape their shuttle-van reality.

To fuel the sense of belonging, MINI takes inspiration from influential fans and re-injects their language, experiences and causes to create identifiers and templates for local replication by self-organized clubs. They use the word 'motoring' rather than the mundane 'driving' and propagate the 'secret' exchange of the 'MINI wave sign' as you pass each other. They create lighthouse 'MINI United Events', which have reached gargantuan proportions. The 2012 three-day event at the Le Castellet racetrack in France gathered over 30,000 fans from over 50 countries, some from as far as Russian towns 6,500 km away. Beyond the official car and stunt shows, races, hip concerts and exclusive model previews, it's mostly the fans that take over and exhibit custom styles on their cars as well as MINI art on their own bodies. These events in turn spawn hundreds of national and local ones every year around the world, from the 'Super Battle of MINI' in Tsukuba, Japan, via the '848.5' crossing of the Mackinac bridge in upper Michigan (848 and a mysterious half MINIs) to the meaning-laden 'MINIs to Monte' touring event from England to the principality. As we have seen in Principle 2, MINI encourages and sponsors the online sharing of these events for everyone else to get inspired, plus the extension of the community in the cloud. Netnographer Bernard Cova counted over 50 MINI-dedicated Facebook sites and over 70 user-managed sites, blogs, twitter accounts, YouTube channels, etc... and that was in the digital Stone Age – 2011 (Cova, 2011). Add to that over 300 MINI-registered off-line clubs and the clandestine 'Secret MINI Clubs' that only 'those in the know' will be able to join and you understand that owning a MINI is as much about belonging as owning a car. The 'velvet rope' principle taken to perfection.

Un-sell: behold the 'not normal'

Your first sighting of a New MINI might have been of one strapped on top of an SUV, 'glued' onto the side of a wall, spiked on a pole to light the street, loaded on a giant sling-shot, packaged in an over-sized toy car box or printed on an equally big box and seemingly discarded with Christmas trash on the curb. Or you might have read in tabloids about the MINI being involved in wild police chases or being clumsily faked by other car manufacturers (these are fake stories). Or yet again you might have seen news and YouTube reporting about MINI challenging Porsche to a race for months, just to lose when they finally gave in (this being a real story). In other words, you are unlikely to have become aware of the MINI via the industry-standard TV ads-cum special rebate offers followed by a hard sell at the dealership.

In fact, you are more likely to have heard that those owning a MINI needed to patiently wait because launch quantities are constrained, or because making their custom model took several months. The local allocation of limited edition models also often sells out before the first car reaches the dealership.

This unconventional approach mixed with a unique language and rituals makes for high memorability, along with word-of-mouth value and spending efficiency (the MINI US launch is estimated to have cost a fifth of that of the Fiat 500, for example). The campaign slogan 'Not Normal' fits in every respect – truly un-selling and under-marketing yet over-achieving exactly because of it.

Yet, as much as they go light on traditional marketing, the BMW designers have gone big on product. They cheered up the feisty bulldog look, added a good dose of German engineering and applied supply chain ingenuity to enable more people to customize. What used to be the purview of some MINI addicts is now within reach of those who dare to select from over 370 interior and some 320 exterior options. Apparently that works out to some 10 million, 10 billion or… 30 trillion possible configurations, depending on who counts. It's all part of the fun and mystery. How about a Clubman Bond Street in 'Cool Champagne' with 'Black Jack' mirror covers and 'MINI Ray' side scuttles? (Note the idiosyncratic language.) And it is rumoured that this model has a hidden inner glove compartment that does not show up in the user manual. The true aficionado can choose to stand out further by making 'mods' post-delivery using special parts from a cottage industry of accessory makers that have sprung up around the MINI. On the other end of the spectrum, one can leave the identity making entirely in the capable hands of MINI and buy one of the reassuringly 'limited edition' cars. Close to a hundred such cars have been conceived, some limited to as few specimens as 250. The MINI Agent Provocateur with laced rooftop and black leather was for the sensually daring while the Goodwood with Rolls-Royce interior and paint job is made for royals and those who already own an equally priced Porsche.

These custom jobs are a prime case of 'exclusivity through complicity'. We know the MINI 'configurator' will yield an industrialized version of what the uniquely psychedelic version of a George Harrison was. But we are willing to play the game for our creative convenience and since MINI pokes enough fun at the idea to prevent it from being unmasked as a desperate attempt at identity making.

Living the dream and moving with gravitas

The MINI organization has been part of the BMW group since 1994, but the management, marketing and dealerships are spiritually and physically separated from the mother house. 'Normally stuffy and orderly BMW lets the people working the MINI brand act majorly strange' reports the *Canadian Globe and Mail* (Cato, 2013). Take the 'MINIstry of Finance' department that provides dealerships financing 'through a heady cocktail of mathematical know-how and endless lashings of tea' (Mini Menzies, 2014). MINI 'intravertises', encouraging employees to imagine, organize and experience the kind of thrilling experiences with the little car that become event programmes. Owning the car and belonging to MINI clubs is not just part of a job, but part of a shared identity. China Marketing Director Izzy Zhu describes himself as one of 'the angry young' and working for MINI is part of tagging yourself as such (Xiao, 2010).

To avoid oversaturation and equity dilution – despite the raging popularity – BMW has restricted the number of MINI dealerships and is prescriptive about their giant toy store look; it has limited annual base-car output, preferring to add volumes via special editions. But most importantly, it strives to keep purchasing a MINI something special. Thus, a MINI convertible buyer might find themselves being asked to sign a 'pledge' to keep the top down, as delivered (and sealed with stickers) for as long as they possibly can to ensure their little MINI has fun…

MINIs and their fans having fun

Photo courtesy BMW Group

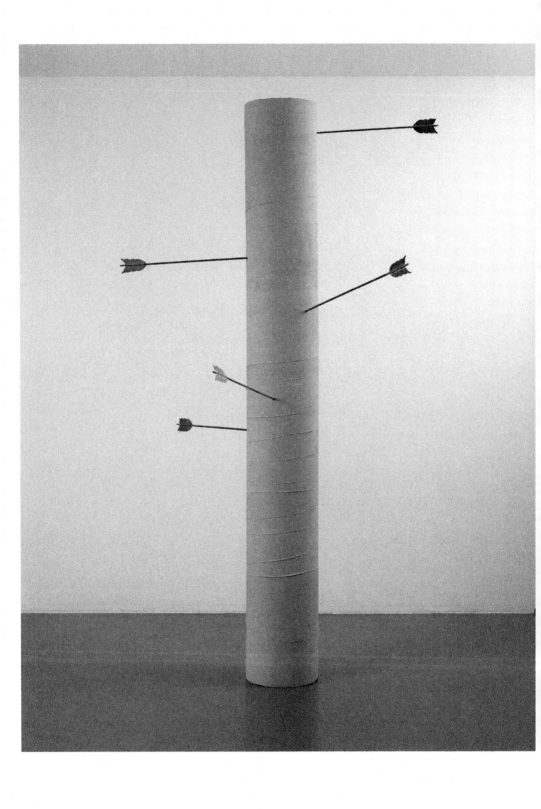

Principle 5
Behold!
The product as manifestation

Of course, even the most prestigious or mythical of brands are nothing without their products. No style will ever survive in the long run without substance. Even modern prestige or Ueber-Brands need good hard physics to reach their metaphysical realm.

This is especially true in our day and age, where we are getting tired of empty shells, supercilious bling and over-marketing. We have been duped too many times, we've had – and thrown away – too many things and we've started to realize the consequences of mindless consumerism. More and more of us, or at least those fortunate enough to be able to do so, are starting to look for the real thing instead of just anything. We are eschewing mundane matter in search of something that lasts, something that means something, something that is worth the waste, so to speak.

And that's where Ueber-Brands fit in perfectly. Not that they are all eco-sustainable, not by any means, but they are all beyond their competition, in a class of their own, a cut above. That makes them special, even when it's in a category or a product that's anything but, like Red Bull energy soda or Method cleaning supplies. They work very hard on it, doing everything they can to secure this feeling of superiority and worth, as we have seen.

The same diligence and conscientious effort is naturally applied to their product: 'The product as essence'. **Because when it comes to Ueber-Brands, products aren't just products, they have to be seen as Ueber-Products. They are never just useful objects to hold and handle; they must be experienced as a manifestation to behold, evidence of their own myth, to be revered.**

Making something very well that delivers what it's supposed to deliver isn't enough to achieve this of course. You have to also treat it accordingly. After all it's the context that makes the king. Ueber-Brands do this mainly in three ways.

In 'Make it a holy grail' we'll show how they take their knack for myth-making and apply it on a product level. They create 'stories to believe' rather than the traditional 'reasons to believe': stories can help mitigate a sales pitch by romanticizing it, making it feel much more seductive (see Principle 3). Beyond this, Ueber-Brands also often appropriate codes from other, higher categories for an 'arts and crafts' feel, and they ultimately try to turn regimens into 'rituals'.

The second route is to 'Make it unmistakable'. Most Ueber-Brands establish a rich, ownable design vocabulary that gets them – and their users – recognized, without being logo-plastered: subtly, but 'unmistakably branded'. An ever-growing number even take it to the ultimate level and enable customization to make things truly one in a million, ie 'unmistakably you and me'.

Lastly, Ueber-Brands always make sure their quintessential products stay at 'The centre of attention', in their marketing and particularly the minds of their customers because 'heroes need a spotlight'. Though they may not always be bestsellers, they are long sellers, and for that they must be kept fresh and current. 'Icons must also evolve' – to be and become 'musts', again and again.

Three routes, one goal: put the product where it belongs, at the core of the myth – and on a pedestal. But all this starts with having a product substantial enough to survive all this 'beholding'…

The product as essence

About 100 years ago, in 1912, the advertising agency McCann established the world's first advertising trademark 'Truth well told' (McCann, accessed August 2014). It's debatable whether McCann or the advertising profession in general always lived up to the idea, but it's a nice way to capture the relationship between Ueber-Brands and their Ueber-Products.

Only if you're trustworthy can you guide. Being credible and reliable is the first condition to provide orientation and aspiration, and that requires being seen as truthful. Logically, Ueber-Brands must be almost more so than most other brands, and try to deliver what they promise or better yet preach – because they certainly do want to guide us. Despite all the things we have discussed and which could create the impression that you're dealing with a bunch of tricksters, prestige and particularly modern prestige brands actually go to quite some pains to live up to their image and make their products stand up to even the most critical tests. Some like Patagonia for instance, even make this their entire premise. The same goes for Swiss bag brand Freitag, with its neo-industrial upcycling and craftsmanship (see case study, Principle 6). Or Whole Foods, who educate about the pros and cons of certain food standards in great detail (Whole Foods Market, accessed August 2014). Beauty brand Kiehl's, on the other hand, became famous for refraining from advertising at all and putting their marketing dollars into excessive sampling, so convinced were they of the superior quality of their products.

This extreme product, manufacturing and sometimes also ethical focus doesn't happen by accident of course. To some degree it's the price you have to pay as an Ueber-Brand, because the higher your position, the higher the expectations of your customers. In the traditional as well as in the new prestige world you're dealing with people who are paying above average and so that's what they want to get. Our level of discrimination is usually proportionate to our level of involvement, which in turn is connected to the brand's level of pricing – no matter if it's a car or a pint of ice cream.

Beyond that, however, we as consumers also have evolved. We're trending towards a 'New Functionalism' where we're turning the old Bauhaus credo 'less is more' into a new mantra for our consumption: More with Less. We want less merchandise and more meaning, less quantity and more quality, fewer unmet promises and more honesty and integrity. That's why we're keen on the background, the story, the details of our brands and products rather than just being bedazzled by lifestyle imagery. This is one of the reasons for the increasing number of brands turning their advertising into 'history lessons'. Just think of Louis Vuitton and how they have moved in recent years from glossy celebrity shots to travelogues to craft stories. Similarly Gucci, the epitome of glam, which suddenly felt the urge to balance their sex appeal with some talk about masterful ateliers. Or in other categories, Bacardi's 'Untamed' campaign and its recent copy, Jim Beam's 'Make History' (Schulz, 2014).

However, as crucial as the truth is as a solid foundation, that alone doesn't make a modern prestige or Ueber-Brand. The 'well told' bit from the old ad slogan is still what makes the difference; not just in the sense of a nice campaign, but a holistic marketing programme from production to packaging, presentation to customization and yes, also communication. All swirling around the product to figuratively and sometimes also literally put it on a pedestal. Presenting it as the thing, not just anything, the ultimate, the epitome, the essence, the ideal substance, which pales everything else to mere matter. **Only if the products are revered, treated and polished as the stars that they shall be, will they really develop the power to shine in the eyes of their beholders. Only then will they have a chance to be admired as 'essence' that fills their form and justifies their brand's myth.**

Yuan Soap is a wonderful example that we came across (see box overleaf). It is a small but exponentially growing TCM-inspired (Traditional Chinese Medicine) brand from Taiwan, which absolutely 'makes truth', but then also 'tells' it in such endearing and engaging ways that you can't help but be completely enthralled, as our little story shows. They literally treat their products as 'essences', which is admittedly a bit easier given their métier. For all our marketing readers to whom this doesn't come as 'naturally' we have also assembled the key points in three 'to do' sections.

Yuan Soap

A story of 'essence'

'Labour of Love' – Yuan Soap founder Jiang Rong-Yuan (top right) and his workers creating essential products to behold

Image courtesy of Yuan Soap

About a year ago we were standing in the middle of a field in YangMingShan National Park in Taiwan. It was a rainy day and only plastic bags over our shoes kept the mud from seeping in. Nevertheless, we stood in awe of the beauty: multiple paddy terraces fenced in by large stone boulders and framed by wild forests and streams cascading down into the valley with a loud roar. The terraces are remnants of stone quarries, as the Yuan Soap export director explained, and have now been converted to supply the mostly indigenous herbs that are key ingredients for Yuan's products.

But let's rewind. It all started in 2005 with ad agency executive Ah Yuan suffering from serious burn-out. He couldn't take the stress anymore and he couldn't stand the way the products he advertised were made. After some time of meditation, reflection and study, Ah (aka Chiang) decided to change direction and find his way back to where his ancestors had left off. His grandfather and great-grandfather were traditional Chinese doctors. Chiang started studying the healing properties and use of home-grown herbs and the methods to create all-natural household and health care products. He began making soaps in his house following an 18-step process that took almost two months from extracting the water to cold-saponifying to moulding, cutting, stamping and wrapping the single pieces by hand.

Fast-forward a few years and this is still the way Yuan Soap workers do it today, all of which anyone can see when visiting their workshop. They pour oils from cooking pots, shape soap balls with their hands, stamp them and let them mature like cheese before cutting them. All this is accompanied by a strong herbal smell: tea, lantana, Asian puccoon, lemongrass, roselle, patchouli… and celebrated and explained in elaborate Mandarin on their website, their marketing materials and an enchanting five-minute video (Yuan Soap on YouTube, accessed August 2014). The products are wrapped in beautiful artisanal papers and cartons, also made locally, and decorated with Ah Yuan's sketches and poetic product descriptions.

We also visited one of their wood-clad stores, where in the back you get to a little terraced garden. On the second-floor balcony, a tablet explains that each terrace is planted with indigenous herbs just like the fields in YangMingShan. We sit down for a cup of Yuan tea and hear about the continued expansion of the brand across Asia. Taiwanese hand-made, herbal household care and beauty products selling at US $9–90 apiece, growing from a few hundred soap bars a month into a multi-million-dollar business with some 500 resellers, producing double-digit

,h the financial crisis? Who would have thought! But
,ittle herb patch outside and the customers listening
,ant's storytelling inside you realize the strong appeal of
nythical yet timeless narrative many of us can relate to,
,e rat race, finding your way back to nature, harvesting
the best in... in one of the most magical places and sharing their
rediscovered wealth. And it's of particular appeal to a Chinese audience
haunted by the destructive consequences of first a 'Cultural Revolution'
and now fast and often ruthless industrial development. The fields, the
farming, the making… they are all an integral part of giving the brand and
its product soul, and making them feel of 'essence', a manifestation of
something bigger, of times past and beauty to come. Truly an essence to
'behold' which people do not just buy but buy into and are willing to pay a
premium for. After all, what is US $30 for finding truth and harmony – even
if it is just a nice-looking string of ball soaps, for now?

Make it a holy grail

Axel Dumas, 6th-generation owner and Co-CEO of French luxury house
Hermès said in an interview recently, 'We are the rare company with no marketing department, because our first goal is the product' (Story, November
2013). And that's exactly how the brand comes across: no over-marketing
but understated yet ultra-luxurious craftsmanship, pure and honest – noble.
Now, for less ultra-rarefied Ueber-Brands it's not really an option to simply
rely on the products selling themselves. Yet that's ideally the impression they
should give. Their marketing must appear so 'un-marketed' (see also Principle 3, Un-selling), as if it was just their passion for the product doing the
talking. They must make their product the 'holy grail', present and treat it
as if it was a revelation. Because only if they show true love for it will they
have a chance to inspire the same in their followers.

From RTB to STB

One way, and perhaps the most important one, to do this is to apply the
concept of storytelling not just on brand but also on product level. **Take
your ingredients, your technologies, the sourcing or manufacturing – what's
usually called Reasons to Believe (RTB) – and transform them into Stories to
Believe (STB). Weave it all into an enchanting narrative, add some flavour
and romanticize the heck out of it.** Because as we've seen, stories are much
better at bypassing rational filters and going straight to the heart – which

is exactly what you want as an Ueber-Brand: *heart selling vs. selling too hard*. Besides, stories are much more conducive to generating something truly memorable and distinctive and defending it in the long run. They work both ways: they emotionalize the product and make you fall in love with it, but they also give our critical minds something to wrap their heads around. STBs are thus the ideal weapon of every Ueber-Brand against substitution and commoditization. They elevate it out of the ordinary into the sphere of that which is worthy of being remembered, told and beheld – and that makes everything else, including price, much less relevant.

A wonderful modern example here is Icebreaker, the active wear brand from New Zealand. They invented what they call the 'Baaa Code', a funny, but very purposeful twist on today's ubiquitous barcodes: all Icebreaker products are made from 100 per cent finest Merino wool. A good selling point, and they could have left it at that, as many others do. But then that wouldn't have been very distinctive. So what they did was let the ingredient come alive, give it a story and a soul, a sheep soul to be precise. Through the 'Baaa Code' every customer can trace the origin of his or her product's wool to the herd and the pastures it grew on: 'see the living conditions of the sheep, meet the growers who raised them and follow the production process through to the finished garment' (Icebreaker, accessed June 2013). The result is that the abstract, generic claim of '100 per cent Merino' becomes 'charged' with lots of beautiful imagery and emotions, the product gets imbued with an almost personally made, artisanal feel and the quality promise becomes very 'real'. Apart from the fact that it's a nice way to provide production transparency and talk eco footprint. In the meantime, Icebreaker has seen such volume growth that tracing the sweater to the sheep has become a tad too ambitious, we were told. But they still want to preserve the ideal 'without needing to identify whether it is Sandy or Zilly that provided the wool'.

Another example is Freitag. Our case study at the end of Principle 6 will tell you all about this interesting Swiss Ueber-Brand and how they are 'Living the Dream' in every aspect. A great detail in this context is how they 'romanticize' their product RTB, recycled truck tarps. Every piece of their material, and thus every bag they turn it into, is necessarily unique, which they celebrate by calling it 'RIP – Recycled Individual Product'. But beyond that they even give it a story – and veracity – by supplying every bag with its little video (online) and a portrait for the box, showcasing its 'previous life'. Now, if that doesn't give your rubberized canvas soul and you a feeling of getting something truly 'special'…

Of arts and crafts

With the likes of Hermès, Chanel, Dior or even Montblanc it's expected that they invest highly in their craftsmanship. So it's no surprise when Montblanc establishes a dedicated and grandiose manufacture for their watchmaking in Le Locle (Montblanc, accessed August 2014) or when Chanel buys up handcraft ateliers on the brink of extinction (Thomas, 2013). Even for a high-end eyewear brand like Smith & Norbu it's almost de rigueur these days to talk of the Tibetan yaks, raised by local farmers, their horn frames are made of. But the love for arts and crafts has moved way beyond the usual suspects – in terms of categories as well as price tiers. Gwen Whiting and Lindsey Boyd for instance founded The Laundress, a high-end laundry and detergent line to 'take excellent care of you, the things you love, and the environment', as they told us and write on their website. It not only promotes hand washing over dry cleaning and provides products that look and feel as if they were made by the two women in their own soap kitchen: the whole brand is designed and presented in a very artisanal way, quite unique in a category so much more known for commoditization. But it's indicative.

Take Lakrids by Johan Buelow, the brand we already mentioned in Principle 1 (Mission Incomparable): 'Johan imagined himself stirring the pot of boiling liquorice and letting people smell and taste his creations while watching the manual production.' And that's exactly what happened. Now his delicious concoctions are sold in all kinds of upscale gourmet shops from Harvey Nichols in London to Chelsea Market in New York to Germany or Dubai, but they still look as if they were just hand-cooked and packed by Johan himself (Lakrids, accessed June 2013). There are many examples to be found, and most of you will know another to add, we're sure.

The point is: even categories that were heretofore staunchly industrial, like detergent and liquorice for instance, are being upgraded and 're-manufacturized', one by one. And Ueber-Brands are at the forefront of

La Maison du Chocolat 'code-poaching' from jewellery with their 'Perle de Ganache'

Image courtesy of La Maison du Chocolat

this – emerging ones or established ones – because it's one of
most respected ways these days to generate prestige, modern
other interesting aspect: in this up-trading **Ueber-Brands regula**
ate prestige or sensual codes, often from other high-craft catego
and creative ways, to express and celebrate their superiority and ᴀ ......ship.
Dorset cereals are packed to look more like a chocolate treat than a healthy
morning standard. La Maison du Chocolat creates a 'Pearl Collection', presenting pralines like fine jewellery. Matilda Pale Ale comes in a bottle that
reminds you of a rare vintage from your wine cellar and Badoit mineral
water stylizes itself into a champagne. No wonder Chobani, the Greek-style
yoghurt that lifted an entire category out of boredom and blandness, spent
a disproportionate chunk of working capital on upping their cup design –
European large mouthed for easy, sensual mixing and scooping and shrink-
wrapped with brighter colours and modern artwork (Gruley, 2013).

In doing all this, however, these brands don't just elevate themselves and
up their margin – the German craft beer of the year charges now 25 euros
per bottle, in store! (Meck, August 2014). They usually also feed our growing
need for the authentic, the hand-made and the genuine – for products with
roots and soul. Symbols of craftsmanship and artisanal 'code poaching' don't
only help Ueber-Brands distinguish themselves, they both express a brand's
ambition and status as well as connect with its customers in a very timely and
highly emotional way. Because modern prestige and the new 'new' are ideally
old and hand-made – and Ueber-Brands have recognized this very well.

The importance of a ritual

Lastly, every myth and certainly every holy grail needs a ritual to take you and
the experience out of the profane and mundane into the sacred and blessed.
Ueber-Brands know this as much as you and I or the Catholic Church.

We already talked about La Mer's rubbing ritual (Principle 4). Something
similar exists with SKII, the Japan-originated premium skin care brand
(SKII Rituals, 2012). Even in a category as 'grounded' as shoes, the Berluti
brand created a ritual – and an insider code – by adapting the Windsor tie
knot into a distinctive way of lacing your Berluti shoes. They even go as far
as organizing posh shoe-polishing dinners involving Dom Pérignon (on the
shoes!) and Venetian leather cloth. The sessions take place during the first
lunar quarter, which is thought to enhance the shine – only by the initiated
and die-hard believers, of course.

Another example comes from Nespresso (see case study at the end of this
chapter). Not only did they develop a whole new way to brew coffee and
a unique artisanal language to talk about it, they also did all they could to
elevate their brand through rituals. They provide all the instruments needed
to turn the everyday act of having and sharing a coffee into a ritualistic,
uplifting experience, for instance with specially designed trays or drawers
to present and offer their capsules as if they were pralines or a pricey cigar
from your humidor.

Finally, let's look at MINI, one of our mythmakers par excellence, for a bit of a chuckle. Upon ordering your car you are registered and a countdown starts, showing you the remaining days until 'delivery'. Seriously. Getting your MINI is being ritualized like having a baby, all the way to the happy 'parents to be' calling themselves 'Expectant Car Owners' (Mini2, accessed August 2014). But, then again, the wait can be just as long.

Rituals have always been an integral part of elevating simple acts into special experiences and creating cults. Prestige brands have known and used this all along, just like any other institution bent on establishing a distinguished and committed collective. Ueber-Brands are only taking this ancient truth into the 21st century, updating it and playing with it to create their modern version of prestige.

Inspiring the modern romantics

Romanticism was a German-inspired movement around the time of the French Revolution, and one could easily argue that at least in the Western world it is celebrating a major comeback. There are four key aspects that defined and define Romanticism:

- Romantics of the 18th century wanted to 'imbue the meaningless with meaning, give the ordinary a sense of mystery, re-connect the known with the dignity of the unknown, and enrich the finite with an infinite glow' as Novalis said (Safranski, 2007). Not so different to what many of us are trying every day – be it through Harry Potter or yoga or even 'magic potions'.

- Art and aesthetics were seen as key in achieving this. 'Beauty leads to liberty' and 'people are only truly themselves when they play' to paraphrase Friedrich Schiller's famous dictums (Safranski, 2007), which could easily be the mantras of our 'modern' entertainment economy driven by marketing aesthetic and blockbuster shows.

- Romanticism was all about reconciling culture with nature, reconnecting with the universe and the 'divine creation' rather than dominating and potentially destroying it, as philosopher Johan Gottfried Herder said (Safranski, 2007). Still, or again, this is our biggest challenge today.

- Last but not least, Romantics were staunch individualists, if not egocentrics. They argued that the key and the secrets to everything

lies in 'me', because only 'I' can re-start and re-create (my) w
any given moment. Sounds familiar?

We, particularly younger generations like the aptly named Me-
llenials, have all become unabashed self-lovers, self-indulgers but
also self-seekers – trying to find deeper, richer, more profound and
hopefully more (instantly!) gratifying and exciting experiences.
Attempting to squeeze the most out of every minute of our lives in
search of meaning – or at least in the interest of having fun in case
we can't find it. We are all still, or once again, on the quest for the
holy grail. Looking to see the invisible and enhance the ordinary.
Longing to re-synch ourselves and our culture with nature. Playing
along as audiences and participants at the same time.

That's exactly where Ueber-Brands and their products come into
play – if they provide enough narrative, but also truth. They can become
the 'holy grail' even if just momentarily, giving us harmony in a soap
or reconnecting us with nature in form of a t-shirt, letting us feel the
power of the sea in a moisturizer or RIP with truck tarps, rekindling our
creativity by i-phoning or opening our minds to see forever through
artistic acrobatics. Or, if all else fails, they at least can make for perfect
playmates and substitutes on the way to all of this.

Sleeps a song in things abounding, that keep dreaming to be heard:
Earth'es tunes will start resounding, if you find the magic word.
(Joseph von Eichendorff)

Make it unmistakable

In early 2013 Selfridges, the venerable London department store, launched
their groundbreaking concept 'No Noise' to celebrate quiet and calm in an
age (and an environment) of over-stimulation. The initiative included 'The
Quiet Shop' in which 'some of the world's most recognizable brands have
taken the admirable step of removing their logos in our collection of de-
branded products' (Selfridges, accessed August 2014). Interestingly though,
all those brands from Beats by Dre to Crème de la Mer, could still be immediately identified and instantly became collectors' items, which is exactly
what the next two points are about: **Ueber-Brands make sure to have a big
enough repertoire of brand cues to be unmistakably themselves without
anything as ostentatious as a logo. And they reach the ultimate level of**

adoration when they allow for the epitome of specialness – products that are so limited that they are singular, for example through customization.

Unmistakably branded – the strength of soft assets

Every brand has a logo and every brand makes sure this logo is protected, celebrated and recognized. Many brands even have iconic assets on top, visual symbols like the Nike swoosh or Tiffany's robin-egg blue or a unique font like Yuan Soap's Chinese calligraphy. Yet, as usual, Ueber-Brands often try to go further, being highly considerate in establishing a large repository of more or less known brand signals that are recognizable without being too obvious. This serves two purposes: it gives the brand more scope and means to play, surprise itself and its followers, while still staying coherent. It expands their vocabulary, so to speak. But, as with any elaborate vocabulary, it will simultaneously limit the number of those who will easily understand it. In other words, Ueber-Brands like to establish a rich, permutable brand language to express themselves without being overly repetitive, a subtle yet distinguished 'insider code', which thus at the same time creates clear borders between those in the know and those not.

Nespresso is a great example here, as the case study shows. Of course there's the logo. Then they also have the iconic wave, the coffee-inspired brown-black colour code and the 'What else?' tagline in a handwritten font. But beyond that there is a whole slew of symbols and signals, which they have created over time, and which they can tap into at any given moment and reconfigure in myriad ways. There are the iconic pods and their colour palette. There is generally a unique postmodern style language that mixes classic shapes with vivid colours. There is a repetitive geometry in the way they showcase their product, creating walls of 'pod art'. Then there is also a sense of self-deprecating humour. And of course there is the suave Euro-American connoisseur personified by George Clooney and Penelope Cruz. Of course, they hardly ever use all of these elements at the same time. They don't need to put the logo next to a wall of pod art; you'd recognize it instantly anyway. It's the same with their commercials. Their playful arrogance, their brown-black colour code, the club-like atmosphere... no need for a logo in the first three seconds. Their branding is much more subtle but also much more powerful.

Another, albeit very different Ueber-Brand example is Cirque du Soleil (CDS), the world's leading and most innovative circus. They also have their logo, their anthropomorphic sun icon, their golden-yellow colour code... but then they also have an endless variety of assets at their disposal. They have the exotic-romantic language of their show titles which many of us immediately recognize, like 'Quidam' or 'Amaluna' or simply 'O'. They've established a modern fantasy world, mixing the artistic with the acrobatic, turned crazy avatars, phantasmagorical figures into one of their signals and made a unique mix of soft music and dreamy twilight their own. Their eclectic stew of different cultures, highbrow and fun, past and future, far and close is instantly recognizable. And 'our icon, talisman and asset is the "Big Top". It is symbolic, practical, a differentiating point. It fits 26,000 people yet feels intimate, like you are visiting our house', says RC Menard, Senior Director, Communication at CDS. And that's the point: iconic yet intimate, this is what Ueber-Brands should make you feel – and an ever-evolving array of assets help do that.

And in some ways even more prominent and obvious example than Cirque du Soleil and Nespresso is probably the Italian fashion brand Bottega Veneta (BV). BV managed, among other things, to turn one of their weaknesses – the fact that their machines couldn't handle supple, luxurious leather – into a global but subtle sign of luxury and sophistication: their signatute intrecciato weave. Everybody who is even remotely fashion-aware will immediately detect a 'Bottega' bag or wallet, without ever having to see the logo. Consequently, Bottega Veneta often doesn't even bother to put their logo on their products, not even inside or hidden – certainly one of the most extreme cases of Un-selling through an iconic but unobtrusive (de)sign language, staying under the radar yet 'unmistakable', with a secret code that their target will immediately decipher.

By the way: Hermès found a fun idea to celebrate the secret, independent life of their 'assets': the 'Observatory of Orange Boxes' campaign lets you see what their iconic casings do after sunset (*Luxury Daily*, 2014).

No story about design language and brand assets these days would be complete without mentioning Apple, the undisputed hero in this discipline. We don't have to go into too much detail, because everybody knows this current king of branding and cultural superstar. Just think of their shape language: round, sinuous curves, sharp and sensual at the same time. Their minimalism: modern, but neither sci-fi nor retro. Their creative irreverence: iconoclastic and yet endearing. Their colour code: white and black, but never in the sense of an absence of colour, more in the presence of all of them, able to break free at any time – which they often enough do. Their humanity: confident and cocky, yet also insecure and a bit nerdy.

We could go on and on, so deep and wide is their vocabulary of design, symbols and styles. In this case it is made ever so much richer because of the beautiful, underlying tensions inherent to the brand and brought alive on all levels. But let's get to the bottom line: Apple is omnipresent but never overbearing. And that exactly is the intention of any Ueber-Brand and the purpose of them creating an extensive brand vocabulary to draw upon. It allows them to pursue their mission and unfold their myth (Principles 1 and 4), but never to over-sell (Principle 3) or become so ubiquitous, obtrusive and thus bothersome and boring that people stop longing to belong (Principle 2).

Unmistakably you and me – the age of tailor-made

Customization used to be a privilege of the chosen few; now it's become one of the choice ways of Ueber-Brands to make all of us feel like one in a million. Welcome to the age of tailor-made and the digitally provided modern mass-prestige of personalized products.

Some years ago, writer-cum-entrepreneur Chris Anderson popularized the concept of 'long tailing', stipulating that the internet would revolutionize logistics and economies of scale, leading to more and more things being and remaining available, even in the smallest numbers (Anderson, 2006). In statistics this is called a long-tail distribution, with a disproportionately large number of occurrences far from the mean. What that means practically, for instance, is that the likelihood of us being able to buy an obscure book with very few sales will increase thanks to Amazon, because distribution and stocking costs are decreasing. That already is great enough and perfect in a time of massive individualization. But many brands, and particularly modern prestige or Ueber-Brands, have taken this even a step further, enabling partial or total personalization or at least individual configuration within a set of parameters.

Of course, this first and foremost happens in luxury categories, where many brands always allowed for custom products, and the high-ticket prices make this economically more viable. But the dynamics are accelerating and it's almost becoming de rigueur. Take Goyard for example, the much older yet until not long ago much less-known competitor to Louis Vuitton. Goyard was founded in 1792 and has always been famous for its personalized design, counterbalancing their colourful canvases with equally colourful monogramming of your choice, thus creating instantly recognizable yet unique products. This 'individual' design made them so popular in recent years that they surpassed Louis Vuitton in status, at least among the metropolitan fashion crowds, and forced the latter to re-instate their own personalization of a limited number of trunks, purses and travel luggage under the initiative Mon Monogram, in 2011. Hermès followed suit with their 'Custom Silk Corner', allowing for the customization of some of their silk scarves, and Prada is set to do the same with the soles of their brogues (Josic, accessed 2014). All of this, of course, came quite a while after the famous 'Art of Trench' project from Burberry, launched in 2009, and which we have already discussed.

Yet, and this is where it gets really interesting, this personalization craze isn't restricted to the luxury lane. 3x1 jeans pushed the idea of tailor-made denim to the fashion forefront. Nike, adidas and New Balance all allow for mass-customization of certain models. And even beyond higher-priced items the idea of tailor-made has arrived, helping to create new Ueber-Brands or give mass ones a shot of new energy. For instance, MyMuesli, the rapidly growing German cereal brand launched in 2007, is all about providing individually mixed mueslis and cereals, putting it first in a recent customer survey (LifePR, accessed August 2014) and well on track to become the new superstar in the grocery aisle. And everybody has probably seen Coca-Cola's 'Share a Coke', which toyed with the whole idea in a packaged goods way.

What this all means: new technologies are allowing marketers to not just speak with their targets in more personalized, individualized ways; they make bespoke the new frontier in production, even in mass. It's the previously-discussed idea of 'arts and crafts' taken to the top, giving products not just 'a feeling' of the personal, the handmade and 'a sense' of authenticity and soul. They have truly become that way again. And that's why this is the new 'must' for any brand wanting to keep or achieve Ueber-Brand status – unless we one day turn around again, becoming tired of the flawed but soulful, and start longing for industrialized yet soulless perfection again. But that is certainly going to take a while.

Make it the centre of attention

We already discussed the campaign for Absolut vodka in the context of Ueber-Brands applying art or art collaborations for a more sophisticated, 'subtle' communication and sticking to the idea of Un-selling (Principle 3). Funny enough, it's equally a great example for the seemingly contradictory point we want to make now: Ueber-Brands need to not just 'un-sell' but also make their product the 'centre of attention'. But this supposed paradox is easily solved.

Putting your product as the focal point doesn't mean pushing or promoting it as hard as you can – and thus potentially compromising its status. It actually means the opposite: putting it on a pedestal, ideally with a glass dome to make it practically untouchable – metaphorically speaking. And thus protecting and 'un-selling' it while at the same time proudly placing it smack in the middle, at the 'centre of attention'. **Ueber-Brands celebrate their iconic products as true heroes, marketing them full force without ever over-selling or undermining them.** They put them at the eye of the hurricane so to say, all swirling around them, but in a hush of calm and control at the same time.

There are two aspects to this: the first one is in some ways more a matter of communication, yet not only that. It's really about a going-to-market mindset, taking into consideration all touch points and channels, always ensuring to not leave behind that product which represents the brand in 'essence' – even if there are times when other, perhaps newer ones, may be 'hotter' and selling better. Icons aren't necessarily always bestsellers, but as most marketers we spoke to confirmed, they are long-sellers. As such that they must be treated like that in order to serve their purpose and iconize your brand. The second point is definitely about product development – how Ueber-Brands must always update and upgrade their icons, dramatizing them in a new, current light, but without ever giving the impression that the 'star' needed a 'makeover', because that would destroy its nimbus of timeless perfection.

Heroes need the spotlight

'Got milk?' There's hardly anybody interested in marketing who has never seen or at least heard of this campaign for the US milk board. It ran for over 20 years until its still-too-early 'demise' in 2014. In the print ads you'd always simply see a celebrity in a characteristic pose, sporting a milk moustache. This put the product quite naturally into the spotlight – while at the same time entertainingly taking a crack at the celebrity's aura of course. Back when the campaign started, a milk moustache was seen by most as an embarrassing sign of having had a 'baby' drink, something the campaign changed in no time. Through its irreverent yet confident and proud display of 'lactal love', a trace you'd rather have wiped off was transformed into a statement of cultural cool – with milk almost achieving Ueber-status for a while.

A campaign that reminds us of this hallmark in a lot of ways is the one for Nespresso (see the longer commercial from 2013 on YouTube). Both share this candid-cocky challenger tone that shows pride and confidence in the product without being unbelievable or off-putting: 'Got milk?' – 'What else?' Both poke fun at their celebrities, and both have turned their brands and products into cultural icons. They use the star shine to draw attention, but at the same time they break it, redirecting the light at the true hero. Yet, even here the hero-halo is somewhat fractured, because it's so obviously and wittily over the top. They truly turn celebrity endorsements on their head (see Principle 3), making the brand the Ueber-Star, which is so self-assured of its impressiveness that it can make fun of itself. It's a multi-dimensional yet well-balanced play on 'who's the boss' or 'who's on top', which lets us 'behold' and store the brand as truly 'Ueber' – one way or the other.

Another, equally memorable and successful, yet totally different product-as-hero approach is the Apple iPod campaign. Apple has always been proud of its product design, celebrating it boldly in their communications. But the iPod spots showing black cutout silhouettes of people dancing in front of colorful backgrounds with the product's iconic white earbuds dangling have been burnt into our collective conscience. They turned the product into an instant hit – putting Apple en route to the Ueber-Brand it would become. Of course it helped that the product was indeed a breakthrough as well, taking what the older ones among us still remember as the 'walkman' to the next level. But the completely new and rarely seen way of 'highlighting' the iPod, celebrating it as the iconic star that it would become, with the wearers as faceless figures, was certainly integral to giving it instant notoriety. This becomes clear if you remember that their first iPod spot with Jeff Goldblum was a short-lived, forgettable flop. What a difference a self-confident yet light-hearted heroization can make: the Goldblum spot presented the product as tool for the self-expression of the celebrity – and tanked. The second one let the product outshine everything else, literally, and brought itself and its hero iconic status (Apple iPod (2001)). 'Thought different', indeed.

But, as we said going in, making the product the hero is not only a matter of communication. It's an overall mindset that manifests itself most clearly in the brand's marketing. Both Nespresso and Apple build their entire world around their products, their iconic design and their impeccable delivery. So them putting this front and centre in their commercials or print ads is just a logical consequence. This is true by the way for many luxury brands, who put most of their money into product and packaging and then spend what's left on celebrating rather than cluttering that. The most famous example is certainly the beauty brand Clinique with their long-running pack shot campaign originated by master photographer Irving Penn. There are endless others in the beauty world, but also in the 'dirty' one, as our last case will show: household appliances revolutionary Dyson.

James Dyson was always fascinated by how things work. And he definitely wanted everyone to see the fascinating technique of his new, cool cyclone vacuum cleaner. Retailers and other partners of course thought he was stupid, claiming people would not want to see the dirt. But they turned out to be wrong. Dyson managed to make the process of 'suction creation and dust separation' intriguing, if not beautiful to watch, and convinced many of us that the machine works, better than any other. He dramatized the beauty in superior technology and performance and catapulted his brand to the top of a category that was until then totally boring, commanding a price point way above any competition and inspiring involvement in vacuum cleaners (and by now also other equally mundane appliances) that had not been thought possible. Of course the fact that his transparent techno-stars were 'popped up' with glossy colours, giving them almost a sculptural quality, helped. The main point, though, is that he made the product and its workings so emotionally alluring that we couldn't help but fall in love with them, all without the need for any accoutrements like life-styling, celebrities or any other borrowed interest. His product was the hero and his technology the story that would give both mythical power and status, turning the Dyson brand into an Ueber-Brand that reigns supreme over a growing number of categories.

The morale: don't be shy as an Ueber-Brand. Be bold and show what you've got. Flaunt it, but don't over-sell it either. **Celebrate your goods in the best possible light, but always make sure that this is coming from a position of strength and pride – not greediness or last-call neediness. Nothing is less sexy than despair.** You have a hero. And heroes don't hide. They are always ready for their close-up, in love with the spotlight – but never too obviously in search of it.

Icons must also evolve

Hero products are usually those that are an instant break-out hit, putting the brand on the map, yet with the endurance of a marathon runner. They don't wear the yellow jersey only for a day but keep on leading and exemplifying the brand in an ongoing, if not permanent way. They are not always bestsellers, as we said, but long-sellers; your brand's *pièce de résistance*.

In order to be able to do this they must, however, be carefully kept in shape so they can keep on delivering. There are some, like Nuxe Hand Cream for instance, or designer furniture from Herman Miller, that have sold untouched for decades, and where any altering would actually be seen as a sacrilege. For most, though, it's important to tweak and update them occasionally, but without giving their users the feeling they were sub-optimal, no longer on a par or losing their lustre. **And that's the challenge: 'new and improve' your heroes without ever making them feel old. And stick to them, even when others may be sexier at times or bring in more money.** Show them respect. They epitomize your brand and you would literally 'cut off your nose' by taking them off their pedestal.

Someone who has done this quite well is Estée Lauder with its iconic Advanced Night Repair (ANR) serum. ANR was launched in 1982 and has stayed at the top of beauty products globally ever since. At first glance it still looks the same as it did more than 30 years ago. Yet the 'little brown bottle' has gone through a number of minor evolutions, the latest giving it a little striped collar. The same goes for the serum itself, which has seen many little updates over time, but without ever truly changing the core or 'the essence'.

Another way of achieving this 'rejuvenation without deprecation' we have discussed already in Principle 3: Louis Vuitton and their art collaborations. Again and again they work with current, of-the-moment artists to 're-envision' their iconic canvas. A strategic double-whammy, because it elevates the brand, cementing its Ueber-Status as cultural arbiter. But at the same time it re-confirms the product's timeless power, continuously putting it at the nexus of all that's hot and cool – as well as the 'centre of attention' of the brand and its fans. On top of that, because of the limited nature of the collaborations, the brand and its products stay 'low', keeping their allure 'up', because there are always more of us 'longing' for one of those rare artifacts than will actually be able to own one (see Principle 2).

How this works not only in the high-and-mighty world of designer fashion but also in an everyday category like bottled water is proved by Evian. Their annual New Year's editions of specially designed bottles have become bona fide collectors' items, injecting the brand with intrigue and energy every 'season' and making it feel special, gift-special indeed, albeit it mostly a gift to yourself. Here's a funny tidbit to finish: Evian likes to call them 'commemorative bottles', though it's not quite clear who or what exactly they want to commemorate – other than the brand and its iconic product itself.

But this, actually, is the reason: commemorate and celebrate your product as the star, the key to the myth that you as its Ueber-Brand hold. Make sure you present and treat your icons as the undisputed 'essence' that you think they are and that you want your customers to trust in. At the bottom line this means that you truly put your money where your mouth will be, and create a product that can withstand even the most critical examination – because nothing kills a bad product faster than good marketing. But then you should indeed treat it as the 'holy grail' that you created, make it and your brand 'unmistakable' and never take it out of the 'centre of attention'. Never stop celebrating and updating it, but without ever calling into question its outstanding, timeless power – and certainly without completely changing its 'essence'.

Principle 5: The rules to 'behold'

1 Create an 'essence'
Or stylize your product into one at least. The thing that's beyond anything. The holy grail.

2 Romanticize the heck out of it
Turning RTBs into STBs to create intrigue, love, adoration and distinction, and to prevent substitution and commoditization.

3 Up-code!
Appropriating ways and signs of higher, artisanal categories.

4 Never forget a ritual
It elevates and unites, creating cults and turning ordinary occurrences into extraordinary experiences.

5 Be unmistakable
But never boring. With a rich language of insider signs and signals for subtle distinction and recognition.

6 Customize
Nothing is more 'Ueber' than making your customers feel so. It's the kindness of kings.

7 Flaunt it
Don't be shy. Give your hero the spotlight it deserves, and your brand the iconic product it needs.

8 And never leave your star behind
Constantly polish, update and upgrade your icon, but without ever making it obvious or seem necessary. Because what you want is the impression of ageless and timeless currency.

Ueber-Brands need substance like any other, even more so. Because they don't just need to prove a promise, they must create something to behold – a manifestation of their underlying myth. That's why they put their products on a pedestal, making them the holy grail, unmistakably and always at the centre of attention.

Ueber-Brand case study 5 Nespresso – coffee as crema de la crème

Rogue researchers at Nestlé had tinkered around with the coffee capsule and brewing technology that was to become the Nespresso system since the 1970s. At that time, Nestlé dominated the soluble category, which made up over 30 per cent of the total coffee market, but that category was stagnating – except for the niche gourmet coffees. It took Nestlé several failed launches, first into hospitality (Switzerland, 1982), then into office catering (Italy and Japan, 1986) until the home-selling business model was tested as a 'last resort' in 1989. Because there were so few users initially, no grocery store was willing to stock the 'pods' and they had to be ordered via phone and shipped directly. What started out as a tactical fix to enable availability quickly developed into a unique service experience that had the allure of exclusive membership. The Nespresso Club was born. From a few hundred, its membership has grown by 25–50 per cent annually ever since, hitting 10 million members in 2010, with about US $3 billion dollars in sales of the colourful pods alone. In addition to the (now online) Clubs, some 320 flagship boutiques and cafés have been opened around the world. All in all, some 1,300 Nespresso employees sell or serve over a third of the global espresso consumption (Nespresso.com, accessed Oct 2014, Arabian Business.com, 2012).

Behold! – So much more than coffee in a pod

With Nespresso everything revolves around the product. From its name to the unique form of delivery to its communication, the brand succeeds in making its coffee perceived as the holy grail, creating a product experience, language, rituals and visual identity – literally a code(x) – that makes it unmistakable. An inimitable cup of coffee that is always fresh – in every sense of the word.

Nespresso's advertising is indicative of this celebration of the product as Ueber-Hero. In the films, George Clooney is shown being out-attracted by a fine cup of Nespresso or mistaken for a valet by Club members (friend Matt Damon, John Malkovich or Penelope Cruz do not fare much better in other films). The print and billboard ads show the star as a Nespresso drinker and simply affirm 'What Else?' in their confident manner. The consistent message: the product is sexier than one of the sexiest men (or women) alive. It's not just any espresso, but espresso in its most unique and truest form, the essence of espresso – as simple and as perfect as that.

The true magic, however, happens when the precious coffees, encapsulated in their mysteriously potent pods, are extracted by the proprietary machines. It is an intricately designed, sensorial experience that involves a muted purr, a room filling with coffee aroma and a distinctive 'crema' forming on top of the small espresso potion. Nespresso celebrates this crowning finish in many of its communications by using glass cups that let the thick froth show through.

All is revered by an idiosyncratic, fine wine-inspired language: there are two dozen 'Grand Crus' ranging in provenance from the popular 'Arpeggio' to the 'Pure Origin Bukela Ka' to the flavored 'Caramelito with notes of the Livanto Grand Cru'. And then there are the many limited editions, like the 'fruity-winey Cauca' of the 'Colombian Terroir Collection', which have their creation stories brought to life on the Nespresso website in sights and sounds. For the Ueber-Target who want to peel the onion further, Nespresso has tasting notes available that describe the 'aromatic complexity and gustatory-olfactory persistency' in minute detail. The 'Nespresso Coffee Codex' book is the inner sanctum, assembling dozens of these notes on the blends as well as teaching tasting and pairing techniques.

Such drama lets the rest of us sip with awe from our little Nespresso cups: cups that are of course also designed for an unmistakable look, just like the pods and machines. The machines almost blur the lines between art and object. The outward simplicity belies a complex micro-chip-guided process that includes grain-adjusted pre-wetting and aeration before extraction. It makes the tech-inclined owners rave and others salivate at the sight of the sensual curves... And just like a high-performance car, there are tiers of machines, from the small, youthful Pixie model, all the way to limited-edition machines designed in collaboration with Shanghai Tang or the 'Racepresso', a concept machine only, built in the shape of an F1 helmet with Ferrari. There are also a plethora of unique accessories to help credential the pods, serve the coffee and even to carry the pods away to recycling, all in the recognizable, post-modernist Nespresso design and with suggestive names like the 'Bonbonierre' and 'Totem' pod holders or the 'Aeroccino' milk frother. On a business level, they serve to ensure households are stocked and to generate incremental sales, but they also make serving the pods look precious and support a habit-forming ritual. The popular Nespresso serving tray for example encases each of the colourful pods like chocolate pralines and showcases to guests the sophistication of the host – provided they have purchased enough varieties.

To keep the icon always fresh, new flavours or machine designs are released at regular intervals, with the kind of hoopla Apple is famous for. And they are greeted with similar enthusiasm. The 'Citiz' machine, for example, was unveiled at the Maison & Objet trade fair in Paris, and social media-induced queues were reported outside Nespresso boutiques where the machines were sold exclusively during the launch.

Mission and myth – inspiring consumers as well as marketers

If Nespresso was an ordinary brand, its mission might simply be described as 'enabling consumers to make an excellent cup of coffee'. But the brand wants more than this. It's elevating coffee to something to be prized and enjoyed, a moment of sophistication and cultural elevation, a spark of *la dolce vita* or *savoir vivre*. The Ueber-Mission is thus more something like 'allowing us to bring out and enjoy our inner gourmet', similar to when coffee was first introduced to Europe in the 17th century and became the drink of the rich, noble and cultured classes. The important distinction now, though, is that Nespresso's system really makes it possible for anyone to become such a coffee connoisseur. It gives the time-crunched modern lifestyle masters bragging rights to serving-up a perfect 'Kennedy' (three shots of the long roasted 'Dharkan' blend of washed Arabicas) with ease and elegance – if they are willing to pay the premium. Note that the fact that the beans are fair trade-sourced and the pods recyclable is not part of the core mission, but rather a way to prevent bon-vivant remorse and get them back into the store to drop pods into the recycling bin and buy some more.

The brand has elevated this element of hedonistic gourmandize and sophistication to mythical proportions, teasing out a distinctly suave and witty character. If you want to out-finesse the upper-Italian lifestyle experienced by George Clooney, then being a Nespresso aficionado is a good start (see also Principle 2, Ueber-Target). The Nespresso myth is thus a 'right-handed' one, in Campbell's terms, guiding us to the highest echelons of culturally conformist living or rather socio-culinary superiority. Didactic tools like the 'Codex', teach how to talk about coffee and food – and thus ourselves – in an intelligent and appetizing manner.

Another interesting aspect about Nespresso mythmaking is that the brand has achieved as much mythical status from a professional POV as it has from a consumer or cultural one. At least this is the case judging by the number of times their creation story and all it entails is being re-told in studies and articles (see also box on page 179, Principle 6).

Nespresso elevates and celebrates its brand as different from the 'common coffee', from degustations, to credentialing and fashion made from up-cycled pods (bottom left by Ellie Mucke)

Image courtesy of Nespresso and Nespresso Australia

Un-selling by making us long to belong to the Club

To inspire, engage and enchant their Ueber-Target, the 'foodie-sophisticate' – a well-educated, well-situated person for whom appreciating and sharing the finer things in life is core – Nespresso runs an elite 'Expertise Program' that includes a global Sommelier Education Program, a Chef Academy, as well as the sponsorship of high gastronomy competitions and events like the 'Bocuse d'Or' and the 'Grandes Tables du Monde'. Very select Club members (less than one in 10,000), VIPs and the media are invited to get a taste of the culinary mastery at those events or in 'Nespresso Atelier' workshops organized especially for them. Here, top sommeliers will educate about the perfect pairing of coffees with liquors, wines and sumptuous food prepared by Michelin-starred chefs. Nespresso also plays patron of haute cuisine to groom expert-ambassadors in the appreciation of coffees in high-end restaurants and to elevate the image of Nespresso in the process. Having graduated from the 'Chef Academy' or being named a 'coffee sommelier' by Nespresso has become a desirable accreditation in the profession. Diane Duperret, PR Manager at Nespresso, points out an important detail: 'The programs do not simply celebrate the aromas like you would expect from regular PR. There is an emphasis on new ways to use our coffee as an ingredient in dishes to make them interesting'. This gains the respect of the select audiences and – through them – of a larger foodie community that wishes it could be there, too.

If the above serves to trigger a 'longing' among the rest of us 'normal' coffee drinkers to upgrade and join the party, then the Nespresso Club is the perfect way to do so and create a strong sense of belonging in the process.

The Club agents are trained and armed with the data to know your name, machine model and preferred blends. They forecast when you need to stock up or when it is time for machine maintenance. Demonstrating dedication was a priority from day one and the club ordering line became famous for always being picked up by a real person – within the first three rings. 'Today, we seek to exceed the expectations by providing mobile ordering services that allow you to choose the delivery time or offer at home pick-up and delivery in lead markets' says Duperret. It does not come as a surprise that over half of all new brand trial is based on referral by other members rather than any form of promotion (Slywotzky and Weber, 2011).

It is also telling that it was the Club members who had the privilege to elect George Clooney as most worthy to represent them, rather than a marketing manager. Duperret confirms this is not a myth and emphasizes that the campaign debuted in 2006, a full decade after Nespresso had started to take off and only outside its biggest market, the United States. That is to say that the endorsement of Mr. Clooney is quite nice, but the brand does not depend on it, a point that the advertisements reflect in their light-hearted arrogance (see Principle 5).

Living the dream and moving with gravitas – full force

According to Duperret over 70 per cent of Nespresso employees in a market work in direct contact with consumers. Club agents interact with tens of thousands of members or 'Nespressi' every day. They are encouraged to develop routines that delight their customers and are given the autonomy to back them up. Agents might mail out machine-cleaning kits with a personalized reminder or add a sample of a new flavour the customer might like. They also share a budget to loan (and on occasion give away) a new machine model to the most loyal and influential of members.

However, Nespresso has learned that discounting the price of the machines or even giving them away to a more general public does not lead to the levels of sustained usage. It is the special Club or boutique experiences that do. Just visit one of the museum-like boutiques or the website. The machines are put on illuminated pedestals like modern sculptures. The tubes of pods are arranged on the shelves to create colourful patterns and the walls are hung with pixel portraits and other works of art made from the pods themselves. Those pods have become so iconic that an entire cottage industry has sprung up which fashions them into jewellery, holiday decorations, lamps and other lifestyle items. Nespresso of course fuels this enthusiasm by inspiring, sponsoring and reporting on these creations.

Of course the personal endorsement from friends, family or from influencers is just as important. That is why Nespresso focuses its trial efforts on making those experiences an ever-more-potent draw and source of word of mouth. They are seconded by the hospitality sampling we talked about earlier and demonstrations at electronic retailers and department stores where the machines can also be purchased. To date, Nespresso's answer to competitive, lower-priced single-serve offerings 'popping' up like mushrooms, has thus been to romance its 'Grand Crus' even more and to add more exclusive 'limited editions' rather than giving in on pricing or pushing harder.

But the direct supply model allows Nespresso not only to stay out of the battles for shelf space and promotions. It also enables them to grow globally and exponentially while still maintaining an air of exclusivity, never feeling over-present. Since Nespresso switched to selling to households in 1989, the growth rate of the brand has ranged from 20 to 30 per cent annually, well above even that of the specialty coffee segment. Reports say that Nespresso is outselling Italian classics like Illy and Lavazza, but also the much cheaper pod competitor Keurig. The former CEO of Nespresso estimated that 'Nespressi' actually brew more cups of espresso than the omnipresent Starbucks around the world (Arabian Business, 2012). Who would have thought? But mostly behind the 'velvet rope' it all happens.

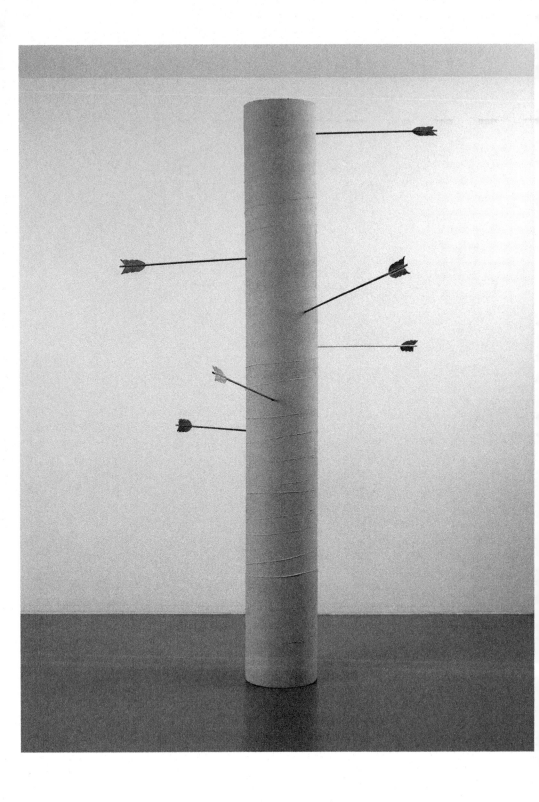

Principle 6
Living the dream
The bubble shall never burst

If you think the concept laid out in the previous principle was gruelling, think again. Because Principle 6 takes it even further: in order to be credible and live up to their own ambition and, more importantly, their customers' expectations, Ueber-Brands have to make sure they truly let their myth and their mission guide them in everything they do. And we literally mean everything – from company set-up through sourcing and production, organization and culture all the way to marketing and – not least – creating meticulously crafted brand experiences across all touch points. It sounds like a lot of work with an endless number of pitfalls and potentials for failure – and that's exactly what and how it is. But there's no way around it. **Dreams aren't all that easy to create, but they are even harder to make come true.** And that's the challenge: live the dream, and make sure that the bubble you created never bursts.

We will start by talking about some of the problems and look at brands that have had their fair share of trouble in 'dreamland' – and consequently in our real world as well. It's the best way to truly understand the level to which the dedication of modern prestige or Ueber-Brands has to go. And it's the best way to learn. After all, that's what mistakes are for, so let's use those already made – then we can make some new ones. We titled the first section in this chapter 'Nothing is as volatile as a dream', and that's especially true in our day and age. Many if not most consumers are having their eyes opened wide, and there is a large number of watchdogs. High degrees of transparency, easy access to information and a growing culture of ultra-vigilance to the point of scepticism and cynicism are making it harder and harder to create and live in your own 'bubble' without it ever bursting. The lines of credit that we give companies are getting tighter and tighter, which means years of commendable work can sometimes be wiped out with one wrong step. So you'd better tread carefully.

We organized the insights we gleaned from looking at successful modern prestige brands creating and living their dream in the three sections that follow.

As with anything, and perhaps even more so in this case, it all starts at the top: 'Of gods and masters' talks about the importance of leadership and how one leader is often not enough. It takes both great creative vision and almost ruthless, pedantic execution to build an Ueber-Brand and keep it alive. That's a lot to ask from one person, so many have decided to split the job.

The next point, 'Radiating inside out', tackles the relatively higher importance of the organizational and cultural set-up in today's prestige world. Ueber-Brands are, for the most part, mission-driven and mythmaking, and this must be reflected in the way their enterprise is structured, their processes are laid out, their products are sourced and produced, their employees are organized and treated etc. At least that's what the most glowing examples teach us. If you're waving the flag of environmental and ethical responsibility, you'd better make sure that all your actions adhere to these standards. Similarly, though a bit easier admittedly, if you're stylizing yourself as the epitome of fashion you can't have your offices and certainly not yourself or your employees look like duds all the time. In both cases this doesn't necessarily mean you have to go to major expenses. It's more a matter of the choices you make than the money you spend. It's about consistency and credibility. Although, as we said already in Principle 1, a principle isn't truly a principle unless you're also willing to pay for it...

In order to allow for this entrepreneurial integrity, many bigger companies like Nestlé or Unilever have decided to give some of their brands that are playing in very unique territories a larger degree of organizational and structural independence. We call this 'ring-fencing' and show some illuminating examples in a box later in the chapter.

At the end it's all about 'The world according to you'. After all, that's what prestige has always dreamt of and made us dream of – a world that's different and ideally better than our daily lives. At least as a momentary transformation or a temporary shift of our perspectives on reality. That's their mission and that's what their myths are made for: and that's what they have to bring alive in seamless brand worlds or experiences. Many Ueber-Brands have today gone the route of vertical integration, literally creating their 'dream worlds', the tip of which are flagship stores or 'brand experience' centres. Even those who don't or can't, because of their way of distribution for example, must take great pains to ensure their products come in their own, unique 'bubble' so to speak, with an imaginary world attached. And again, that's not an easy task. It takes slavish attention to detail – because that's where the devil is, and not every detail is created equal.

Nothing is as volatile as a dream

The higher you rise, the harder you fall. That's particularly true for Ueber-Brands, and the worst is, it doesn't even take much. All it sometimes needs is the sliver of a doubt or getting close to supposed 'dark forces' and the dream vanishes quicker than you can explain yourself. And, as we all know, that can lead to a very hard landing, which you won't always survive. At a minimum it will take a lot of time and effort to get 'up' again. Myths are no magic; they mostly adhere to a very strict logic, and so must their managers. Just how strict is the subject of the following pages.

Learning from the mistakes of others

The Body Shop, mentioned in Principle 4, is the best case. Most of the allegations that arose after Anita Roddick's death were never completely proven, but, they went so much to the core of what her brand (owned by L'Oréal since 2006) stands for, that just the suspicion was enough to affect its status. Roddick had so much made herself 'The Queen of Green' (MailOnline, 2007) that all her fans and followers were up in arms, calling for boycotts etc, simply because they didn't even like the affiliation with supposedly dubious practices or agents. The brand was seriously tarnished and its stratospheric rise came to a screeching halt. Growth, if any, has been anaemic ever since.

Like The Body Shop, Snapple, the poster child of alternative drinks, rose to Ueber-Fame on a wave and an image of counter-culture. But then it also sold itself, in this case to Quaker Oats, in 1993. Quaker, encouraged by their success with Gatorade, tried to replicate it with Snapple, taking it big. However, they completely misjudged the importance of soft factors. 'Quaker's failure can be put down to a fatal mismatch between brand challenge and managerial temperament', is how John Deighton, Professor of Business Administration at Harvard Business School, summarized it (Deighton, 2002). Quaker let go of Snapple's spokesperson Wendy Kaufman, straightened the labels, streamlined its portfolio and distribution and did many other things, none of them particularly wrong or even detrimental in themselves. Taken together, though, they managed to ultimately kill the spirit and the appeal of the brand. In 1997, just four years after the purchase, Quaker sold Snapple to Triarc for a mere pittance – US $300 million compared to the US $1.7 billion they had paid. US $1.4 billion burnt, 'simply' by not understanding how adhering to the mission and the painstaking execution of details makes the myth – and the value – of an Ueber-Brand.

Fortunately, Triarc managed to turn the ship around, re-hired Wendy Kaufman among other things, and re-cultivated the brand's original spirit of genuine imperfection and authentic artlessness. They sold Snapple for US $1 billion to Cadbury in 2000 and it has done quite well since then.

One brand that only recently emerged as an Ueber-Brand and may be about to lose this status just as fast is Lululemon. We previously explained their unique, club-like approach that gives their target a feeling of belonging, while still keeping them and others longing for more. But, as with any Ueber-Brand, this is a very fragile eco-system, which can quickly be destroyed.

Lululemon was always plagued by questions of product quality (Story, 2007), but in 2013 this boiled up into a true scandal. Some of their black pants turned out to be almost see-through when stretched. That alone was damaging enough, literally exposing women and thus undermining the brand's whole 'sisterhood' feel. The worst, though, was the reaction of founder Chip Wilson, who blamed this to a large degree on 'some women's thighs', basically saying that Lululemon doesn't work for plus-size women (Bloomberg TV, accessed August 2014). The brand never had a very nurturing attitude towards its customers, pushing them to 'elevate the world from mediocrity to greatness', something which was often critiqued by those who didn't feel up to Lulu's standards. But the outright shunning of women with bigger thighs made the whole careful balance of being 'empowering yet embracing' flip – and some of their targets flip out. Suddenly what used to be for the most part seen as encouraging came across as overpowering and dismissive; what was meant and taken as activation turned into arrogance. Wilson later apologized, but the damage was done and he and his long-time CEO Day had to resign. Lululemon had to recall 17 per cent of its bottoms and the brand's image as well as the company's stock suffered significantly.

Letting dreams thrive

A brand that avoided all this is Kiehl's. The consummate apothecary brand and Ueber-Success of recent years was bought by L'Oréal in 2000, almost 150 years after it was founded in New York's East Village in 1851. But in contrast to their not-so-successful acquisition of The Body Shop, L'Oréal did a great job of ensuring they understood and protected the brand's core values, driving principles and executional idiosyncrasies. They only integrated what made sense to integrate and let alone what should be left alone. Shortly after the take-over, then-L'Oréal CEO Lindsay Owen-Jones said in a *Fortune* article looking at Kiehl's iconic shaving cream: 'It leaves a mess in the basin... and the label on the tube occasionally doesn't stay on... But it just happens to leave your skin smoother than anything else I've ever used' (Tomlinson, 2002). Kiehl's culture was always quirky, cherishing the personal, thriving on imperfection – except when it came to its products. And this is exactly what L'Oréal understood. They made sure to keep what was unique and essential about the brand and improved only where they could without clashing with the brand's myth and ethos. They integrated R&D, production and logistics for example, because here they wouldn't hurt but strengthen Kiehl's commitment. They didn't, however, touch the brand's 'soft' side: the excessive sampling and 'try before you buy' policy, the hotch-potch store style, including motorbikes and skeletons (lovingly dubbed Mr. Bones), the extreme customer service, endearing humanness amongst many other things. To this day, for example, every Kiehl's store looks slightly different, specific to its neighbourhood. Not because L'Oréal doesn't understand the importance of creating a consistent brand world (see also 'The world according to you'). Just the opposite: it is because they do understand it. Kiehl's world is one of peculiarity, locality and individuality. It would go completely against the brand's core if their shops were to look and act exactly the same in Hong Kong as in Berlin. Even the places in New York's Upper West side and Lower East side (which happens to be the original store) are different in tone and feel. And that's exactly what unites them, defines them and sets them apart. They are all dedicated to their customers and that means being dedicated to their neighbourhoods – to the point of every store getting a certain budget for local support and activities. Sticking to this, protecting and developing it, allowed L'Oréal to turn the little apothecary from the East Village into a global player without diminishing its cult status, thus letting it thrive into an Ueber-Brand.

All these examples show that it's not the major strategic decisions that make a dream come true and a myth come alive. It's often the seemingly insignificant aspects that can make or break an Ueber-Brand. Sure enough you also have to respect the brand's core, its mission, but HOW this is being expressed and executed is what often gets overlooked by managers on a quest for efficiency and improvement. Modern prestige brands and their myths aren't a rational thing. The 'right' thing to do can thus often turn out to be very wrong indeed.

Of gods and masters: the question of leadership

Nobody would ever argue the importance of leadership in any organization, certainly not when you want to build anything 'Ueber'. But how to best instal the leaders or what you must do to set them up for success can be passionately debated.

In the case of Ueber-Brands this is of particular concern. Very often these brands have been founded by a strong, visionary entrepreneur and they sooner or later run into one of two issues, the first being how to grow beyond the original founder's capacities or abilities. A classic case of late is TOMS and their decision to sell a stake to Bain Capital – for the capital influx, but also because founder and Chief Shoe Giver Blake Mycoskie's 'abilities to scale the business were naturally limited', as Allie Tsavdarides, manager in charge of EMEA markets put it. The other issue is that at some point they must find successors and set them up to stay true to the founder's style or vision and thus the brand's mission and myth. The alternative situation would be that the brand is part of a bigger organization from the get-go or is integrated into one, in which case the question is always how much freedom and protection to give the leader, and how to best allow him or her to thrive.

Looking at our 100-plus Ueber-Brand case studies and talking them through with experts we have found two main leadership set-ups that work: an organizational approach we discuss in the box later in this chapter.

The dream team

There are strong Renaissance men or women who can envision a brand and then take it to the highest level as well, who know how to dream but also deal with all the nitty-gritty details of reality in running a growing enterprise. Dietrich Mateschitz, founder of Red Bull, or Yvon Chouinard from Patagonia are certainly up there. Also Guy Laliberté, owner of Cirque du Soleil: '(He) is a hands-on owner, artist and operator. You can almost see him split into the child-like observer role looking at a new show and then switch, judging it, evaluating its long-term potential etc.', said RC Menard, Senior Director, Communication at CDS. But those are far and few in between, and even in these cases one could argue that they don't really do both – drive their companies creatively as well as commercially. Chouinard and Laliberté have both recruited strong financial and organizational partners or teams they rely on.

And that's the point: it's almost impossible to find a person equally entrepreneurially imaginative as he or she is managerially strong, someone who totally balances left and right brain and excels in both creative inspiration and cunning implementation. More often you'll find a congenial duo or the above-titled 'dream team' at the helm, running the show together. One of the best-known examples of recent years is probably Tom Ford and Domenico De Sole, who took Gucci from a '70s has-been to the fashion Ueber-Brand we all know today. In fact, their partnership has been so successful and strong that they are still working together, almost 20 years later, now in their latest venture Tom Ford International. Other and earlier famous pairings include Max Braun and Dieter Rams, who made Braun the ultimate reference for design in electronics, to this very day, with Apple's Jonathan Ive explicitly and obviously taking a lot of inspiration from Rams. Or Yves Saint Laurent and Pierre Berger, whose partnership has just been celebrated in two feature films. One of the latest couples to rise to business as well as cultural prominence was certainly Burberry's Christopher Bailey and Angela Ahrendts, though their relationship broke up recently with Ahrendts' move to Apple, which proves that professional pairings can be just as unstable as personal ones. Remember the famously fraught relationship between Steve Jobs and Steve Wozniak, or, much earlier, Coco Chanel and Pierre Wertheimer?

By and large, however, it's easier to find and pair a couple of different strengths than to find one person able to both continuously inspire creatively and steer the ship commercially.

This is particularly true when the brand has reached a certain size or must deal with the additional complexities of becoming part of a larger organization. In those cases, a lot of Ueber-Brands that we looked at chose wisely to keep the original visionary on board, but buffering or coupling him or her with a complementary partner. We already mentioned the partnering of TOMS with Bain Capital, though their success remains to be seen. One company that has managed to show how this works is L'Occitane, where investor Reinold Geiger made it a prerequisite that the brand's founder and creative visionary Olivier Baussan re-join before he purchased the company.

Now the two are leading together. It's the same with many Estée Lauder companies like Aveda and Bobby Brown, or Olio Lusso, one of their latest acquisitions, where Linda Rodin stays on as CD.

The protective mentor

Talking about Ueber-Brands growing within or becoming part of a larger company, they usually need a third person to protect and guide the couple, a kind of mentor. Lindsay Owen-Jones, ex-CEO of L'Oréal, we have already mentioned. He successfully protected Kiehl's from being swallowed or dissected by its new parent in search of savings or synergies. In the case of Nespresso it was then-CEO Peter Brabeck-Letmathe and SVP Camillo Pagano who held their hand over the experimental venture, which was for the longest time anything but a sure-fire success. The visionaries here were Eric Favre in the R&D department and Jean-Paul Gaillard the marketer (see box). Both were considered 'nuts' and outsiders by the majority of the mother organization and mostly survived because of the support of Brabeck-Letmathe and Pagano, who were frequently challenged by the rest of the organization as well as the board for sponsoring and holding on to such an incongruent, incompatible but expensive innovation. Fortunately, though, they had the power and the conviction to withstand the pressures and gave the project the 10-plus years it needed to grow until it became successful. Which brings us to the growth trajectory of Ueber-Brands, but we will discuss that in the next and last principle, Principle 7.

For now let's just summarize. Like most brands, certainly prestige ones, Ueber-Brands usually need both unrelenting creative imagination and inspiration as well as profitable yet painstaking management operation and execution. But they need them even more so than most brands, and as great as it is to find both in one person, it is highly unlikely. That's why most successful Ueber-Brands have opted to share responsibilities between a creative 'god' and a commercial 'master'. In case of being part of a supra-organization they often also establish a high-powered 'mentor' to give those two sufficient room and leniency to grow. Because nothing can be more damaging and suffocating than an overly 'loving' and 'embracing' parent – in life as in work.

Together apart

The concept of ring-fencing

Laliberté, Chouinard and Mateschitz all reportedly declined numerous offers to sell their brands that would have made them instant billionaires. Invariably, their reasoning reveals a fear that integration into a larger company and the pressures to deliver competitive returns to external shareholders would somehow threaten the uniqueness of their brands and organizations. Does this suggest brands like Cirque du Soleil, Patagonia or Red Bull have to be privately owned to protect their authenticity, desirability and future?

We certainly have found Ueber-Brands that are part of some of the largest public corporations around and that nevertheless flourish. One thing their corporate owners seem to have in common is that they found ways to ensure critical parts of the brand myth and mission are protected, rather than 'normalized' away for the sake of scale and higher short-term returns. We call it 'ring-fencing' and it may occur from the birth within a large corporation or as an Ueber-Brand is acquired. The acquiring company may incubate a small start-up before admitting it or hold developed Ueber-Brands in a network of largely independent 'houses'. All will review their portfolio regularly to find efficiency gains in integrating 'back-office' processes and operations that they see are not core to the brand myth. Sometimes they might undo these changes if they find them to have gone too far, as the Ben & Jerry's example shows on page 183.

Separated at birth – Nespresso and Nestlé

Nestlé's CEO, Peter Brabeck-Letmathe, intuitively understood that the fledgling idea of selling single-unit gourmet coffee made in special machines needed a business model and culture different from the main mass-packaged goods business at Nestlé. He sought early on to separate the new Nespresso unit organizationally and culturally. Agreeing to a separate physical location was relatively easy since a purpose-built plant was needed anyway. Licensing the machine design and sale to outside suppliers also made sense to everyone, given the corporation had no experience with small appliances. Hiring a total industry outsider, Jean-Paul Gaillard, to lead the new unit created an internal stir. However, Gaillard had proven unconventional thinking before when he launched a fashion line under the Marlboro brand, and he did the same again at Nespresso. It was he who turned the original business-to-business idea into a prestige consumer brand model – on a hunch and against Nestlé's forecast and many internal stakeholders (see case study 5 on p 165). Brabeck had to defend these and other departures from the Nestlé norm repeatedly over the next decade and fight off suggestions that he divest the 'non-strategic' unit. Today, of course, the billion-dollar brand is a jewel in the Nestlé crown. Recent Nespresso CEOs are Nestlé-grown and numerous back-office operations like buying, payroll or IT have been integrated with the mother corporation. However, Nestlé has learned to protect and nurture unique elements of the Nespresso model, such as the 'Club' member care organization, which make up the differentiating edge of this Ueber-Brand. Nestlé certainly learned from their experience in creating their own prestige brand as they ring-fenced others they acquired, like Italian fine-dining water San Pellegrino in 1997. But it is beauty giant Estée Lauder that has mastered the art of acquiring prestige brands and letting them shine as part of their universe.

Network of houses – The Estée Lauder Company

The Estée Lauder brand is a legend in its own right and, together with other prestige brands it developed like Aramis, Clinique and Origins, it forms the core of this 10 billion dollar-plus corporation. But since the mid-90s, the company has also been on a hunt for unique brand stories from the outside. In the autumn of 2014 alone, Lauder acquired boutique perfumers Le Labo and Frédéric Malle and skin care icon Olio Lusso. It has shown skill in selecting, acquiring and letting them grow as part of a network of semi-autonomous 'houses' – with most consumers unaware that Bobby Brown, MAC or Smashbox (all make-up), Jo Malone, Aveda or Bumble and Bumble are part of the same holding. The last, a fashion-forward hair-care brand, literally operates out of 'The House of Bumble', which includes brand headquarters, a salon and a stylist school and is located in the hip Meatpacking district of New York. That is across town from Estée Lauder Group headquarters but a culture-shock away from the opulent, upper-crust elegance and hushed atmosphere that reigns there. Estée Lauder is careful to preserve the 'smell of the place', often retaining the brand founders as creative leaders – for example make-up artist Bobby Brown – or at least as 'spiritual guides' like the late Horst Rechelbacher. The latter was a pioneer in introducing the ideas of aromatherapy and Ayurvedic healing to hair and beauty care through his brand Aveda in the '70s. He sold the brand to Estée Lauder in 1997 but was convinced by chairman Leonard Lauder to stay on for another six years and transmit the legacy to the organization. Today, Aveda still operates out of a holistic wellness campus in Minneapolis and has become a centre of expertise for nature-related brands in the group, like the home-grown Origins. Expertise that is not essential to the essence of the brand, on the other hand, is housed at other offices of the group. For example, the global director for Aveda e-commerce is co-located with other brand colleagues in New York.

The incubator approach – Coca-Cola Co

Coca-Cola's interest in 'quirky and niche brands' does not stem from a desire to add unique stories to a premium brand portfolio. In Coke's case it is the realization that many new trends start with such brands, which can create mainstream segments if they garner enough influencer support, told us Deryck van Rensburg, President of Global Venturing and Emerging Brands (VEB) at the Coca-Cola Company. So Coke's VEB division is managing a portfolio of initially non-controlling stakes in what could be a next Red Bull. Their insight is that the authenticity of a small team of founders on a mission would be hard for Coke to replicate. Rather than absorb or copy the brands, Coke ring-fences the 'seedlings' and provides measured amounts of funding and expertise on request. The ultimate goal is that the brands grow enough in scale that it – literally – make sense for them go on the Coke truck and be distributed together with the other big brands. When that happens, the company will take on full ownership. This has been the pattern with investments in Innocent smoothies in the UK or Zico coconut water and Honest Tea in the United States. As the name implies, Honest Tea is about transparency in the use of all-natural ingredients, a limited amount of cane sugar in particular. High-fructose corn syrup, the key ingredient of most soft drinks, is frowned upon, and the brand makes this very clear on their kid packs and to mums – at a premium of 2–3 times the price of those regular soft drinks. However, allowing the tiny brand to continue this campaign and with it the potential to hurt their infinitely bigger mainstay brands, shows that Coke understands the importance of this point for the integrity of Honest Tea – and possibly the future of the Coca-Cola Company as a whole, since consumer concern in this area is rising. Coke boosted their stake from 40 per cent in 2007 to 100 per cent in 2011 and Honest Tea is now an independent unit operated by one of its remaining co-founders. Read van Rensburg's paper (2014) for more detail on how large corporations can harness disruptive brands and their entrepreneurial spirit.

Radiating inside out: it all starts with the culture

When we contacted an employee at MINI recently we got the following reply: 'Greetings Motorer! I am motoring cross-country with hundreds of MINI owners starting in San Francisco on Sunday, July 26 and finishing in

Boston on Sunday, August 10...' Now that's truly taking the brand's spirit to heart and 'Living the Dream' – language and all.

You'll find more about MINI and how they totally radiate their myth and their mission inside out in the case study adjacent to Principle 4. The same goes for Patagonia, which is certainly one of the most purist and perfect in this regard (see case study Principle 1). From internal board meetings in wet-suits (as in surfboard meetings) and mountain climbs to supporting employees' cause-related activities to sharing new eco-technologies with its competition and incorporating Patagonia as a 'benefit company' committed to a 'positive effect on society and the environment' (Patagonia, accessed August 2014), you will be hard-pressed to find anyone more dedicated to practising what they preach than Chouinard and his team.

Now, arguably, Ueber-Brands with a socio-eco agenda often don't have much of a choice anyway. They are mostly run by people with a strong sense of conviction, and their targets are generally much more vigilant. What is truly amazing in the case of Patagonia is the level to which they equally pursue their ecological mission and translate this into a thriving, new standard-setting way of doing business – without any outside help, actually rejecting various offers for investment or takeover. A brand that hasn't always been as 'straight' or successful in this respect yet managed to churn ahead and is still – or again – a stellar Ueber-Brand is Ben & Jerry's.

The tale of the double dip

Ben Cohen & Jerry Greenfield started their eponymous ice cream brand and business in 1978 in an old Vermont gas station, after first trying their luck at finishing their studies, driving cabs and starting a bagels and newspaper business. Driven by a love of food, they took correspondence courses on making ice cream. Within 20 years they had made it into a multimillion-dollar publicly traded company that became the subject of a bidding war between food conglomerates, with Unilever taking away the grand prize in 2001 for US $326 million.

The problem: the brand's myth and success were always built against traditional economics, not in synch with them. Rather than focusing on shares and shareholder return, the hippie company became famous for their 'double dip" idea, making profits and people a double bottom line. Beyond creating great ice cream, they wanted their company to be a fun and equitable place to work that would help further social equality and peace in its community, the nation and the world. And that 'dip' often took over, making the profit line more than once dip deep, into red.

So when Unilever took over, they were almost 'forced' to clean up and straighten out the economics. Judging by all reports they were quite respectful towards the company's social agenda, yet they invariably ran into some touchy topics – most famously the discontinuation of the iconic but unprofitable product 'Wavy Gravy', an homage to the entertainer-activist of the same name. The biggest issue, though, wasn't any major blow to the company's ethos, spirit or executional eccentrics; as with Snapple it was the gradual erosion of its culture. Bit by bit, spoon by spoon, the crazy-curly-counter-cultural vibe turned corporate, simply by instating minor – and by themselves sensible – processes like asking for pre-approval of cause donations for instance. The mood soured and employee morale as well as business went down, until in 2006 Walter Freese became CEO and managed to lure the company's founders back 'on board' with the infamous 'American Pie' initiative (Sneyd, 2006). Freese said at the time: 'There was always the commitment… to honour the social mission. (But) Ben & Jerry's was less courageous for a period of time, post-acquisition' (NBC News, July 2006).

Since then the company has slowly regained the grassroots feel inherent to its myth and mission. It probably helped that many big businesses have begun to acknowledge the importance of a fundamental shift, like current CEO Jostein Solheim does: 'The world needs dramatic change to address the social and environmental challenges we are facing. Historically, this company has been and must continue to be a pioneer to continually challenge how business can be a force for good and address inequities inherent in global business' (Food Processing, accessed August 2014).

Today, Ben & Jerry's is back in full swing, uniting delicious ice cream and social vision in the form of their foundation, their 'partnershops' and supporting thousands of activities from the Occupy movement to the US Institute of Peace. They still don't use milk containing growth hormones, and they mix their flavours in a hippie-tie-dye fashion, naming them 'Karamel Sutra' or 'Hazed & Confused'. They have special editions to advocate for specific causes, like 'Rainforest Crunch' or 'Hubby Hubby' (in support of gay marriage). They also try to avoid big, paid media, rather starting or inspiring counter-cultural conversations and cults as they did with their 'Late Night Snack' versus 'Americone' debate (*Huffington Post*, 2012, accessed August 2014). One thing they did give up though is their original 'David against Goliath' sentiment. But that's the price of growth. Overall they still – or again – live their dream in full force and with flying colours, feisty and fervent, inside and out.

The moral: it's as Ben Cohen said early on in the story: 'It's not a question of making great ice cream, making some money and then going and doing socially responsible things. Caring about the community has to be imbued throughout the organization so that it impacts every decision we make' (Lager, 1995). Modern prestige brands are built on a mission, and in today's vigilant world they can only become a true Ueber-Brand if they stay true to that mission. They must take it to heart and translate it into a myth by celebrating it in many unique ways, even if they are unprofitable or polarizing, and make sure that nothing undermines this core dynamic. **Every business needs to grow and needs to make money, but Ueber-Brands also need to make sense, and radiate this sense, unbridled and uncompromised, from the inside out.**

Be it, don't execute it

Another great case of living the dream is without a doubt the 'King of Cashmere' and his 'humanist capitalism' (Amed, 2014) gone soft-yarn-ultra-luxe in the bucolic setting of the Umbrian hills. We are talking about Brunello Cucinelli, of course. You'll find all the details in the case study on page 193 of this chapter, so let's just focus on two aspects here. First, how the whole idea of having a mission, turning it into a myth and then living it wholeheartedly, is in no way limited to brands with a socio-ecological core. Cucinelli is absolutely no tree hugger. He has a social conscience, but he primarily sees himself in the heritage of Hadrian, the Roman emperor and Renaissance man *avant la lettre*, feeling 'responsible for the beauty of the world' (Eder, 2013). He admittedly took inspiration from Benetton, but only their sense of focus and colour, not their political activism. He is an entrepreneur first and foremost, with all his heart and his eyes clearly on growth and success, albeit a bit more sustainable than others perhaps. His ultimate goal is to create beautiful things that last and have a soul, and yes, do this in a way that respects people and the environment.

Ueber-Brands need to have clear values beyond their value and they need to abide by them stringently, but these values can absolutely also revolve around the quality of the yarn and the beauty of classic, humane craftsmanship.

Which brings us to the second point that's amazing about Brunello Cucinelli: his sense of place. It's good for any brand to have a clearly identifiable origin, giving it roots and history and often enough, as in the case of all those 'Parisian' labels, status and cachet. Cucinelli has taken this idea to the ultimate level. He gave his Ueber-Brand a true home and its myth a time and place as real as anything in the world: Solomeo, a little town outside of Perugia. That's where he works and lives, where most of his beautiful things are produced and where he's slowly reconstructing his ideal version of a working collective for the 21st century – clad in cashmere. It's a bit like going to Disneyland, but it's very real and of course much more refined. And it comes with an enticing outlet. It makes the whole brand tangible, but without diminishing its status – perhaps because Solomeo is literally perched on top of a hill. It provides authenticity, but at the same time it enhances the brand's aura (see case study at the end of this chapter).

This is something that most Ueber-Brands have done, though not all as spectacularly as Cucinelli, and without milking it as astutely in their communication. Method, the cleaning supply Ueber-Brand we mentioned in Principle 4 for their mythmaking skills, made their headquarters in San Francisco not only a reflection of that myth – they designed them to inspire it. From its colourful chaos to the quirky playfulness to the ping-pong tables and their infamous recruiting process, focusing on the cultural fit of the applicant as much as his or her competence, you can always expect the unexpected. Or, as their 'Green Chief' Geetha Solheim says on their website, 'We are one living breathing organism' (Method (b), accessed August 2014). 'People against Dirty' indeed!

Similarly their brothers in spirit: Innocent, the British fruit juice brand (now owned by Coca-Cola, see earlier in this chapter). They are in a totally different category and a very different world than Method, namely London, yet they share a similar spirit of playful conviction. If you don't know them, look at their website (innocentdrinks.co.uk). Thomas Delabriere, a marketing leader at Innocent, over the phone gave us a pretty good picture of how it feels to walk their halls. Green astroturf, quirky sun umbrellas, table football, healthy cafeterias… even their 'common grounds' are fairly uncommon. All a far cry from your corporate office, which is exactly what they want to be and project – and which helped make them an Ueber-Brand.

Ueber-Brands live their dream. They don't just execute it, they are it. And that is much easier in a true time and a true place.

The Innocent brand lives their dream – innocent fun all the way to 'Grassy Van' sampling mobiles

Image courtesy of Innocent

Most of the Ueber-Brands we visited and know take great pain in stylizing and organizing their headquarters in a way that is not only reflective of their myth and mission, but drives them. They may not always go to the extreme and buy an entire village, but they make their 'home' the brand's nucleus. They literally 'work' the brand from the core, and not just for integrity, also for inspiration. As Angela Ahrendts from Burberry put it: 'Everyone talks about building a relationship with your customer. I think you build one with your employees first' (Leahey, 2012). Very true. Only then can you convincingly radiate it inside out.

The world according to you

Ultimately 'Radiating inside out' means shining out into the market, out to your consumers, out to the world. You start at the core, the company culture and its employees, but the goal is to reach and convince your clientele, existing or prospective.

To that degree many if not most modern prestige or Ueber-Brands have, in recent years, started to integrate vertically, opening their own mono brand stores rather than just being present in traditional retail channels like department stores or specialty shops. Of course they've built an online presence, initially hesitantly, but lately with a vengeance, including e-commerce.

Two seminal moments in this were certainly the launch of Niketown in the early '90s and then the first Prada and Apple stores, tellingly both in New York's SoHo neighbourhood in 2001 and 2002. These ventures set new standards in 'retail theatre' and kicked off the race for the fantastic flagship, which still doesn't show any signs of slowing down. Ralph Lauren, another Ueber-Brand, which is certainly a guiding light when it comes to creating a brand world from scratch, had been in the Rhinelander Mansion since 1985, but that was something else. With the grandiose store on New York's Madison Avenue and 72nd Street, the brand had basically created its own heritage home: Ralph Lifshitz' Solomeo, so to speak. Nike, Apple and Prada now went a step further and pushed the idea of creating brand worlds, or 'epicentres' as Prada likes to call them, into a global programme – risking the outrage of their established retail partners and taking imaginary brand worlds 3D.

In the meantime many brands have followed, certainly in the traditional world of prestige, but also in the new one. Sometimes with multi-media mega-experience centres like Louis Vuitton's Tokyo store on Omotesando or Burberry's Regent Street store, sometimes with multi-brand concept centres like Comme des Garçon's Dover Street Market in London, Tokyo and now New York and increasingly as pop-up shops for anything from Birchbox, the sampling phenomenon, to Illy coffee.

There are basically two reasons to do this. First and foremost it gives brands an opportunity to create their own world, much more so than shop-in-shops or areas in tradition retail ever allowed. Ueber-Brands love to be in control of themselves and their environment and this is the best way to do it. It is for this reason that Tesla refuses to go through traditional dealerships, preferring to forfeit potential sales, but keep the brand's ethos, spirit and way of delivery unique, 'on equity' and high margin to fund its grand plan (see p 63). Others use this to create the idealized version of their brand, the ultimate way to experience it. Nivea, the global, mid-priced beauty brand, started to create spa centres, trying to elevate their brand, imbuing it with a pampering feel, but also showcasing their products' abilities and giving them almost an air of pro-grade quality. Equally Chobani and their made-to-measure yoghurt shop on West Broadway, New York, a concept they are intending to roll out.

This brings us to the other aspect of why creating their own world is so intriguing to brands, and particularly modern prestige or Ueber-Brands. It gets them closer to their customer, quite literally cutting out the retailer in the middle. They can use some of their stores as quasi-labs or test kitchens, as Chobani does (Fawkes, 2012). And even those Ueber-Brands that don't use their retail space to overtly experiment and try out 'new flavours' will always have a chance to feel out the consumer as well as themselves. Or, as Cucinelli said recently, it wasn't until they went retail that they truly started to develop the brand's taste, its tone and feel, the total look (Amed, 2014).

The devil is in the detail

> Our performances are timeless, made to last. There are no oversized costumes that make you feel there is a stand-in for the night. No chipped-off paint, no broken hats. We design these shows to last 20 years. Everything about them is minutely planned, designed and high quality.

This excerpt from our conversations with the directors of marketing and communication from Cirque du Soleil says it all.

Obviously, no matter how or why an Ueber-Brand starts to unfold its brand world, it is of utmost importance that it does so with an incredible eye to detail. Being less than exacting will do more harm than good, as Ueber-Brands obviously don't do this for reach, which could be achieved more easily through traditional distribution and isn't their key interest anyway. They do it to make their myth and their mission come alive in a multi-sensorial environment. And that requires taking care of all those supposedly minor impressions, which together create the big picture. **Crafting an Ueber-Brand world means being considerate of all the things, which we may never consciously register, but which make us sub-consciously feel right or wrong.**

A great example of this scrupulous attention to detail is the fastidious construction of the Aēsop shops. They make it look simple, but 'it is massive work just to look normal', says Matteo Martignoni, Aēsop's General Manager Marketing. Like their 'shelf art': Aēsop displays products only in odd numbers, as if they were a bunch of roses, for the visual appeal. Now, if that's not pacifying the detail devil… (see also the case study, Principle 3).

Equally minimalist, but perhaps a bit more high-touch than high-brow, are the Apple stores, which all of us know. While the brand claims to design each one according to the location and its surroundings, that doesn't ring quite true – not in the way of Aēsop or Kiehl's anyway. Of course the spaces are defining to some degree, so that some will have a staircase and others won't, but basically every Apple store looks the same, no matter if you're in Rio or Tokyo: rows of Parson-style tables with lots of people fingering lots of products and somewhere a genius bar. Other than that, there are white walls and glass. Apple stores are almost the absence of a world, with all attention geared to the products and getting your hands on them, and not much else. Kind of like the design version of an IT nerd's home or office – 'look at the monitor, never mind real life'.

Yet another world again is Chipotle, the fresh-mex take-out chain. Their idea is 'Food with Integrity' and that's how their joints are designed: modern-minimalist yes, but not in a cerebral sense. Here it's all about simplicity, reduction, focus and transparency. Every detail of Chipotle is designed to signal quality and value for money. Not cheap, because Chipotle is anything but for fast food, but focused on the product and the high-grade ingredients rather than fancy surroundings. Smart prestige in other words, and thus very modern prestige.

Lastly let's look to Asia; Japan, specifically. Given that the entire Japanese culture is extremely detail focused and exacting, it doesn't surprise that the brand worlds created here are setting new standards as well. Even Western prestige brands are more choosey in their store design, materials and maintenance in Tokyo than they are in New York, for instance, or in Paris. Japanese luxury resort brand Hoshino takes this to an extreme level, especially since their whole mission is to 'capture the essence of Japan. Not traditionalist, but pure. Not a nostalgic imitation but its own, parallel dimension', as their PR Manager Tansawa-san explained. Let us give you a little taste. You are whisked away onto a barge. The street noise disappears behind lush vegetation. You hear the water gently being pushed away and the soft sound of a gong announcing your arrival. You smell an unusual incense and taste an unfamiliar yet pleasant welcome tea. You have escaped the outside world and started to experience the 'fifth dimension' as Hoshino-San, the founder, likes to call it.

We love Hoshino's concept of the fifth dimension in itself, but also because it perfectly captures what every modern prestige or Ueber-Brand has to do: create a parallel world, a bubble that expresses their dream in the most perfect way. Celebrate their mission and their myth in a manner that is as equally meticulous as it is multi-sensorial. Never leaving anything out of sight, not even (or especially) that which is invisible, because *God sees it, and we people may certainly sense it – or see it with our hearts.*

Some details are more equal than others

Lastly, let's make it a bit more difficult yet: just taking care of even the tiniest detail would have been a bit easy. The additional challenge is not to take care of any but the right details.

As with Ueber-Brands as a whole, their executional details aren't created equal either. Ueber-Brands must have a 'Mission Incomparable', and that means they also have to find their 'details incomparable'; not just anything, but the things that are material to their world, their myth, the things that make them unique and bring their core to life. Doing everything perfectly is never a sign of superiority but, if anything, one of feeling inferior or at least insecure. And that is clearly not an option. **Ueber-Brands must obsess over those elements and aspects that set them apart and above their competitors, the ones that make their very own dream come true.** This can be a 'New-World-meets-Old-World' coffeehouse feel (eg Starbucks) or the capturing and re-fracturing of light (eg Swarovski) or the 'Art & Science of Nature' (eg Aveda) or a very brainy beauty (eg Aēsop)... the examples are as endless as the world of branding.

To make this point more tangible let's look more closely at Hoshino. Their resorts are as much defined by what they are and do as by what they are not and don't do. They take extreme care in creating a unique, timeless and stress-free environment. They don't, though, give you all the creature comforts we've become used to, because that's the whole idea. If you look at Hoshino's amenity kits, for example, most of us would consider them basic, to say the least, especially considering the price. It's the same with the service, which many judge (too) slow, or the strict no smoking policy (in Japan!). But those are not important aspects for Hoshino to score on: if anything it's important for them to be seen as too simple, too slow... by many, because only then will you focus on those aspects that are important to the Hoshino world. Consequently the resort has developed a strong confidence in its choices. 'Cheap' or 'disrespectful' are unacceptable, but 'simple' or 'subtle' are virtues. The resort has, on occasion, even suggested that Hoshinoya (as the resorts are called in Japanese) might not be the right environment for some. They recommend that guests stay at least a week to fully immerse themselves into the experience, according to Tansawa-San: 'We don't like, in fact we discourage, the "weekend luxury dipping" other resorts promote to optimize revenues'. A true Ueber-Brand attitude. And, indeed, the group seems to have been successful in attracting a profitable crowd that can afford a one-week stay at a cost of US $8,000 or more, having them come back and keeping them shielded from those who can only afford a taste.

We went into quite some detail about Hoshino because we feel that in this case one in-depth look explains the principle better than many short dips can. Nevertheless, let us quickly give you some other examples. Jo Malone, the London fragrance brand owned by Estée Lauder, puts a lot of money and effort in creating a precious gift feel, with every purchase packed in tissue, boxed, ribboned and put in bowed bags. Yet their bottles are stock, because it doesn't matter. The brand is about mixing and layering their scents, and in that sense the true product will only be created by the buyer – beyond the flacon. Same with La Mer, the high-end beauty icon we looked at earlier. The simplest packaging, not changed for years, but every shop-in-shop is outfitted with gorgeous and costly aquariums of exotic fish, albeit often fresh-water, to imbue the potions and lotions with that 'power of the sea' feel – something that expensive bottling could never do as effectively. Or Aēsop: all products in what looks like simple, stock bottles and containers, tinted brown to protect against UV rays and bagged in paper, yet carefully proportioned and adorned with poetically written copy, punctiliously laid out and attached with the architectural exactness the brand wants to exude.

To sum up, Ueber-Brands must and do take great pains to build their own worlds – for the consumers to experience their myth and their mission in the most ideal, pure and perfect way. To constantly learn, fine tune and further their brand – to stay on top, of themselves, their competitors and their consumers. And this requires great attention to detail: not just any detail, but exactly those that make or break the brand and let it thrive, or not. It requires almost the same fastidious neglect of the details that are not important or are the opposite of the brand's core. Because just like Hoshino, we are always defined by what we are not and don't do as much as by that which we are and do. Often even more so.

Principle 6: The rules of 'living the dream'

1 If in doubt – don't
  Never compromise. Even getting close to anything that undermines your myth and your mission can be lethal.

2 Divide et Impera
  Ueber-Brands need imagination and precision in execution, which is usually better served by a congenial duo.

3 Ring-fence and protect
  Companies must take care not to hold their Ueber-Offspring too close. They usually require different standards, processes and structures and flourish better on a long leash.

4 Radiate from the core
  Let your mission drive your culture and build your myth. Inspire your employees to ignite your customers – for integrity, credibility and loyalty.

5 Make it your world
  You're not selling a product but a dream, or at least an ideal. And it's nice to see that become reality – occasionally.

6 Take care – a lot of care
  The dream is in the detail, as is the devil. Utmost attention is required – but not to everything…

7 Be dismissive
  Of those details that are not material to your dream. What you are is equally defined by what you are not.

There's no faking it when it comes to modern prestige. Ueber-Brands must live the dream they try to sell. Only when they truthfully build their own world inside out, not compromising on the details that matter, can they radiate with the credibility and authenticity they need today.

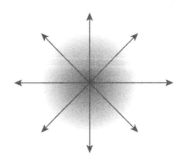

Ueber-Brand case study 6   Living it like Brunello Cucinelli or the Freitag brothers

What might an Italian brand known for luxury sweaters and a debonair clientele have in common with a Swiss brand that makes messenger bags from recycled materials? Freitag, the bag brand, hardly sees business in its Davos store blip during the ritzy World Economic Forum, while the Brunello Cucinelli store in nearby (by helicopter) St. Moritz almost sells out during this time. What makes these brands similar, nevertheless, is the detail and depth with which they bring their respective brand myths to life, elevating them to Ueber-Brand status.

Brunello Cucinelli started his company in 1978 when he was surprised by an initial order for 53 of the unusually colourful cashmere sweaters he was proposing. At that time, Cucinelli had no money, no factory and no plan for how to actually deliver. Today, his brand generates close to half a billion dollars in annual global sales (estimate for 2014) and is valued at over three times that much on the Italian stock exchange. His iconic sweaters are priced around US $800, but buying into the total Cucinelli look can set you back thousands of dollars, depending on how many layers you want to put on. And people do layer. The company has grown in double digits every year, including in 2008 when the rest of the luxury industry lay flat on its back.

The story of Freitag begins 15 years later in 1993, when young brothers and design students Markus and Daniel Freitag were in need of sturdy and rain-proof bags for their bicycle commute in Zurich. Inspired by trucks with colourful covers zooming past their window, they constructed a bag from old truck tarp, with a piece of seat belt as a strap. Quite unintentionally, they landed a hit with fellow students, bike messengers and, eventually, the individualistic and environmentally conscious at large. Although they never sought boosters like outside financing or advertising, the brand has grown to recycle some 400 metric tons of tarpaulin into over 400,000 bags and accessories in 2013 (the private company issues no sales numbers). The mainstay shoulder bags retail for around US $200, but special edition bags can reach multiples of that and are unlikely to grace the shoulders of a humble messenger.

Living the dream – to the top

As different as the dreams of Cucinelli and the Freitag brothers are, they are both living them wholeheartedly. Freitag uses every opportunity to celebrate the 'out of the bag' beauty of recycling and 'recontextualizing' – which is also the title of a book and retrospective by the Zurich Design Museum. The brand teaches its art of giving products a second life through internships, lectures and professional workshops. It demonstrates green living by offering free bike sharing for employees and shoppers or by demonstrating urban underground gardening. On a more ideological level, Freitag has teamed up with the equally eco-conscious and non-conformist Swiss magazine *Reportagen* to fund documentaries and host discussions on the beauty and challenges of objective reporting.

Much of the above happens in or around the dozen Freitag stores. They are at the same time the end point of a unique and closely controlled supply chain and monument to the world according to Freitag. The Zurich flagship stands tall at the same busy interception of roads and railway that inspired the brothers. Just like their products, the store is made of repurposed material: 19 rusty steel shipping containers that were gutted and rigged to create a towering vertical brand gallery. Arriving on the rooftop, visitors can have their own Freitag moment. The landscape below is gritty and industrial and the passing trains and trucks are noisy. But a change of perspective can transform this scenery into a cacophonous and colourful urban art experience. 'Re-contextualization is a joy to behold' (www.freitag.ch/fundamentals, accessed September 2014).

Consequently, store interiors are designed to 'contextualize' the rough beauty of the bags. Naked walls of industrial steel or concrete are lined with tightly stacked white cartons, making the few bags on display look like modern art. Once you approach the wall, things get more vivid and personal as each carton is labelled with a colour picture of its unique content, a 'Recycled Individual Product' ('RIP' in Freitag speak) with a tag that tells of its provenance.

Freitag wants its audience to discover the detail behind the re-birthing process and the ultra-eco design of the factory where it takes place to lend the product authenticity and soul. On their social media pages one can follow 'Heartcore Thomas', the '23-year-young truck butcher', dissect a tarp or 'Dirt Buster Mustapha' wash it in rainwater-fed machines (freitag.ch, accessed May 2014). You can't help but notice the challenging social background many employees share – refugees, high school dropouts – or the fact that Freitag operates one of the last places for blue-collar workers in the decidedly white-collar Zurich. It's an ideological statement the brand invests in via higher manufacturing costs. The payout can be measured in the factory tours, which are always solidly booked by the kind of alternative living types that make up the brand's design target and an influencer audience that will add testimony to the unique fabric of the brand and spread the gospel.

Freitag manifestations are gritty by design: the container flagship tower, the brothers and CEO (Hans Haefliger in the middle) all casual and a 'Tarpbutcher' at the F-abrik'. But note the bag beautifully elevated in the showroom

Courtesy of Freitag. Photos: Roland Taennler (bros), Joël Tettamanti (tarpbutcher)

The leadership of this peculiar neo-industrial organism is split between 'the bros', as everyone calls Markus and Daniel Freitag, and a CEO. The bros are owners and creative leaders, but they decided early on that they were neither particularly skilled nor interested in managing the company. However, they also make a point of not paying themselves more than the CEO. While they no longer wash tarps in their bathtub, they still come to work on bikes, and still enjoy hanging out with their young employees and customers, as Elisabeth Isenegger, spokeswoman at Freitag, confirms.

One can observe equivalent efforts to create this kind of a brand-specific socio-sphere at Brunello Cucinelli, except that Mr. Cucinelli's ethics, aesthetic and ideology are inspired by the thinking of Aristotle and St. Benedict rather than by ideas of environmental engineering. Cucinelli is staging a singular take on enlightened patronage and humane manufacturing on top of a hill in his native Umbria, surrounded by fields and forests. Rather than in a carbon-neutral industrial complex, his ateliers are housed in a medieval village, Solomeo, which he buys up piece by piece and lovingly restores. There his workers craft the luxury knitwear in a beautiful, wholesome environment. They take communal meals of fresh regional produce in an elegant tavern on china bearing the Cucinelli crest. In their leisure time they are encouraged to nurture mind and body at the company's own Forum of Arts, Accademia Neoumanistica, its gardens or its gymnasium. David LaRocca, scholar of moral theory, described it in our conversation as 'a sort of campus for the human spirit' (scan QR code in Preface for a link to David's film *Bruno Cucinelli – a new philosophy of clothes*). Loyalty, discipline, creativity – humbly presented – are valued and rewarded with above-average salaries. Arrogance, on the other hand, is frowned upon. The townspeople are often clad in the cozy clothes they make, which is enabled by a serious wardrobe subsidy. One can see them depicted in Cucinelli brochures and print ads strolling through the village and fields or picnicking in front of a Renaissance palace. Even if most consumers may not recognize the 'models' as Cucinelli and his employees or the village as Solomeo, it gives the idyll authenticity and makes for a great conversation starter.

Of course, all the stores have a sense of Solomeo as well. They are decorated in white but are elegantly appointed with pictures of the village and Umbrian landscape and with wood fixtures that are well stocked with both the noble wool garments as well as antiquarian books by the great thinkers that inspire Cucinelli's world. Shoppers are invited to indulge in the sartorial craftsmanship and to get comfortable on a leather chair with a copy of Rousseau's *Discourses* – at least that is the dream. A dream that could hardly be lived more perfectly.

Myths and missions – rooted in the making

The mission that guides Cucinelli is summarized in a Dostoevsky quote that headlines the brand website: 'Beauty is our salvation.' Cucinelli wants the garments to be an expression of the good character of the wearer, rather

Brunello Cucinelli creates his own brand of enlightenment whether through his special approach to entrepreneurship, town building, lifestyle or lectures (real and reflected in print ads). Select classics are around for reference and Solomeo is at the centre (see crest)

Photos by David LaRocca and Dr Brigitte Walz

than costumes expressing a short-lived trend. He wants them to be worn with 'sprezzatura', the humble, nonchalant ways described by Baldassare Castiglione in his 1528 Renaissance manual for the perfect courtier (Castiglione, 1528). But he seeks this 'truth in beauty' not just regarding the wearer but also in the manufacturing process. Cucinelli so religiously pursues this mission that the phenomenon has become a myth studied by philosophers, theologians and the media alike. The brand itself describes it as a combination of 'neo-renaissance values of craftsmanship [with] neo-humanistic capitalism' (brunellocucinelli.com, accessed 2014). Beyond fair wages and good working conditions, it is particularly concerned to protect the dignity of the worker and to nurture their souls.

The creation story retold in innumerable blogs and articles is that Brunello was born into a poor family, and was chagrinned to see his father suffer the indignities and bodily strain of working in a cement factory. Enlightened by his strong faith, the self-study of philosophy and armed with a beautiful product idea, he embarked on creating the kind of manufactory and village he would have wished for his father to work in. This consistent and inspiring narrative naturally nourishes a steady stream of word of mouth from those who discover its depth, plus an influential group of disciples.

In this sense, Cucinelli is very much like Freitag, except that the brothers focus on industrial production and what it should be like in an environmentally conscious, modern world. Then there is also a mythical, almost alchemistic side to the process of taking worn parts of a truck and giving them an entirely new form, function and identity-giving halo (or 'charisma' as Glenn and Walker would say, see page 122). It adds a pinch of the metaphysical magic to the sociological guiding myth. And that is priceless, no matter if you're selling high-end sweaters or recycled bags.

Un-selling, longing and belonging – the more you know

Inviting your shoppers or investors to read a 16th-century edition of Aristotle's *Nicomachean Ethics*, as Cucinelli has done on occasion, hardly qualifies as selling. No word about the garments or where to buy them, but a belief that the right customer will be seduced by the beauty of it all. In their book-like brochures one can see Brunello Cucinelli in front of a class of philosophy students apparently lecturing about 'Knowledge, Wisdom, Tolerance' rather than seeing supermodels in seasonal fashion (see image above).

'Promotions' focus on elite customers and select media. They take the form of exclusive invitations to Solomeo or noble venues like the Fortezza da Basso during the Pitti Uomo trade fair. Guests will be treated to a seemingly casual but meticulously choreographed lesson in Cucinelli lifestyle. Reporters like Richard Nally swoon: 'Of that party's several hundred studied attempts at dressing with artless sophistication, even I could see that Cucinelli was in a league of his own' (ForbesLife.com, 2013).

These kinds of exclusive experiences, lessons and tools of refinement are most crucial for those who already own all the material goods that might set them apart. For the rest of us, the fortress doors and substantial price tags may be enough to make us long. But it still all feeds the dream of rewarding ourselves and slipping into that rarified world at the next special occasion.

It seems a stretch to see parallels with the regular get-togethers the Freitag 'bros' have with likeminded eco-conscious friends and fans. But the same principle of associating the product with a desirable lifestyle and ideology is at work. At Freitag, messengers, students and journalists are the design target and an important part of the image, even if some of them will have to graduate to more senior jobs before they can afford the more expensive items in the line.

In line with their unconventional image, there is no mass-media advertising or promotion at Freitag, just word of mouth, Isenegger tells us. 'We produce quite laborious stop-motion movies for every single Freitag product.' The mix of online videos ranges from the serious to the artful-quirky documentation of the recycling, design and re-contextualization process involved (see some links in the bibliography). The stores, the internet and the 'F-abric' (see below) have been identified as appropriate and powerful media magnets and tools. They are often paired with the bike as a central element of the creation story, whether it is in the form of YouTube clips of crazy traffic scenes around the world shot from mounted cameras or sponsoring the Italian Cycle Messenger Championships. While the more cerebral events like the *Reporter* meet-ups (see above) are largely in (Swiss-) German, this visual storytelling speaks a universal language. The proof: local brand fans camped out in anticipation of the first Freitag store opening in Tokyo in 2012.

Behold! And grow with gravitas: principles over profit

As we saw, the products are a focal point of both Cucinelli and Freitag and they are imbued with values beyond function. Clearly, it would be cheaper for Freitag and its customers to make and buy a bag made from new synthetic materials. But then, the magic of 'recontextualization' would be lost along with the outcome of giving every bag its unique colour, graphic and wear pattern. Additionally, the fact that there is a finite and decreasing amount of used tarps in the world creates an element of natural rarity. In many ways, one is reminded of the rare skins and

The process of and organization around making Freitag bags from
used truck tarps is a central expression of the brand's 'raison d'être'

Image courtesy of Freitag, www.freitag.ch

dedicated craftsmanship that go into a Hermès bag – except that Freitag is talking
to people at the opposite end of the ideological spectrum. A premium 'Reference'
line has been created to hunt certain seasonal colours to satisfy the more stylish
avant-garde among its following and extend the brand up in price and 'hipness'.
But the original 'F-undamentals' messenger bag is still the icon, foundation and
strongest seller. The name was not randomly chosen. 'F-words' have a special
place in Freitag's unique language. Just as with Mini, Freitag's e-mail to us stood
out, telling us about a new 'F-abric' that will be made in the 'F-abrik' (plant).
It's another way to add to the 'custom-madeiest, individualisticiest truck-tarp
protection you can get', as a Freitag Facebook post observes (Freitag, 2014).

Of course, things are a bit more refined and romantic on the Cucinelli side,
but the storytelling around the product and its sourcing are just as central. The
centrepiece is still the cashmere sweater, the brand's icon. Print ads show
Brunello Cucinelli visiting Mongolian and Tibetan goat shepherds to purvey the
fine neck-wool that goes into it; 'Anima Mundi' the ad states, making reference
to an occult belief that everything in the universe is connected by a world soul.
It's the Cucinelli version of Icebreaker's 'Baa Code' (see p. 151). The diligence
of Solomeo's workers is also woven into the product and expressed through
a promise to maintain and repair the garment they sold to the owner for life.
Cucinelli is not shy to point out that some 25 per cent of the cost of goods go
into the free maintenance service, as David LaRocca told us. *All this signals to
customers that they are not buying (disposable) clothes but are making a lasting
investment, almost like the Patek Philippe 'heirloom' approach (see Principle 5).*

Finally, collections are always limited and shipped to retailers on a 'while
supplies last' basis, with the goal for them to run out. There are no logos on
the breast but a crest on the inside tag where you can discern a gryphon, a
tower and '1391', the founding year of Solomeo – but it might just as well be the
spiritual founding of Cucinelli.

Introducing the 'total look' and accessories has allowed the brand to continue to grow, while aiming further up. The jackets, coats or suits sell for ten times more than the already high prices for the knitwear. Cucinelli wants this growth to be 'gracious', as he told his investors before the IPO (Amed, 2014). He laid out humanity and high quality as the guide, not profits. He also created a structure that guarantees a family stake in the company and the continued operation of the 'Accademia Neoumanistica'. Nevertheless, the IPO was oversubscribed. As William Hutchings of Goldman Sachs explained to us: 'The story and provenance all support the very premium price. It positions the brand well to benefit from growing global demand for high-quality, authentic luxury products.'

Over at Freitag the growth has been appropriately organic as well, determined by the rate at which the word of mouth spreads (initially all in German), the unique sourcing infrastructure and availability of materials and by the refusal of 'the bros' to discount their products or inject external 'F-inancing' (which reminds us of Red Bull). They have worked on an alternative 'F-abric' made of natural, fully compostable material, over the past five years, not knowing if it will work out in the end. 'We don't do market research – we trust that the products we make according to our own needs will find new fans and clients', says Isenegger. So far, growing according to their own rules and speed seems to work, judging by annual growth that Freitag indicates as being in the 15–20 per cent range over the past 20 years. Asia is another growth engine. A Korean TV star shouldering the bag made it sell out there in a heartbeat (Barmettler, 2013). 'No bling', 'green living' and a dose of visible influencer use are what create increasing demand for the brand in Asia – just like in German-speaking Europe 20 years ago.

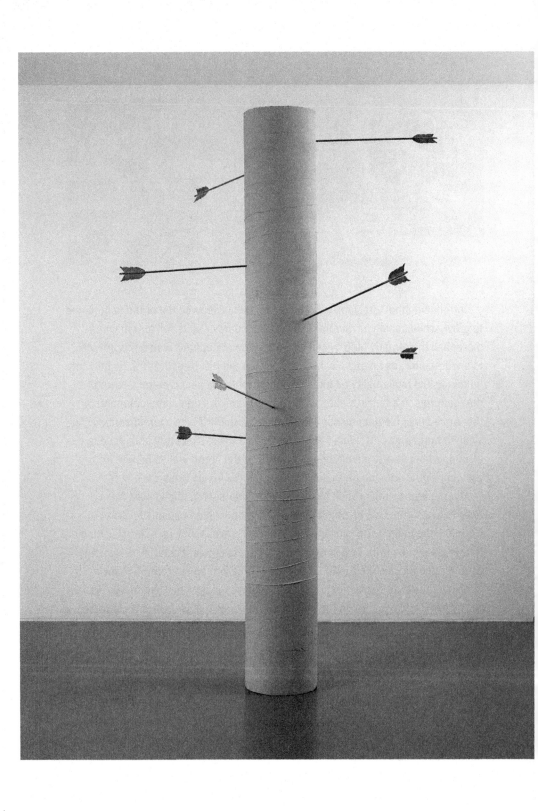

Principle 7
Growth without end
The ultimate balancing act

At the end of most journeys you're back where you started, and yet it all looks different. The same applies to this journey into the world of modern prestige and Ueber-Brands. The last principle is in a lot of ways not so much a new one, concerning itself with a special topic. It's actually more outlook and summary at the same time. It picks up one of the core themes running through the whole book – balance – and shows how this is the ultimate rule in building prestige brands in this day and age – forward, without end.

To 'grow without end', Ueber-Brands must continuously and carefully balance opposing forces – their need for profit and popularity with their need for rarity and mystery, their consumers' demand for access and their desire for exclusivity, their stakeholders' interest in growth and the ultimate goal of keeping that growth sustainable. They must develop their 'Star Power' in other words, which is what the first part of this last principle is all about: how crucial it is for Ueber-Brands to achieve the perfect equilibrium between radiating out and pulling in, like any good star does – the 'real' ones up in the sky and the proverbial ones up on our stages.

The implication: sustained growth is possible! The traditional prestige dictum that accessibility is the death of desirability seems to be less true in today's prestige world. Of course you still need to carefully manage your exposure and balance your growth, but grow you can. Modern prestige brands are less restricted or doomed to an eternal life of scarcity and rarity than their ancestors it seems. Most of them, however, show 'A Different Trajectory'.

Ueber-Brands tend to grow exponentially, where most mass brands grow more along the lines of a linear or square-root equation. To achieve this and keep their balances in check even as they scale, Ueber-Brands apply five different growth strategies based on all the analyses, interviews and reviews that we undertook:

1 **Grow with gravitas.** This is the ideal, but not always realistic way of growing slowly. Very much in tune with the zeitgeist of deceleration, but for the most part only possible if the brand is privately held – or has ultimately generous 'holders', like Shang Xia does in the form of Hermès for example.

2 **Grow back.** This is about pruning for growth. A very healthy, even natural way, but also for the most part in need of very understanding 'shareholders' and thus mostly applied by only a chosen few.

3 **Grow sideways.** The most popular alternative practised by pretty much every Ueber-Brand except for very few examples. It's a very simple idea: if you don't want to grow down too much, grow out – into other directions and categories.

4 **Grow up.** The golden route, because it's a strategy that has been around for a long time, and because it literally has to do with 'gilding', most famously of the golden credit cards we all have. But it has turned into a two-way street now: grade up as you trade down.

5 **Grow with passion.** Lastly something we all should do, which is however indispensable for Ueber-Brands: keep the fire alive. They must, at all cost, stay close to their Ueber-Target and keep their enthusiasm and support for the brand burning or they run the danger of losing the rest of us as well (see also Principle 2).

All five strategies are of course not mutually exclusive; actually quite the opposite. Most are wildly combined since they more or less complement each other. But let's first look a bit closer at the ultimate strategy and the ultimate goal: star power and balance.

Star power – it's a matter of balance

Most Ueber-Brands have it all, and actually, that's part of what makes them Ueber-Brands. For them, the lifecycle rule that states a peak is followed by a decline seems to not apply. They go up and up and one would think they have already long passed their zenith. They are almost ubiquitous and yet manage to keep their desirability. Look at Apple for instance, widely considered the number one brand of our times, which can yet create the excitement and engagement usually reserved for small, cult heroes. Or take Armani, the Italian fashion empire that serves everybody and their grandson with multiple sub-brands, yet still commands the red carpets around the world. Or think of Red Bull, the 25-year veteran, US $5 billion behemoth that still manages to be the darling of the very fickle youth market, which usually dismisses something as 'my mom's' brand way before it's reached shift workers and truck drivers, some of the energy drink's heavy users.

How do Ueber-Brands manage to do this? How come they don't die of their own success? How can they maximize reach and respect simultaneously?

One simple answer: balance! Of course, there are other factors, like luck for example, being in the right place at the right time, or innovation, having a great R&D force, or good foresight and great instincts. By and large, though, the continued growth of Ueber-Brands and the fact that they manage to stay at the upper echelons of their categories can be based on one core principle: balance. **They manage to keep things in check. They stay grounded as they take off, open themselves but never reveal too much, are out there yet always up, move forward but sometimes also laterally, are inviting but never forget who their true fans are.**

And in that it seems they are evolving the old dictum of growth as the death of prestige, making it less absolute. Modern prestige has become more about managed or considerate growth as opposed to none or little. Today you can have millions of customers around the world and still be perceived as prestigious – and harvest a premium. Just look at the above examples. There are many reasons as we outlined in Part 1, like our matured marketing world, where we are not so purist anymore, or social media platforms, which have made us reconsider our attitudes toward popularity and sincerity, or the internet as a whole and our globalized world, in which connectivity, flexibility and creativity are becoming more important values than dominance, orthodoxy and restriction.

Whatever the exact reasons in any single case, today's Ueber-Brands show a different approach to prestige in which the 'velvet rope' still rules, as we discussed in Principle 2, but in more idiosyncratic, intelligent and ultimately more inclusive ways. Growth and popularity are no longer auto-killers of prestige and aspiration.

Pushing out, pulling in

The old mantra, 'known by many, owned by few', seems to be moving towards a more social media attitude of 'linked with many, fond of a few'. We don't keep 'the others' out as much as we used to, and Ueber-Brands don't either. They can be more accessible yet still exude a sense of prestige – in a modern way. Naturally, scarcity and rarity are still key strategies for some, especially at the very high end of the market, but for others like Red Bull, Hoshino or Aēsop it's more sincerity, integrity and intimacy that make the difference. And those are emotional, interactive values, not physical or restrictive ones.

Speaking of intimacy, the other thing prestige experts used to say is that 'exclusivity is like virginity; impossible to regain once lost'. We don't think that's really true anymore either. If anything, today's exclusivity is more like celebrity. You can lose it but also regain it, and certain 'scars' don't make you 'kaput' but sometimes rather more attractive. Yes, desirability is still important, but it's a desirability that is at least partially also earned and proven rather than inherited, 'by royal appointment' or artificially created through restrictiveness. It's one that is warmer, more touchable. Today's prestige and Ueber-Brands are more and more glowing from within and with a soul. This is not always the case, and the way this glow is polished is definitely still as important as it always was, but it's no longer just about sitting protected and guarded. It's also about engaging and acting. Ueber-Brands must deliver – as we explained in Principle 5 – and they must 'live it' as we showed in Principle 6. Their myth must be substantiated and regained every day again. It must have a soul and a face, not just an 'immaculate' body. That's all more work than just being 'a virgin', but it's also less irrevocable – and perhaps a wee bit more substantial.

All in all today's prestige and Ueber-Brands are thus much more related to 'stars' than to virgins – the ones above as well as those on stage. They are about exuding charisma more than projecting untouchability. They shine inside out and create an emotional force field, which they use, manage and grow. They have an inner power, a star power, which expresses itself and lets them radiate. They know how to balance – even on high heels – and how to use this balance to stay on top. They can pull us in as they push us away. They are as magnetic as they are expansive. They attract their followers while they're already all over the place. They guide us and unite us. And they connect with us, but still always stay a little mythical and out of reach.

A different trajectory

What do Armani, Ben & Jerry's, Chanel, Cirque du Soleil, Nespresso and Red Bull have in common? Yes, they all are what we call Ueber-Brands and share most of the principles laid out in this book. But there is more: they all have a similar past, a specific growth trajectory, which made them become the multi-billion-dollar businesses they are. **Most Ueber-Brands, if not all, grow differently to the way mass brands do. They start slowly, very slowly sometimes, taking their time to establish themselves until they break out and through.** To go back to our star metaphor, one could say that they first go and test run their act in proverbial Pennsylvania until they get it right and finally decide to open on the big stage on Broadway. Of course, a lot of times this type of growth isn't necessarily a conscious decision on behalf of the founder but driven by lots of other factors like limited funding, market readiness, capacity etc. But before we get into this in detail let's quickly look into some other forms of economic growth to make the difference a bit clearer.

There are probably as many different growth curves as there are ways you can draw a line. For us, there are only three of particular relevance. The first, and some might think the most normal one isn't actually a curve at all – it's a line, a straight line. You grow regularly in the same way, the same amount from day one until infinity. Step by step up the hill, a perfect diagonal smack between your x and your y axis. As you can probably guess, this geometric beauty may be ideal, but it has not got much to do with reality, certainly not with economic reality. It's the base line but there aren't many cases that ever stick to it.

The second line is called either 'square root' or logarithmic growth. That's the one most marketers long for, at least in the beginning. You are off to a fast start and spike up with extreme growth, but eventually you level out, your growth rate declines until you are potentially looking down the hill. It's preferred as the quickest way to scale, maximizing use of production, logistics, marketing, amortizing all start-up investments and helping you to break even and enjoy the fruits of your labour, as you rocket into higher margin land. This calms investors of course and anybody who is 'vested' in the venture. Naturally, the question is always how long this growth will be sustainable, when you will plateau, if you will plateau at all or if you'll go straight from growth into an equally rapid decline. But in the beginning all looks good and all the signs are up, way up. And since our perspectives are getting shorter and shorter and the pressures higher and higher this is very often all that matters.

The third curve is the one that we want to focus on, because it's the one most Ueber-Brands show – and actually also prefer. It's an inversion of the traditional mass-marketing model and of its square-root curve and is called exponential growth. Any mathematician could go on for hours about the details and differences, but for us the main point is that its absolute growth starts out very slowly, extremely slowly, to the point of being impercepti-ble, but then, seemingly suddenly, begins to explode – doubling, tripling in shorter and shorter intervals.

Financial model comparison

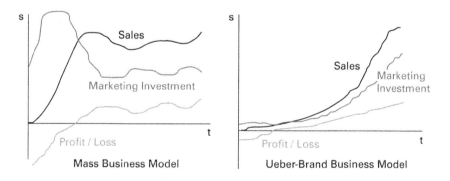

Why is this growth pattern so typical, and arguably even preferable for Ueber-Brands? For one it is often a function of the circumstances we have already alluded to. Given that Ueber-Brands for the most part are started not by big conglomerates with deep pockets but by visionary entrepreneurs with limited funds, they simply don't have the means to invest big time and go in with a bang. They are forced to take it one step at a time, try themselves out, make some profits and then re-invest to grow further, and so on. Also, apart from capital means, they often work with otherwise finite resources – small production capabilities, limited supply of materials or ingredients that are rare or need to be developed, few skilled or trained labourers, and of course the capacities of the founder-entrepreneur him or herself.

Attract instead of attack

But all these limitations also have one big advantage that makes up for all the hardship and headache, which they certainly entail: they allow for a more 'organic' growth. They give these brands time to grow roots before they branch out. And that is why most Ueber-Brands that we spoke to actually preferred this growth pattern – irrespective of the fact that most of them didn't have much choice in the matter. It allows these brands to evolve gradually, walk before they run, learn and improve themselves and their products step by step. It gives them soul, heritage, substance and a feel of authenticity, not to mention the struggle that is so important for any good story or myth, as we explained in Principle 4. Yes, the eventual explosion of their brand often caused a lot of problems and forced many to 'sell out' to bigger corporations or find other ways to keep up with the 'gold rush', often compromising their original mission and the culture of their brand as we've seen for instance in the case of Ben & Jerry's (Principle 6). But that can be dealt with, not least because of the solid core and foundation they've built.

There is yet one other, perhaps even more important aspect. **The slow initial growth doesn't only give the company time to find itself and its story, it also enables its potential customers to find the brand bit by bit.** It allows the brand to attract their fans rather than them feeling attacked by it, as so often is the case with mass-marketing bonanzas. Because of their exponential growth trajectory, Ueber-Brands can develop gradually from first-hour veterans through early adopters to trendsetters to a broader and broader part of their potential target, allowing them to foster a cult and slowly grow into a movement. They create a core and a strong base that gives them validity as well as helping them grow out and convince others. They are cooking things at minimum temperature until they mesh rather than creating a bonfire that risks burning everything down in the long run. They don't just grow slowly and softly, in other words, but also quietly. They move and unfold under the radar of the public at large, which endows them with an extra sense of intrigue and myth. It gives them prestige value and makes them a 'secret', despite their success. Which is exactly what Ueber-Brands want.

That's why even those brands that didn't need to, like MINI, re-launched by the BMW group, or San Pellegrino, owned by Nestlé, decided to take it slow and grow with their brakes on, so to speak. Try things out, let their fan base develop gradually until they felt things were stable enough to let loose a bit. Let their early aficionados and Ueber-Targets (see Principle 2) do the talking while they keep themselves a bit veiled and 'un-sell' (see Principle 3).

This also helped them to appear smaller even once the growth had kicked in, despite the fact that they – just like Kiehl's, bought by L'Oréal, or Ben & Jerry's, acquired by Unilever – also employ a lot of other tactics to manage their growth and keep their sense of specialness while becoming bigger and bigger, as we've seen throughout the book and will look at in the rest of this principle. All this to keep the desire high as they reach out, their fans 'longing to belong', their myth and their mission in control and themselves and their growth balanced with depth, anchoring them as they take off.

Grow with gravitas – the ideal, but not always real

To follow the exponential growth curve with its long initial period of little growth is the ideal for most Ueber-Brands as outlined above. Some even take it slower yet, trying to decelerate take-off as much as possible because it offers them the best way to follow Principles 2 and 3, to 'Un-sell' and keep their budding followers 'Longing to belong', which in turn of course drives their myth and helps them sharpen their mission. One of the most recent cases is the new kid on the sneaker block Buscemi. The US $800-a-pair brand (the industry average is US $65!) was founded by ex-stockbroker Jon Buscemi in 2013 as the sneaker-world equivalent to the Hermès Birkin bag (see Principle 2). The aspiring Ueber-Brand limited its supply from the get-go and thus stoked demand. Their initial run was 600 pairs, sold through prestigious, fashion-forward outlets like Barneys NY or Colette Paris. They were gone in no time, thanks to a quiet, word-of-mouth campaign. Then Justin Bieber and Sean 'Diddy' Combs got in on the game, posting and tweeting about their latest infatuation, starting a whole brouhaha. Consequently, the brand has been sold out more than it's been on shelf. Yet, Buscemi wants to keep it this way, producing 'only' 8,000 pairs this season and adhering to his core strategy of 'not just selling to anyone that wants them' (Karp, *Wall Street Journal*, 28 July 2014).

Obviously this approach is easier when you're a small brand without many responsibilities towards employees or production lines to keep running. And if it's your own money that you're spending – or not making. Private money buys you patience as well as liberty, which is one of the reasons so many Ueber-Brands have resisted the urge to sell, by the way. But ultimately and in the long run this strategy is really only viable for two groups: 'The high priced' and 'the high minded'.

The high priced

The poster boy of this category is certainly Hermès, the Parisian luxury house founded in 1837 and still family owned and run. So much so that we actually dedicate a case study to them at the end of this chapter, showing how they 'grow with gravitas' but also 'back', 'sideways' and 'with passion'.

Another example is Brunello Cucinelli. Before Cucinelli went public in 2012 he wanted to speak to investors personally, in Solomeo, and reportedly said, 'Are you looking for a company that grows very rapidly? Because that is not us. Do not join us... We want to a make profit, that's for sure, but a healthy, fair profit' (Amed, 2014). Despite – or because of – this, his stock was over-subscribed in a matter of days and the whole IPO became one of the most successful in recent history, making Cucinelli a billionaire. What this shows, however, apart from the propensity of super-high-end brands to show this kind of 'gravitas' and the need for financial independence to defend yourself and stick to your mission, is also that times seem to be evolving and there are more investors understanding that 'quick' money isn't always the best, certainly in the long run. But it definitely still takes visionaries and patrons with chutzpah and conviction like Cucinelli to pull this off.

The high minded

These brands are not necessarily as high priced, but certainly as determined to slow their growth. They also usually have a superior motive beyond the ulterior one of making their success sustainable – namely the sustainability of our world. We're talking about Ueber-Brands with a strong ethical grounding of course, which often enough have a very critical attitude towards capitalism, consumerism and the effects of rampant commercialization on our environment and ourselves.

The first one to mention here is definitely Yvon Chouinard, who to this day owns Patagonia and has done pretty much everything he can to curtail and channel his company's growth, all of which you can read up on in our case study in Principle 1. He has empowered his competition, literally 'un-sold' by reminding consumers not to replace clothes that are still perfectly fine and has eventually turned his company into a 'benefit corporation' requiring 'consideration of non-financial interests when making decisions', among others (patagonia.com, accessed August 2014). He has explicitly and almost aggressively followed a path of qualitative over quantitative growth – if growth at all – from the beginning being more concerned with upgrading and up-trading his products, mostly from an eco-footprint perspective, rather than furthering penetration or intensity of consumption.

Cirque du Soleil's motivation to grow with gravitas and not sell out, on the other hand, has been less environmental, but more about the company culture and the well-being of its employees, as owner Guy Laliberté stated repeatedly when rejecting offers: 'I was not going to make 4,800 employees hamsters in a wheel working to pay off debt' (Miller, 2009).

Whatever the motivation though, staying high priced or being high minded, thinking first of the sustainability of your prestige or that of our environment, taking care of your employees or your integrity, 'growing with gravitas' is and will always stay the most ideal path for prestige brands – including the modern ones. It allows them to follow all the principles laid out in this book, with minimum compromise. But it costs – as any principle that truly is one should.

Grow back – the way of the rose as royal privilege

'When one of our products sells too much we discontinue it', said Patrick Thomas, the first non-family CEO of Hermès (Simonet/Virgile, Admap 2013). This perfectly captures the attitude of 'growing back'. It's a very simple and convincing idea, yet again mostly realistic for brands at the luxury end of the spectrum, and/or those not having to answer to stockholder demands for continuous growth. This is why we've also called it the 'royal privilege'.

The idea behind it is as old and perfect as nature: it's like growing roses. Every gardener knows that in order to make your roses bloom their best you need to cut them back regularly; prune them in other words. This pruning principle holds the same for Ueber-Brands, perhaps because they are the equivalent of the 'Queen of Flowers' in branding.

One of the most recent and prominent examples of this idea of growing back to grow forward in action is probably Dior's and Louis Vuitton's 'upmarket drive', where Bernard Arnault, CEO of holding company LVMH, vowed that 'rather than opening new stores, we are concentrating on ameliorating and enlarging existing ones' (Szmydke, 2011). The whole programme is intended to shrink the brands back to the top and counter-balance their excessive expansion of recent years, especially in Asia, but also in the West, where a growing number of upper-middle-class consumers have flocked to the luxury houses, if only for a little sense of stability and the scent of indulgence in times of recession. LVMH is publicly traded, but Arnault holds the majority stake, which is probably the only way he could push such an ambitious programme through.

The other, somewhat older but still famous case is Burberry. When Angela Ahrendts took over the company as CEO in 2006, one of her first actions was to cut back on licences that had proliferated to more than 23, selling anything from dog leashes to baby bibs (Finke, 2013). Ultimately, but not before 2012, she even took the quite large and profitable fragrance and beauty licence back in house, at no small cost. All with a dual goal: cut back on businesses that hurt the brand more than they benefited it, and take back control. Both goals were designed to grow the British heritage house back into the Ueber-Brand it is today.

Interestingly, Ahrendts additionally 'grew back' in some other way, beyond cutting business and over-extensions. She re-focused not only through reducing dilutive portfolio items, but also by putting the brand's hero 'back' where it belonged, at the core. Through this, reinstating the trench coat at the heart and glorifying it with the innovative and interactive 'Art of the

Trench' campaign, she not only gave the whole enterprise a renewed sense of purpose and confidence, she also re-energized its myth.

And that's ultimately the idea of any Ueber-Brand 'growing back'. At first degree it's about weeding out products that literally pull a brand down and weaken its image. As an additional benefit it can create a context to drop items that hurt the bottom line or create too much complexity and confusion. **But the ultimate objective is and must be to re-centre and re-invigorate the brand and its myth, internally and externally.** Elevate its reputation, yes, but even more so spike its vision, its mission and its ambition. Prove it still has the strength of a true leader not afraid to chart its own destiny and project its Ueber-Power to convince all of us of its rightful position at the top.

Grow sideways – the most popular alternative to drive profit

This is the opposite principle to the one we just talked about in a lot of ways. Where Burberry bought back licences and re-focused its brand to 'grow back', we will now talk about what happens before that: growing with licences or generally expanding into other categories. Ideally only adjacent ones, though, because we certainly don't want to promote the over-inflation and over-extension, that 'ruined' many brands in the '70s and '80s.

We've all seen this happening across many luxury brands, particularly in fashion or accessories. A prestige brand starts out with one core competence and before you know it you'll get a fragrance, an eye shadow, sunglasses or watches, purses and umbrellas, sportswear or lingerie, furnishings... pretty much everything including the proverbial dog blanket, all plastered with the same logo. Armani and its move into Armani Casa, Armani Hotels, Armani Dolce, Armani Fiori... is probably one of the most extreme cases in recent memory.

The logic behind it is quite, well, logical and seductive. On the one hand it happens almost naturally if a brand is successful. Customers will ask for more and more from their favourite because they like its design, its craftsmanship, its attitude or simply its allure. If Bottega Veneta makes great leather satchels, why not also a leather coat or jacket, or at least belts and shoes? And once you're there it's a quick step into a fully-fledged fashion house, including the almost obligatory accoutrements like fragrances.

On the other hand most Ueber-Brands have an inclination to express themselves holistically anyway, because they have a mission and a vision, and they like these to become reality, no matter if that vision is ethical-environmental or aesthetic or both. Of course the latter cases like fashion houses, for instance, are particularly prone to this. Every designer must envision his or her design target, the woman (or man) and her style in totality anyway, with every collection. So why not 'live up' to it and make sure your vision truly comes alive – as a lifestyle. Even staunch 'singularist' and 'principlist' Cucinelli got 'sucked' into it, having expanded his business beyond cashmere to include women's and men's fashion with knitwear almost down to a third of his business compared to the 90 per cent it originally held (Amed, 2014).

Of course, beyond customers asking for more and designers envisioning more there's also always the simple economic reason of needing more – profit, scale, reach. And if I don't want to grow 'down' and devalue my brand, why not grow laterally? It's certainly better than becoming over-present in one category and stretching myself vertically, potentially all the way down to the bottom. Moving sideways is thus very often simply the more 'natural', 'logical' and 'equity-friendly' alternative for successful Ueber-Brands to grow without 'reaching down'. Or, as Dennis Paphitis, founder of Aēsop said, 'I felt and still do that it should be possible to grow in a lateral way without prostituting the essence of what the company is about' (Dezeen, 2012).

Not that there's anything wrong with this per se. **It's indeed better and more appropriate for Ueber-Brands to grow in scope rather than scale. It unfolds their mission, their myth and their magic more than it creates the danger of milking and undermining them and over-saturating certain categories or markets.** Yet it's also a slippery slope, as we've seen with all those 'victims' of the past, including the ones that recovered to find big success in recent years like Gucci or Burberry.

One example, outside of fashion, which has done a great job in growing sideways not only without endangering but actually strengthening its core, is Cirque du Soleil. Over the years Guy Laliberté has taken the brand from street fair to circus artistry to artistic and circensic events to fascinating TV shows to acrobatic workout programmes and gear and even into imaginative fashion lines in partnership with Desigual. All still very much on equity, all celebrating the brand's myth and its mission rather than just merchandizing or outselling it.

One brand in danger of over-growing left and right but unfortunately not centre, is from our point of view Ladurée, the famous Parisian patisserie and celadon-coloured tearoom, home of the macaron. Ever since Groupe Holder bought them in 1993, the brand has been on quite an aggressive expansion course, lately pushing the brand not just in scale and presence but also in scope. The first idea of sweet-scented candles still bore some connection to a brand famous for candy-coloured meringue cookies. But now fragrances, make-up, body and bath toiletries...

As we have said, the idea of growing sideways makes a lot of sense for Ueber-Brands looking to extend themselves without compromising their myth, their mystique or their position. But it requires great consideration, because what starts as a way to mediate interests of growth and strength, expansion and equity protection, can easily lead to a case of proliferation vertigo. And that's the opposite of balance.

A propos: Ladurée's initial geographic expansion is a strongly recommended and often first-considered alternative to the path of growing sideways. Before growing in categories Ueber-Brands often prefer to grow in countries. In the interest of avoiding over-saturation, they prefer to have one door in 100 markets rather than having 100 doors in one. Yet again, the very opposite of mass-brand behaviour.

Grow up – the golden route to balance expansion

Tiering is probably the most common and classic practice by which prestige brands try to expand and maximize reach while at the same time protecting their appeal and allure. Fashion houses have done it since Yves Saint Laurent (and Valentino) introduced the concept of prêt-a-porter in the late '60s with his Rive Gauche line, as have credit card companies, hotels and many others.

The first time this strategy is usually applied is on the 'way down', when an Ueber-Brand tries to expand but protect its status at the same time. That's when fashion houses start so-called bridge lines for instance, lower priced and usually also a bit younger and more casual in spirit than the main one. Marc by Marc Jacobs is an example or Polo by Ralph Lauren. Examples in other categories include Grand Hyatt/Park Hyatt/Hyatt Regency or American Express Blue. The point is generally to leverage the established equity and grow, allow the new line to cater to a lower-tier target while enabling the established master brand to retain its higher-end position, perhaps even bolstering it by virtue of refocusing it on its core and contrasting it with a more affordable offspring.

All well, all common, all no problem. But, even more than the previous idea of lateral expansion this vertical expansion holds an inherent danger. **Before you know it your brand may be giving into gravity – and start losing its gravitas.** The 'bottom feeders' often develop such a strong dynamic and presence that they easily and quickly start overpowering and undermining the main brand, apart from the fact that this approach invariably runs the risk of over-penetration and saturation. A recent example is Kate Spate Saturday, which the mother brand reintegrated soon after launch, apparently for this very reason. In the end, often the reality is that you're mostly exploiting the brand despite your attempt to protect it by creating a sub-line or brand. And that's what your customers see as well. You're trying to cash in, not build up. You are not really feeding your brand's myth – you're milking it.

That's why it's key and more and more common practice for modern prestige brands to look at tiering not just as a one-way street leading downmarket, but also as a path to glide up and rebalance potential over-democratization by launching a higher tier. **Grow on top and sharpen your tip as you grow down and out, tighten the reins as you loosen them, build distance and aspiration as you increase proximity and approachability.**

Armani, despite over-growing a bit laterally in our opinion, has mastered this up/down balance quite well, by giving his vast empire – ranging from the eponymous Giorgio Armani to the youthful AX Exchange – a graceful lift with the launch of the Haute Couture Armani Privé. American Express went, over the years, from green to gold to platinum to black as the brand and credit cards in general became more common and widely distributed, also through the previously mentioned blue down-tier. They indeed upped the levels and services as they – and their competitors – eroded the existing ones. The most recent venture, the Centurion Card, is also a good case of 'Un-selling' and letting your customers 'Long to Belong', given that it builds itself up as so exclusive that you can't even apply. You will be asked to join. Another, most recent example is Starbucks' Reserve stores and product line, trying to counter the gourmet coffee craze they themselves helped to foster.

Note that many of these up-tierings might not be financially attractive in isolation, but they are once we consider how they rebuild the brand's core promise ('membership has its privileges' in the case of Amex). They strengthen the 'base' and protect or even lift the margins of the main business, similarly to other 'upgrading' measures Ueber-Brands take, such as stunning 'flagship stores' or high-end technologies (Yulex plant-based wetsuits by Patagonia). **All these are not primarily introduced to 'make money' but to 'make myth' and protect the pricing power of the entire brand.**

Johnnie Walker, the almost-200-year-old whisky brand, is a slightly different case in that it shows how it's possible to build prestige and re-energize an Ueber-Brand from the bottom up, all by tiering higher and higher. There are (as of now) the standard Red label and the increasingly aged Black (complex), Double Black (smoky), Gold (indulgent), Platinum Reserve (sophisticated) and Swing (balanced) labels. Then there is the Blue label (rare) at the top. And if that wasn't enough, there are the Blue label George V editions (only from distilleries that were already operating during the reign of the king) that range from special and expensive (hundreds of dollars) to the 'actually not for sale but estimated at tens of thousands of dollars' John Walker 1805 commemorative blend (Olmsted, 2013). Not bad for a whisky that not long ago was scraping the bottom of the barrel.

This successful example has apparently inspired others, who are now trying to tier up as well, albeit not with a sub-line or even sub-brand but with special, higher-end products. Absolut Vodka, obviously pressured by high-end competition like Belvedere or Grey Goose as well as the trend to upscale 'brown' liquors like Johnnie Walker, recently launched an amber vodka 'that is rested in oak barrels' and one that is blended with Sauvignon Blanc (Voight, 2013). Similarly in fragrance: J'Adore, the scent from French fashion house Dior, does it in spectacular ways with over-the-top limited editions. Cooperating with Baccarat they bottled the widely available fragrance in hand-blown crystal decorated with the iconic Massai necklace in 18 carat gold. Only eight bottles were made and sold for up to US $42,000.

Or think of Apple adding a US $17,000 'Edition' model in 18 carat gold to its watch line (starting at US $349).

The list of examples could go on forever – the sky is the limit, so to speak. And that's the whole point: Ueber-Brands have a legitimate need to grow, down as well as sideways. However, they also have to take care to balance this by growing up, so that their myth stays nicely at the centre and doesn't get worn down or out. And the brand itself retains the position it wants at the upper end of its category.

Grow with passion – the need to stick to your Ueber-Target

Principle 2, 'Longing to Belong', is key for any Ueber-Brand, balancing in and out through targeting and distribution. Tip too much towards 'all access, everybody in' and you're eroding your cool and your mystique. Go the other way, and you're running the risk of becoming too elite, something which works for luxury, but not so much for modern prestige. The last, and perhaps most crucial point in keeping this balance, is thus sticking with your Ueber-Target, because if you lose them, the rest of us will follow pretty swiftly.

'Innocent Big Knit Charity' is an annual charity promotion to re-inspire both the brand and its Ueber-Target alike

Courtesy of Innocent

In the case of MAC, the colour cosmetics brand from Estée Lauder, this means keeping make-up artists their biggest fans, because that's what their equity rests on. (After all, MAC stands for 'Makeup Art Cosmetics', as the initiated will have found out.) Not an easy business for a 30-year-old brand in a category built on constant change, with a target as fickle as 'artists' can be. And yet they manage extremely well. First of all they do foster a special pro-customer community, giving professional make-up artists unique discounts and offers as well as promoting them on their website, at events and in store as teachers, trainers and semi-celebrities. Beyond that they ingrain themselves in the industry, advocating and inspiring make-up artists like no other. They were the first major brand to take on the fight against AIDS, a key concern in their community, which heavily over-indexes towards LGBT. All proceeds from their Viva Glam lipsticks go into supporting AIDS research and treatment projects (MAC, accessed August 2014). They truly live their purpose of 'creating cosmetics for all ages, races and sexes' by constantly pushing boundaries through congenial collaborations with the likes of Lady Gaga, Iris Apfel or *Vogue*. And, not the least, they stay at the edge of fashion, innovating with daring colours that would make others blush.

Another stellar example is MINI. Reconnecting to their infamous past of Formula 1 builder John Cooper, they have started to partake in world-class races like the Dakar Marathon Rally again. Perhaps this is not as unique and daring as MAC, given that the idea of fuelling a car brand's equity and innovating ahead through professional racing is as old as the car industry itself. However it's certainly successful in firing the passion of 'MINI Motorists', as proven by all the locally organized amateur rallies around the world, over 100 in the United States alone since 2008 (North American Motoring, accessed May 2014).

In other categories, staying connected to your Ueber-Target isn't so much about sticking with a specific part of your consumer target but literally staying in a certain distribution channel, because that's where your competence and your cachet is created. A lot of 'prestige' hair care brands like Redken for instance take great care to still be seen in salons (and tout this in their communication) despite the fact that the bulk of their business has long been in retail. The same goes for a lot of beverage brands. Absolut Vodka recently 'crafted a collection of vodka flavours hand blended with herbs that will only be sold to bartenders' (Voight, 2013), obviously not only in an attempt to drive their on-premises business, but also to regain their original 'advocates' and re-energize them as their Ueber-Target. Others like San Pellegrino make it a key part of their business model to always launch in white space through restaurants first, before extending into retail. They make sure they very much stay linked with and respected by the industry, for instance by being top sponsors of the prestigious 'World's 50 Best Restaurants' awards.

All these cases show how seriously Ueber-Brands are concerned with fuelling their cult and their Ueber-Targets, especially when the larger base is reaching more or less mass-movement proportions. They must stick with the elite, not necessarily the social elite, but their specific elite, those that set the standards in their category and in relation to their mission. They need to stay anchored in the top to make sure they're not losing their ground while growing out. They must balance upward and forward against the natural tendency of life and business to pull us downward. **Only if you stay firmly above and ahead can you lead. And only then will the rest of us continue to follow.**

Growing without showing – the advantage of the web

Finally, modern prestige brands have discovered that the ubiquity of the web isn't the enemy they thought it was, but can actually be their best friend – because it allows them to be all over the place, yet technically still only in one spot. The web gives Ueber-Brands maximum reach without anybody seeing it. It lets them be omnipresent without ever seeming over-extended. Truly 'growing without showing', and even at a lower cost.

A highly selective brand like Bumble and Bumble, with its price premium, used to have only the option of distributing through salons and specialized, higher-end beauty stores if they wanted to preserve a level of brand credential. Not anymore. Now a small-town customer can bring a piece of the action and product to her home, without the brand needing to extend physically in ways that were un-economical and would dilute the sense of exclusivity. On top of this, B&B is able to provide her with tips, stories and experiences (albeit virtual) as if she was at their flagship salon in Manhattan, something that even higher-end salon partners could hardly replicate. The hair Ueber-Brand gained more reach and more control at the same time. They've expanded their world and sharpened it simultaneously, at a fraction of the cost of expanding physically – never mind the saved margins and reduced diversion (www.bumbleandbumble.com).

As we've seen in the case of Nespresso Club (p. 165) this stealth way of growing can generate many billions of dollars in sales and category-leading consumption while the perception remains that of a sophisticated prestige brand. Consequently everybody is jumping on the web-wagon. Many go a step further, combining their interest in making money with their need for mythmaking, because our web-wide world has become a global showroom as much as it is a stage – thanks in no small part to shoppable videos:

- Gucci introduces new fashion and accessory collections in the kind of opulent environments you imagine their Ueber-Target to live in – yet only a click away from making it yours (Gucci, accessed January 2015).

- Burberry's creative director Christopher Bailey talks to consumers on Youku (the Chinese YouTube) about the inspiration for his first perfume – and makes an almost 'personal sale' (Burberry Prorsum, accessed January 2015).

- Diane von Fuerstenberg (DVF) celebrates the 40th anniversary of her iconic wrap dress by sending it on a global relay to celebrity friends, who document their experiences and invite us to share the joy of owning a DVF dress – for a bit of money (DVF's Journey of a Dress, 2014).

- 'Oscar PR girl's' hip blog explores the rich history of the venerable brand and its late founder Oscar de la Renta, reporting on his and the brand's exquisite travel, events and social encounters – again allowing us to witness and 'buy into' this rarefied world right then and there (Oscarprgirl, accessed January 2015).

It's actually amazing that it took the prestige world so long to figure this out, because it doesn't get much better for Ueber-Brands. They can grow their cake while eating it, so to speak. They never have to worry about dilution as they rake in the profits – unless you of course think about the brand's presence in the hands or on the bodies of all those internet shoppers. But then you can always use modern technology to rebuild the myth on the go and on every street as Ben & Jerry's does with an augmented reality mobile app that shows pictures of its home state Vermont on every pint, even when you're holding it in a supermercado in Cartagena or Krakow (Orsini, 2010).

Principle 7: The rules to 'growth without end'

1 Balance – like a star
   Create an emotional force field. Push as you pull in. Connect, but always remain a bit out of reach.

2 Earn your prestige
   Modern prestige is more meritocratic than aristocratic; it's also inclusive rather than merely exclusive.

3 Attract, don't attack
   It's the ideal way for Ueber-Brands, and it gives your followers time to discover and thus cherish you.

4 Grow with gravitas
   If you have or are the luxury and can afford to put respect and recognition before reach.

5 Grow back
   Pruning is the most natural and the healthiest way to ensure future flowers. But it also takes courage – and independent capital.

6 Grow sideways
   It's always better to expand into adjacencies than go all the way down. Geographic or categoric expansion is definitely preferable to over-penetration and over-saturation.

7 Grow up
   Tiering shall never be a one-way street. It's easy and tempting to just slide down, but the prudent brand builds up as it reaches out.

8 Grow with passion
   Never leave your Ueber-Target behind. Never ever. It's at the core of your myth and helps you realize your mission. Without it you'll soon be without anything – and anyone.

Ueber-Brands can grow and become big, bigger than traditional prestige brands used to be able to, without forfeiting their allure. But they must grow rather exponentially, starting slowly and always ensure they balance reach with equity.

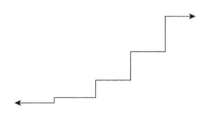

Ueber-Brand case study 7   Hermès and his offspring

Thierry Hermès opened a store to sell harnesses for horse carriages in 1837. He quickly became a preferred supplier to nobility around Europe. The next generation added saddles and carrying bags and by the third, the business covered 'leather, sport, and a tradition of refined elegance' (Martin, 1995). In a move typical of Hermès, the family became interested in the craft and creative possibilities of silk screening just as the industry started to disappear. Then the company expanded into bespoke accessories – boots, luxury tableware and other artisanal goods – by growing its ateliers and acquiring venerable manufacturers, ultimately ending up 'making anything one could possibly need to feel prince of a world where beauty and functionality, practicality and pure indulgence are in perfect harmony' (wikiluxurybrands.com, accessed 2014). In 2010 the company introduced its first ever 'sub-brand', petit h (little 'h'), which makes playful objects by 'up-cycling' left-overs from Hermès production. And, in a second such move, it started to invest in reviving centuries-old Chinese craftsmanship by making timeless objects for modern households under the Shang Xia brand name.

Annual sales when Jean-Louis Dumas became head of the firm in 1978 were reported at US $50 million. By 1990 revenue had increased to US $460 million and in 2013, when his son took over, the group's consolidated revenue totalled about US $5.2 billion generated by 30 manufacturing facilities (mainly in France) supplying 315 own stores worldwide. That is an enviable compound growth rate of almost 15 per cent over the past 34 years and one that accelerates as Asia, which now represents over 30 per cent of global sales, grows at an even faster clip.

Growing back-, up- or sideways – always with gravitas, passion and thus without end

Nobody seems in a hurry at this 175-odd-year-old institution. On the contrary, no effort is spared to make its enviable growth compatible with the exclusivity and desirability that allows Hermès to command (very, very) premium prices. This Ueber-Brand master constantly builds its star power, giving it soul and keeping it fresh. It takes time for itself and its offshoots to become deeply rooted in their mission and create a myth (growing with gravitas). It prunes back production or distribution that starts to feel too commonplace (growing back). And it adds new product categories and countries instead (growing sideways) as well as ever more superb ideas, products and services (growing up) while always ensuring that their Design Target is surprised and delighted by every step on the way (growing with passion).

Shang Xia, Hermès' latest venture, is a core example of the company's measured approach to growth. The brainchild of Patrick Thomas, then-CEO of Hermès and Creative Director Jiang Qiog'er, Shang Xia means 'Up-Down' in Mandarin, describing the concept of applying ancient craft to objects that serve modern customers in the East and West. Of course it is also a perfectly poetic way to express the concept of 'growing with gravitas', letting the brand grow roots first before branching out and up.

Years were spent on scouting artisan masters and creating a collection until finally opening a first boutique in Shanghai – without much fanfare. Even then the store was more a temporary pop-up, albeit an exquisitely designed one, hidden in a corner of a luxury mall. You could hardly be more under the radar, which is exactly what the brand wants. Customers will discover it and appreciate it in the larger context of rebuilding a culture that was lost in the revolution and industrialization, as Shang Xia Retail Director Clara Lin explains it. This is also why they've spent the past few years rebuilding a traditional Shanghai mansion, which will ultimately not only allow Shang Xia to present itself, but will become an educational centre, teaching customers about ancient rituals and customs, something they currently must outhouse in a hotel suite.

It's truly as Jiang told the *Financial Times*: 'Shang Xia is […] a cultural investment project … [at other brands] the life of the project is five years or 10 years, at Shang Xia the dream is 100 years, 200 years' (Waldmeir, 2012). Then again at prices around US \$6,300 for a cashmere jacket or US \$54,000 for a small side chair, looking at longer time spans comes almost naturally.

Hermès has invested about US \$13 million a year on Shang Xia since 2008 and opened two more boutiques in Beijing and Paris. It plans to break even in around 2016 but has no plans for further expansion (Wendlandt and Denis, 2013).

Like this latest offspring, the 'maison-mère' does not seem in a hurry to canvas China with stores either. Hermès has opened some 25 stores in China since 1997, nothing compared to brands like Louis Vuitton or Gucci. Similar to Shang Xia, it took the mother brand years to find the right location for a 'Maison Hermès', but when it did (in 2010, only its fifth in the world) it was in exactly the kind of historic mansion in Shanghai's former French Concession that befits the brand's heritage. A good indicator of how beyond reproach Hermès' reputation for rarity and restraint is, is the fact that the Chinese government has cracked down on almost all foreign luxury brands in its anti-ostentation campaign, but has spared Hermès.

At Hermès, time is never of the essence; craft and perfection are – to the point that royal weddings were supposedly postponed rather than Hermès artisans being rushed. An attitude which Hermès 'crowned' with a watch called 'Temps Suspendu' that lets you suspend time on the press of a button to take in the beauty of a moment, until you reactivate it.

However, even the slowest of growth ultimately reaches a point where it is advisable to 'Grow Back' to strengthen the brand, something which Hermès is also aware of like no other and has done repeatedly over the years. As the company 'grew sideways' through the '80s and '90s into new categories, its collection exceeded 30,000 pieces at one point. But Hermès balanced this by deepening control over its products and vertical supply chain, buying back some 50 licences, bringing production in-house, limiting volumes, reducing third party distribution and replacing it with own stores.

Despite its name, the 'little Hermès', petit h, is a great example of Hermès 'Growing Up' – all the way through to its motto, 'Quand je serais grand, je veux rester petit' (When I have grown up, I want to remain small).

Petit h is the dream come true of Pascale Moussard, great-great-great-granddaughter of the founder. As a girl Moussard would play artisan, hidden under the workshop tables with scrap materials. Later, as she went into the business, she started collecting curious cast-offs. After several years of developing a prototype collection from these materials in hiding, she finally 'came out' and obtained the family's approval to introduce her experimental brand. What petit h objects share with each other and their mother brand are the exacting craft, noble materials and a precious elegance that does not forgo utility. What elevates them to mythical levels is the creativity that goes into 're-enchanting' each of the items, as petit h calls it; their playfulness and the fact that each piece is unique, as Corinne Dauger, Ex-Directrice des Metiers at Hermès, explained. The company website states that 'the essence of Hermès is the joy of the workshop'. Petit h represents that very essence, or a laboratory of unexpected things, as Dauger calls it, and commands the price premiums that prove the point, whether it is well over US $10 for a postcard, over US $10,000 for a toy boat or over US $100,000 for an origami squirrel-shaped leather bookcase.

Of course, 'big' Hermès also practises the classic ways of growing up, such as offering ever more expensive versions of its products – up to the absurd but much talked-about Birkin in albino crocodile with 18-carat-gold hardware encrusted with 242 diamonds, selling for some US $200,000. And Hermès tiers both ways. When it acquired John Lobb, the bootmaker only made shoes to measure for around US $4,000 a pair for customers like Lord Mountbatten or the Duke (Ellington). Hermès gently introduced off-the-shelf lines at about a third of the cost, but at the same time it was careful to maintain the bespoke services and ensured that the Prince of Wales or the Prince of Underwear (Calvin Klein) kept coming.

Mission and myth of reaching beyond – time and space

Hermès believes in the values of craftsmanship, creativity, skill, integrity, patience, precision and that they are ever more valuable and worth preserving in a world that is fast paced, often low quality, automated. Dauger put it this way: 'Hermès is not a fashion house. There are no recipes, nothing is formulated. The power is with the different "metiers", which unite more like a jazz band than an orchestra: Everybody's playing his or her tune and yet it all comes together beautifully'.

The myth of Hermès lies in the humanity it attaches to its creations and its power to suspend time and logic and make us dream. Which other brand would post a three-minute video romancing the 'Etrivière' buckle in its hundreds of uses since its original creation for horse harnesses complete with a subtle neigh over the accompanying hip-hop tunes (scan QR code in Preface to get to the film). Artistic Director Pierre-Alexis Dumas is certain the customer 'feels the presence

Little sister brand 'petit h' shares the DNA of ingenuity, craftsmanship, fine materials (and high prices) with Hermès, but adds a playful side to the venerable 'Maison', reaching the younger-at-heart without diluting the brand

Images courtesy of Navaz Batliwalla at Disneyrollergirl.com and Laura and Sara Lim at SGsisters.com

of the person who crafted the object, while […] the object brings him back to his own sensitivity, because it gives him pleasure through his senses' (Anaya, 2014). The myth of Hermès is that of a creator who 'reaches beyond' by making objects so perfect and precious they entrance you – whether it's an apple-shaped bag with integrated horn-handled knife for your picnic or a solar-powered, floating island with a hardwood covered 'beach' and a 6000-square-feet ultra-modern house. Dumas puts it like this: 'I believe anyone can reach eternity in an instant… I want our customers to indulge in a moment of pure lightness, because it is in those moments of dream where you have insights into life' (Anaya, 2014).

The same holds true for the offspring: petit h creates playful dreams that will make you feel like a child again – albeit a rather privileged one with perfectly crafted toys. And Shang Xia is a quiet agent of healing the wounds of the Cultural Revolution – at least for the rich and the artisans. The brand's 100-page-thick 'brochure' (in the form of a traditionally bound book), which Lin gave us at the end of a wonderful tea and incense ceremony during our last visit, presents the products in the context of design director Jiang recounting her personal family memoires and illustrating them with romantic present-day family scenes that mix the traditional and new. You can explore the art of Pu-erh tea rituals or listen to hymns about rural life of Taiwanese tribes in their native Paiwan language on an enclosed CD.

Un-selling and longing to belong by putting the product above all

While Hermès' manifestations are quiet and void of the typical hustle, they are never boring. The print ads tell visually arresting stories ready for framing, just like its scarves. One might admire an imposing yak carrying Hermès goods up a snow-swept mountain or a beautiful Indian girl in a Hermès sari kissing a brightly tattooed elephant. The Hermès shop windows are legend. Artistic director Leila Menchari, the magician behind the fantastic decorations for over 35 years, regularly creates custom items vied for but never for sale. Hermès' events (the word PR is frowned upon) will centre on imagination and the crafts. VIP soirées will feature horse-racing games, 'dancing bags' performances or fortune tellers reading Hermès scarves. The 'Festival des Métiers' (festival of crafts) tours the globe bringing parts of the workshops to the stores.

Hermès has also embraced digital to tell its stories and to 'surprise', which is an aptly named section on its website: there an unusual product like a bike might be on offer, or an invitation to join a game of chess or a risotto cooking class. 'The World of Hermès' invites browsers to get lost in an amazing firework of films, music and accounts around the products, the artisans and their dreams. There are doodles on how to create your own paper Hermès bag, an interview with leatherworker Michael about how leather 'sings', a romantic fairytale about a boy, a girl and their scarves told by 18-year-old photographer Olivia Bee or an epic film about man, earth and the sky. YouTube shows many of these films getting 100,000 or 200,000 views. The Hermès dream reaches far, far beyond those who can afford to live it.

Maintaining an august clientele is obviously key for all of Hermès' brands and it almost comes naturally with so much love, art and dedication going into each product. Yet, as Dauger assures us, Hermès does not outfit celebrities for free as is custom among most luxury houses, and it makes very subtle but clear differences in the roles famous customers play. While Victoria Beckham, for example, is undoubtedly a valuable customer and influencer – she is said to own over US $2 million worth of Hermès bags – (Abraham, 2009), the ex-Spice Girl's collection is rather an expression of wanting to belong than proof of her belonging to the brand's design target. The brand's Ueber-Target is powerful and often famous, but quiet and refined, shining through restrained elegance. Grace Kelly and Jackie Kennedy Onassis must be the most iconic and admired ones. And Kate Middleton, picking up on her mother-in-law's tradition of wearing Hermès scarves, will also be welcome as well as the multi-talented muse and (ex-) Première Dame Carla Bruni.

A Hermès Birkin. Most women will recognize and admire this iconic bag in a glimpse – no label required

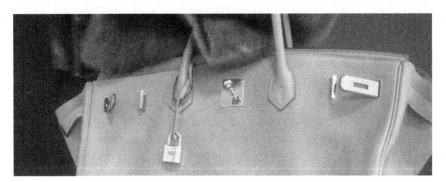

Photo by W Schaefer

In the end, Hermès is always careful to never advertise celebrity customers. You are left guessing, which makes it all the more intriguing and ensures the rich but reserved continue to call on the brand. And that all the rest of us want to.

Beholding the product and living the dream

'We don't have a policy of image, we have a policy of product', is how Jean-Louis Dumas put it in *Vanity Fair* (Jacobs, 2007). Every Hermès product intends to be the holy grail, the dream come true through imagination and craftsmanship beyond compare, the perfect essence. Many of them are without a clearly visible logo, yet Hermès has developed many 'soft assets' that make buying, gifting and using a Hermès item unmistakable:

- **Imagination.** 'Faites nous rêver' (make us dream) is Hermès' call to invite 'artistically atypical orders'. Whether an old Citröen 2CV decked out in fine leather or a little leather chewing gum holder made for a Texan socialite to match her handbag, they are welcome challenges to the craftsmen and can be relied on to be talked about. There is a collection of the most fascinating objects in the former offices of Émile-Maurice Hermès (grandson of Thierry). It's an archive and source of inspiration where you can find anything from parasols to 'paperole' models made of hand-rolled paper to various spyglasses. This treasure trove is also open to the public as the 'Musée Hermès', making it part and parcel of the brand's manifestation.

- **Craftsmanship and provenance.** Shang Xia's eggshell porcelain tea set is so exquisite it is translucent, and the bamboo weaving around it is so thinly sliced and tightly woven it feels like fabric. It is a precious elegance shared by all objects from Hermès, as is the use of materials with intriguing provenance, be it lizard from Malaysia or silk made of 250 mulberry moth cocoons. That silk makes the carré feel extra thick or it may become pillow stuffing. Whether pillow, scarf, bag or saddle, all these items will be hand stitched, as the Hermès shop assistants will make sure to point out. Knowing that an artisan laboured for 18 to 24 hours to make them, makes both bag and customer feel privileged.

- **Choice and iconic detail**. Customers can find some 350 different dog collars at the Faubourg Saint-Honoré flagship store. They are one of the items Emile-Maurice was fascinated with and have become part of a recognizable language of the brand. They have become iconic bracelets that women the world over will recognize like most of us would recognize a Coke bottle. Then there are the famous orange boxes all Hermès items are stored in, with their thin, printed border, brown ribbon and hand-folded silk paper padding. They come in some 200 shapes and sizes and are made to exacting specifications.

It takes an independent organization, unrelenting orchestration and unparalleled patience to create such a world of unique brand manifestations. Hermès forgoes the easy sale. Neither a website designed to get lost in nor an archive occupying prime real estate in your flagship store are likely to optimize sales. There are no promotions to accelerate growth, either. Instead, a lot of money is spent on all those films, glorious show windows and other artistic manifestations, which are unlikely to show an immediate payout. But then, dreams don't come true over night and cannot be measured in money alone. Or, as Pierre-Alexis Dumas puts it, 'a company that makes only money is quite poor, that's for sure' (Anaya, 2014). So Hermès protects itself from short-term financial pressures by keeping the company in family hands both in ownership as well as in management. (There was a brief scare that LVMH might attempt a hostile take-over.) Each new generation is exposed to the company from a young age and select members groomed to take over positions in management or artistic direction. Axel Dumas is the latest CEO after 20 years of 'apprenticeship'. His cousins Pierre-Alexis and Pascale Moussard are among the artistic directors together with a dozen others who share decades-long associations with the brand.

But beyond management, it is the workshops that radiate the brand from the inside out. They are organized in clusters of a maximum 200 artisans under one roof. Wherever possible, a single person will create a Hermès object from beginning to finish – mostly by hand and hand-tool – and apply their personal artisan seal at the end of the process. As a result, only about 15 models of a certain handbag can be made in a month, for example, and supply to the stores is appropriately sparse and random. In their 'Hearts and Crafts' film, artisans talk proudly about being artists, not 'workers', and how giving a silver jewel the final polish is 'like giving birth to something beautiful after a long labour'.

Instead of a summary: 77+ questions

Although it may sometimes appear as if we think we have all the answers, we don't. We don't even know all the questions. Ueber-Brands, like all brands, are as manifold and unpredictable as life. Besides, the context is in flux. How we define and build prestige in the 21st century is shifting, as are the ways we experience it.

So don't expect the next few pages to give you a surefire 'best practice' list to check off *en route* to Ueber-Success. If it was that easy we wouldn't be working anymore. The only thing you can count on is that predictability is not the way. Ueber-Brands need to be 'beyond compare' and that means beyond rules or standards. Otherwise they would soon be seen as just that, standard: and that's the opposite of Ueber.

All that being said, a 'business book' comes with some expectation of an 'executive summary'. So, we took a crack at it after all. But we would like you to look at the following questions more as path planner than a road map. They are meant to stimulate your own thinking on where to go, how to take brands forward and onward, lifting them out of the price wars and on to a higher, more fun and fulfilling level of being and marketing.

In that sense we also refer to many of the examples used throughout the book, to encourage some flipping back and forth, help your memory, but most importantly spark your imagination. Because as we said going into the first principle: it all starts with an idea. Your idea.

Principle 1: Mission incomparable

First it's all about the WHY. Why does your brand exist? And why should anybody care – to pay a premium? Ueber-Brands must project a sense of purpose, towards the world at large or at least their category. Take on responsibilities befitting someone who wants to be a leader. And/or go well beyond existing expectations and standards.

- What was your brand's vision upon founding? What is your mission now?
- Does your brand have goals – beyond making money? (eg TOMS' One-for-One.)
- Have you ever thought what dream(s) your brand might have?
- Is your purpose relevant and desirable to your core target audience? (Ben & Jerry's social activism and its young target.)
- Does the purpose have staying power or does it risk being a fad? Do you take it forward?
- Does it allow your customers to be, do or have something they otherwise couldn't as easily?
- What does your brand believe in? What do your employees believe in? What do you believe in?
- Does the brand project a distinct style and attitude? (Nespresso for suave-connoisseurs, Aēsop for the urban intelligentsia.)
- Are you pursuing your mission with a determination that is felt as authentic inside and out and motivates people to become missionaries? (unlike The Body Shop.)
- Does it cost you?
- Is your brand character different enough or even provocative? (Tom Ford for Gucci and Tom Ford for himself.)

The ultimate question: does buying your product or services allow people to buy into something or are they 'just' consuming?

Principle 2: Longing versus belonging

This is 'The Balancing Act', aka 'The Velvet Rope'. Ueber-Brands need to walk a fine line between accessibility and exclusivity, proximity and distance. To give their customers a feeling of belonging while letting them as well as all of us long for more.

- Do you have a 'Design Target' to guide proposition, design etc? (The Abercrombie & Fitch jock.)
- Is this Design Target distinctive and inspirational to your core buyers, your 'Strategic Target'?
- Can they be 'activated' or are they naturally influential missionaries? (Harley – HOGs.)
- If the Design Target is limited or imaginary, does it inspire disciples to amplify the message? (Fashionistas blogging about Karl and Coco Chanel.)

- Does it take more than money to 'get' your brand – physically and intellectually?
- Is a certain level of brand knowledge or allegiance required? ('Applying for a Birkin' at Hermès.)
- Have you 'spiked' the sense of longing by leveraging an element of randomness?
- Are you creating a feel of complicity between your brand and its strategic target?
- Are you sharing a stratagem that your target can approve of? (Tesla's car future.)
- What and/or who are you against? Or who is against you?
- Are you explicitly or implicitly demarcating your brand territory against outsiders to help your fans feel privileged? ('Luluheads' versus sedentary folk.)
- Do you have a healthy differential between sympathizers and buyers, ie are there more wanting to buy your brand than can or do?
- Are you leveraging limited editions, seasonality, special distribution etc to stoke desire? (Amex Centurion or Berluti 'Initiated by'.)

The ultimate question: would your target 'wear the brand's tattoo' or go to other lengths to know about you, associate with you and not feel left out?

Principle 3: Un-selling

How are your brand interactions? Confident and calibrated? Ueber-Brands don't sell, they seduce. They communicate and connect with their targets without ever seeming too eager or needy. Pulling us as they push the envelope.

- Does your brand exude pride and strength (ads, stores, events, etc.)?
- Have you ever taken a clear stance on anything?
- Do you execute inaccessibility and intransigence? (MINI limited volumes and editions.)
- Do you accept its economic consequences?
- Could a measured dose of arrogance boost respect? (No return policy at Hermès.)
- If you are leveraging celebrities, are they understood as users and admirers rather than paid endorsers? (Mandarin Oriental – 'He's a fan'; Nespresso – 'George Who?')
- Do you risk being discounted (in image and value) for 'trying too hard' to be popular?
- Does your 'functional factsheet' pull people in or really just 'close the sale'? (Patek Philippe.)

- Is your brand considered part of our culture or – even better – a muse or source of art?
- Does the art you support fit with, further and bring to life your brand myth?
- Do you put enough focus on the execution of your interactions? (Chanel spot.)
- Can even non-customers get a feel for or experience your brand? ('The Art of the Trench' by Burberry.)
- Beyond paying for media, can you become the event and be the medium? (*Red Bulletin* or *Porter* magazine by Net-a-Porter.)

Ultimate question: Can you describe a group of potential customers that might have difficulty understanding you?

Principle 4: From myth to meaning

Telling a compelling story that is relevant, relatable, memorable and sharable is key for any brand. But to become an Ueber-Brand you need to elevate your story to a 'myth'. Answer to a higher truth or guide with social value.

- Have you done a deep dive into your brand's history, the founder's vision, the organization's culture and other elements of your brand?
- Ever looked at the semiotics of your brand name, symbols or associated rituals? (Cirque du Soleil.)
- What are the key elements of your story? The hero, the hurdle, the seven steps?
- Is your story true to your roots and your vision? (Freitag or Yuan Soap.)
- Do you have an evocative name? (Aēsop for 'brainy beauty'.)
- Do you allow the target to become part of the story and have a sense of intimacy and ownership? (Patagonia, the 'piton revelation' and their adventurer-activist battle.)
- Are you bringing your stories to life through your actions? Consistently? (Moleskine collective creativity projects; Red Bull stunts and competitions.)
- Have you elevated your story beyond the factual to mythical proportions? (The Renaissance philosophy and world of Brunello Cucinelli.)
- Is your brand myth helping to 'reach beyond' our physical or intellectual limitations? (Red Bull's super-human powers, Crème de la Mer as source of life.)

- And/or is your myth a guiding one, offering social currency? (Harley's outlaw or Ralph Lauren's preppy.)

- Do you evolve your brand myth to stay relevant yet respect its core to become iconic? (Chanel's emancipated elegance.)

The ultimate question: Could your consumers (and non-consumers) tell your myth in three sentences? Could you?

Principle 5: Behold!

Only a product and service that is unique, substantial and superior or at least not inferior is good enough to manifest and support a lasting myth. Ueber-Brands put their goods at the centre of attention and on pedestals (at least metaphorically speaking) so they are paid tribute to and receive the respect they deserve.

- Does your product exceed expectations in areas that are central to your myth? (Porsche on performance, Patagonia on ethics.)

- Have you transformed your 'Reasons to Believe' into a 'Story to Believe' to romanticize your proposition and allow consumers to bond with it? (Freitag's identified tarps.)

- Do you visibly revere your product or service in ways that reflect and inspire respect? (Hoshino resorts' hushed atmosphere.)

- Do your products feel like they have a soul? Do you tell their stories? (The Laundress' personal testing, Icebreaker's Baa Code.)

- Are there rituals associated with your brand? (La Mer 'warming' cream between fingers, Singapore airlines attendants kneeling down to listen to seated passengers.)

- Have you developed assets that make your brand unmistakable beyond a logo? (Bottega Veneta weave.)

- Did you consider appropriating codes and languages of other (higher) categories or of your own? (Maison du Chocolat – jewellery; Nespresso Grand Crus.)

- Did you or could you allow for customization – at least on certain lines? (MyMINI.)

- What is your iconic product and is it always part of your plans? (Chanel No.5.)

- Do you regularly update those icons to keep them current? (Louis Vuitton monogram bags.)

The ultimate question: Is your product or service considered the 'holy grail' of its own myth – and your category?

Principle 6: Living the dream

A mission must be lived to be taken seriously. A myth must be embraced wholeheartedly to work. Ueber-Brands are such because they reflect what they believe in – inside out. From their leader through their organization to all their actions across touch points and times. God is in the details. And so are Ueber-Brands.

- Is your brand led by a visionary who executes with pedantic precision? (Aēsop.)
- Or is your leadership split between Artist and Operator? (L'Occitane.)
- Are structure, processes, culture, and ethics proof of a mission fully embraced? (Method.)
- Do your purpose, brand, organization and target align synergistically? (Patagonia.)
- Is your work environment not only reflecting but inspiring the brand's mission and myth? (Innocent's Fruit Tower with its 'common ground'.)
- Do you make tough choices to support your beliefs? (Patagonia becoming a b-corporation.)
- If part of a bigger group, does your brand benefit from 'ring-fencing' unique aspects and the protection of a high-ranking management mentor? (Nespresso.)
- Are you preventing a chipping away of core organizational or execution aspects through minor 'tweaks' that 'make sense' in isolation but undermine the brand in total? (Snapple.)
- Do you control brand creation and experience all the way into the hands of the user to ensure nothing essential gets 'lost in translation'? (Stonyfield, from field to factory to family)
- Can perfectionism and passion be felt in your execution? (No hair on the ground in a Frédéric Fekkai salon.)
- How is your POS? Is your world clearly distinct and recognizable? (Aēsop's shelving.)
- Do you go beyond the expected or known – at least occasionally – to let organization and customer keep dreaming? (Chanel 'mobile art container'.)
- Are you as clear about what you are not doing? (Brunello Cucinelli never goes 'on sale'.)

The ultimate question: Rather than needing to 'recruit' your employees and customers, can you choose among a group of soulmates and disciples who long to join?

Principle 7: Growth without end

How to constantly grow without over-saturating and undermining your pricing power? Ueber-Brands only become so if they manage the ultimate balancing act. Avoiding over-penetration through horizontal or stealth expansion – and occasional cutbacks. Counter-balancing any reaching down by reaching up. And always staying close to their heroes and their heart.

- Are you consciously managing your manufacturing and marketing investments to align with an exponential growth curve? (Hermès' Shang Xia.)
- Do you avoid deep early losses (as typical in the mass business model) that would create pressure to 'scale up' faster than the brand can grow organically without dilution? (Heavy discounting to drive volumes.)
- Do you allow yourself to 'walk before you run' – to hone your skills, your product, your service, your communication and loyalize your design target before broader exposure? (Aēsop boutique-guided roll-out, San Pellegrino entering in white space through restaurants.)
- Do you leverage e-commerce to grow stealthily, capture the long tail without the need for physical omnipresence? (Bumble and Bumble, The Laundress, Burberry.)
- Are limited editions, seasonal offerings or other ways to curtail supply used to keep demand, desire and prices up? (Dior J'Adore special editions, Ferrari production quotas.)
- Do you tier up as you grow out? (Amex, Johnnie Walker.)
- Have you exhausted horizontal growth before expanding vertically? (Yuan Soap across TCM-related categories, Hermès across crafts.)
- Are you pruning back before perceived inflation sets in? (Dior or Hermès discontinuing items that are 'too popular'.)
- Do you make sure your credentialing community feels uniquely and intimately connected with the brand as you grow? (MAC make-up artist community engagement.)

The ultimate question: Is your design target still singing your praises after years of expansion and growth?

If questions remain or you would like us to participate in your branding project, please contact us at info@ueberbrands.com

BIBLIOGRAPHY

Abraham, Tamara (2009) Bag lady Victoria Beckham's 100-strong Birkin bag collection that's worth £1.5 million, *Mail Online* [online] http://www.dailymail.co.uk/femail/article-1184169/Bag-lady-Victoria-Beckhams-100-strong-Birkin-bag-collection-thats-worth-1-5m.html [accessed Aug 2014]

Aēsop.com [accessed July 2014] http://www.aesop.com/usa/article/who-we-are-usa.html and http://www.aesop.com/usa/about_aesop/

Aesop on Pinterest [accessed January 2014] https://www.pinterest.com/myinsprition/brand-aesop/ and https://www.pinterest.com/pin/129548926751878856/

Ahrendts, Angela (2013), The Future of Storytelling, *YouTube* (accessed January 2014) https://www.youtube.com/watch?v=krQG2Hceov4

Amed, Imran (2014) CEO Talk, Brunello Cucinelli, *Business of Fashion* [online] http://www.businessoffashion.com/2014/07/ceo-talk-brunello-cucinelli-founder-chief-executive-brunello-cucinelli.html [accessed August 2014]

Amos, Gerald [accessed 14 June 2014] The most important right we have is the right to be reasonable, *Patagonia.com / Becoming a Responsible Company* [online] http://www.patagonia.com/us/patagonia.go?assetid=2329

Anaya, Suleman (2014) The humanity of Hermès, *Business of Fashion* [online] businessoffashion.com/2014/04/humanity-hermes.html [accessed August 2014]

Anderson, Chris (2006) *The Long Tail: Why the future of business is selling less of more*, Hyperion, New York

Apple iPod (2001) Jeff Goldblum ad, *YouTube* [online] https://www.youtube.com/watch?v=nX1V8WL2m6U [accessed August 2014]

Arabian Business.com (2012) Richard Girardot interview: Nespresso Coffee, *arabianbusiness.com* [online] http://m.arabianbusiness.com/richard-girardot-interview-nespresso-coffee-453163.html?page=1 [accessed 12 June 2014]

Ariely, Dan and Norton, Michael (2009) Conceptual consumption, *Annual Review of Psychology*, 60 pp 475–99

Barmettler, Stefan (2013) Daniel und Markus Freitag: Wir waren nie auf dem Ego-Trip, *Bilanz*, Switzerland [online] http://www.bilanz.ch/gespraech/daniel-und-markus-freitag-wir-waren-nie-auf-dem-egotrip) [accessed July 2014]

Barthes, Roland (1981) *Camera Lucida: Reflections on photography*, Farrar, Straus and Giroux, New York

Benefitcorp.net [accessed 12 June 2014] 'What is a benefit corporation? [online] http://benefitcorp.net/quick-faqs

Berne, Eric (1964) *Games People Play*, Ballantine, New York

The Bible, Standard English version, Collins, London

Bloomberg TV [accessed August 2014] Lululemon Pants don't work for some women [online] http://www.bloomberg.com/video/lululemon-pants-don-t-work-for-some-women-founder-ATKjgs7jQduIr_ou1z8XYg.html

Bowman, Jo (2010) The Fabled Guys, *CNBC Magazine* [online] www.cnbcmagazine.com/story/the-fable-guys/1526/1/ [accessed 8 October 2012]

Brooks, David (2000) *Bobos in Paradise*, Simon and Schuster, New York

Burberry Prorsum [accessed January 2015] *Youko* [online] http://v.youku.com/v_
    show/id_XMjQ0NTY3MDIw.html
Campbell, Joseph (1972) *Myths to Live By*, Viking Press
Campbell, Joseph (1978) *The Hero with a Thousand Faces*, Suhrkamp
Campbell, Joseph (1988) *The Power of Myths*, Anchor Books
Cassies.ca (2006), Cassies Canada Case Study: Mini – Sustained Success –
    Silver Canada, *cassies.ca* [online] http://cassies.ca/content/caselibrary/
    winners/2006pdfs/_549_MINI_Web_DR.pdf [accessed April 2014]
Castiglione, Baldesar (1528) *The Book of the Courtier*, Penguin Classics
Cato, Jeremy (2013) What is it about Mini that makes it so popular?, *Globe and
    Mail*, Canada [online] http://www.theglobeandmail.com/globe-drive/reviews/
    new-cars/what-is-it-about-mini-that-makes-it-so-popular/article13560747/
    [accessed April 2014]
Chatwin, Bruce (1987) *The Songlines*, Penguin, New York
China Times (2012) Shang Xia, 'Hermès Made in China' arrives in Paris, *China
    Times* [online] http://thechinatimes.com/online/2012/02/2134.html [accessed
    May 2014]
Chouinard, Yvon (2006) *Let My People Go Surfing: The education of a reluctant
    businessman*, Penguin Books, New York
Chouinard, Yvon and Brown, Michael S (2008) Going organic: converting
    Patagonia's cotton product line, *Journal of Industrial Ecology* 1 (1), pp 117–29
Chouinard, Yvon *et al* (2013) *Climbing Fitz Roy 1968*, Patagonia Books
Chu, Kathy (2013) How Aēsop plans to expand without China, *WSJ Live* [online]
    http://live.wsj.com/video/how-aesop-plans-to-expand-without-china/73841B0C-
    6A2F-4D8E-AEA0-3720F966BB90.html#!73841B0C-6A2F-4D8E-AEA0-
    3720F966BB90 [accessed 12 Nov 2013]
Cirque du Soleil [accessed August 2014] http://www.cirquedusoleil.com/en/home/
    shows.aspx
CNBC [accessed May 2013], Moleskine CEO on IPO: Investors have nothing to
    fear [online] http://www.cnbc.com/id/100612006#
CNN (2014) Aerin Lauder: Every woman can be beautiful [online] http://edition
    .cnn.com/2014/08/05/business/aerin-lauder-every-woman/ [accessed January
    2015]
Coca-Cola.com, various sub-sites (http://www.coca-colacompany.com/stories/
    happiness-without-borders, http://www.coca-colacompany.com/videos/
    happiness-machine-for-couples [accessed May 2014]
Cole, Bethan (2008), Aēsop: fabled beauty', The *Independent* newspaper, 14 April
Cone Communications (2013) Cone Communications/Echo Global CSR Study
    [online] http://www.conecomm.com/2013-global-csr-study-release [accessed
    May 2014]
Cooney, Matt (2006) Meet the man who gave Red Bull wings, *Idealog* magazine #7
    [online] http://www.idealog.co.nz/magazine/7/meet-the-man-who-gave-red-bull-
    wings [accessed May 2014]
Cova, Bernard (2011) Advance strategy and marketing for sports organizations,
    slideshare.net [online] http://www.slideshare.net/LaJos11/mini-coopers-
    community [accessed April 2014]
Curry, Andrew and Stubbings, Andy (2013) Brands with a purpose, *Admap*, June
de Saint-Exupery, Antoine (1995) *The Little Prince*, Wordsworth, London
Deighton, John (2002) How a juicy brand came back to life, *Harvard Business
    School* [online] http://hbswk.hbs.edu/item/2752.html [accessed August 2014]

Demeter Group (2013) State of The Craft Beer Industry 2013 [online] http://
demetergroup.net/sites/default/files/news/attachment/State-of-the-Craft-Beer-
Industry-2013.pdf [accessed September 2014]

Denizet-Lewis, Benoit (2006) The man behind Abercrombie & Fitch, *Salon* [online]
http://www.salon.com/2006/01/24/jeffries/ [accessed December 2013]

Dichter, Ernest (1964) *Handbook of Consumer Motivations*, McGraw Hill,
New York

Döhle, Patricia, (2012) Richtig Dosiert, *Brand Eins* magazine, February

DVF's Journey of a Dress (2014) *YouTube* [online] https://www.youtube.com/
watch?v=N3Q9ENKPqKs [accessed January 2015]

The Economist (22 April 2010) Shareholders vs. stakeholders: a new idolatry
[online] http://www.economist.com/node/15954434 [accessed August 2014]

Edelman.com (2012) Introducing Good Purpose 2012 [online] http://purpose
.edelman.com/slides/introducing-goodpurpose-2012/ [accessed May 2014]

Eder, Florian (2013) Ich will nicht der Reichste auf dem Friedhof sein, *Welt am
Sonntag*, 1 December

Eliot, T S (1943/1971) *Four Quartets*, Harcourt, Orlando

Eng, Dinah (2013) Mopping up with Method, *Fortune* [online] http://fortune
.com/2013/10/10/mopping-up-with-method/ [accessed August 2014]

Fairs, Marcus (2012) I was horrified at the thought of a soulless chain, *Dezeen*
[online] http://www.dezeen.com/2012/12/10/dennis-paphitis-aesop-interview/
[accessed August 2014]

Farrow, Boyd (2013) Aesop: brown and botanical, *Billionaire* [online] http://www
.billionaire.com/body/skincare/422/aesop-brown-and-botanical [accessed June
2014]

Fawkes, Piers (July 2012) Food brand tests new flavor combinations through
retail concept, PSFK [online] http://www.psfk.com/2012/07/chobani-store-soho
.html#!bwCaKD [accessed August 2014]

Finger, Evelyn, Jungbluth, Rudiger and Ruckert, Sabine (2014) Die Moralapostel,
Die Zeit, 9 January

Finke, Bjoern (2013) Operation Karo, *Sueddeutsche Zeitung*, 14 November

Food Processing [accessed August 2014] Division President Jostein Solhem [online]
http://www.foodprocessing.com/ceo/jostein-solheim/

Freitag (2014) Post on facebook.com [online] https://www.facebook.com/
freitagstoredavos/posts/150198175136281[accessed June 2014]

Freitag Backstage, produced by 'Brand Expeditions' [accessed January 2015] http://
www.youtube.com/watch?v=cLYIVX_nyD8

Freitag.ch [accessed September 2014], Individual recycled Freeway Bags,
http://www.freitag.ch/fundamentals/freewaybags, Heartcore Thomas,
http://www.freitag.ch/about/feed/thomas and Highlife Mustapha,
http://www.freitag.ch/about/feed/mustapha

Freitag fringe backpack [accessed January 2015] http://www.highsnobiety
.com/2011/06/30/video-freitag-f49-fringe-backpack/

Freitag Stop-Motion videos [accessed January 2015] http://www.vimeo
.com/102953056

Frenzel, Karolina, Müller, Michael and Sottong, Hermann (2004) *Storytelling –
Das Harun-al-Raschid-Prinzip*, Hanser, Munich

Friedman, Thomas L (2005) *The World Is Flat*, Picador, New York

Friedman, Thomas L (2013) Welcome to the sharing economy, *New York Times*,
20 July

Fryer, Bronwyn (2003) Robert McKee, Storytelling that moves people, *Harvard Business Review* [online] http://hbr.org/2003/06/storytelling-that-moves-people/ [accessed March 2012]

Gamerman, Ellen (2014) Are museums selling out? *Wall Street Journal*, 12 June

Gehl, Christian (2014) Mythos Harley Davidson: power sucht Frau, *Werben & Verkaufen* [online] http://www.wuv.de/blogs/markenschau/marken/mythos_harley_davidson_power_sucht_frau [accessed August 2014]

Glenn, Joshua and Walker, Rob (2012) *Significant Objects*, Fantagraphics Books, Seattle

Gottschall, Jonathan (2014) The science of storytelling, *Fast Company* [online] http://www.fastcocreate.com/3020044/the-science-of-storytelling-how-narrative-cuts-through-distraction [accessed January 2014]

Gruley, Brian (2013) At Chobani, the Turkish king of Greek yoghurt, *Bloomberg Businessweek* [online] http://www.businessweek.com/articles/2013-01-31/at-chobani-the-turkish-king-of-greek-yogurt [accessed August 2014]

Gucci [accessed January 2014] *Shoppable* [online] http://www.gucci.com/us/worldofgucci/shoppable_video/shop-this-video

Guerlain (2013) 'La legende de Shalimar', *YouTube* [online] https://www.youtube.com/watch?v=vL6XJw8Oe5M [accessed October 2013]

Harley Davidson (2008) Harley Davidson Experience – Living by It, *YouTube* [Online] https://www.youtube.com/watch?v=jyocDeGh7Qs [accessed August 2014]

Havrilesky, Heather (2014) The brilliant, unnerving meta-marketing of The LEGO Movie, *New York Times* Magazine, 28 Feb

Hearne, John (2012) How Red Bull got its wings, *Irish Examiner* [online] http://www.irishexaminer.com/lifestyle/features/how-red-bull-got-its-wings-217715.html [accessed May 2014]

Henneman, Todd (2011) Patagonia fills payroll with people who are passionate, *Workforce.com* [online] http://www.workforce.com/articles/patagonia-fills-payroll-with-people-who-are-passionate [accessed May 2014]

Holt, Douglas (2004) *How Brands Become Icons*, Harvard Business Press, Boston

Huffington Post (2012) Stephen Colbert and Jimmy Fallon's ice cream war continues on 'Late Night', *Huffington Post* [online] http://www.huffingtonpost.com/2012/02/15/stephen-colbert-jimmy-fallon-ben-jerrys-ice-cream-war-video_n_1278743.html [accessed August 2014]

Humanistic Capitalism, Wikipedia [accessed September 2014] http://en.wikipedia.org/wiki/Humanistic_capitalism

Icebreaker [accessed June 2013] Trace Your Baacode [online] http://uk.icebreaker.com/en/why-icebreaker-merino/trace-your-garment-with-icebreaker-baacode.html

Intermarché [accessed August 2014] Inglorious Fruits, *YouTube* [online] https://www.youtube.com/watch?v=p2nSECWq_PE

Ivory Soap, Wikipedia [accessed August 2013] http://en.wikipedia.org/wiki/Ivory_(soap)

Jacobs, Deborah (2013) How to buy your first Birkin bag, *Forbes* [online] http://www.forbes.com/sites/deborahljacobs/2013/09/19/how-to-buy-your-first-hermes-birkin/ [accessed May 2014]

Jacobs, Laura (2007) From Hermès to eternity, *Vanity Fair* [online] http://www.vanityfair.com/culture/features/2007/09/hermes200709 [accessed May 2014]

Jessop, Alicia (2012) The secret behind Red Bull's action sports success, *Forbes* [online] http://www.forbes.com/sites/aliciajessop/2012/12/07/the-secret-behind-red-bulls-action-sports-success/ [accessed 9 May 2014]

Jing Daily (2013) Heathrow braces for Chinese New Year rush [online] http://jingdaily.com/heathrow-braces-for-chinese-new-year-rush/23648/ [accessed May 2014]

Josic Media [accessed August 2014] Prada's customized shoes cause a rise in personalized fashion [online] http://www.josic.com/pradas-customized-shoes-cause-a-rise-in-personalized-fashion368

Judah, Hetty (2013) Fashion's art fair love affair, *Business of Fashion* [online] http://www.businessoffashion.com/2013/12/art-basel-miami-beach-fashions-art-fair-love-affair.html

Just Auto.com (2013) Germany: BMW group sales continue to climb in April [online] http://www.just-auto.com/news/bmw-group-sales-continue-climb-in-april_id134294.aspx [accessed May2014]

Kahnemann, Daniel (2011) *Thinking, Fast and Slow*, Penguin Group

Kapferer, Jean-Noël (2009) *The Luxury Strategy*, Kogan Page, London

Karp, Hannah (2014) The key to selling an $800 sneaker, *Wall Street Journal*, July 28

Klingman, Jeff (2014) Art and the Academy: Red Bull elevates the corporate music festival, *The L Magazine* [online] http://www.thelmagazine.com/TheMeasure/archives/2014/05/01/art-and-the-academy-red-bull-tries-to-elevate-the-corporate-music-festival [accessed June 2014]

Krueger, Dr. Cordula and Schaefer, Wolfgang (1995) *YoYo: Youth Observes Youth Obsessions*, Lintas

La Mer [accessed August 2014] http://www.cremedelamer.com/heritage

Lager, Fred (1995) *Ben & Jerry's: The Inside Scoop*, Random House USA

Lagerfeld, Karl (2013) Once Upon A Time... by Karl Lagerfeld, *YouTube* [online] https://www.youtube.com/watch?v=0o9dTCl0hkY [accessed July 2013]

Laguiole [accessed November 2013] Laguiole History [online] http://www.laguiole.com/laguiole_history_village.php

Lakrids by Johan Buelow [accessed August 2014] The story of Lakrids by Johan Buelow [online] http://liquorice.nu/pages/about-us

LaRocca, David (2014) Brunello Cucinelli: A humanistic approach to luxury, philanthropy, and stewardship, *Journal of Religion and Business Ethics*, July

The Laundress [accessed August 2014] http://www.thelaundress.com/our-story/

Leahey, Collen (2012) Angela Ahrendts: The secret behind Burberry's growth, *Fortune* [online] http://fortune.com/2012/06/19/angela-ahrendts-the-secrets-behind-burberrys-growth/ [accessed August 2014]

Leibenstein, Harvey (1950) Bandwagon, snob and Veblen effects in the theory of consumer demand, *Quarterly Journal of Economics* **64** (2), pp 183–207

Liessmann, Konrad Paul (2010) *Das Universum der Dinge: Zur ästhetik des alltäglichen*, Paul Zsolnay Verlag, Vienna

LifePR [accessed August 2014] Kundenbefragung: Müsli-Marken 2014 [online] http://www.lifepr.de/pressemitteilung/disq-deutsches-institut-fuer-service-qualitaet-gmbh-co-kg/Kundenbefragung-Muesli-Marken-2014/boxid/497286

The Local (2013) German retailers embrace ugly fruit [online] http://www.thelocal.de/20131013/52371 [accessed August 2014]

Luxury Daily (2014) Hermès gives orange boxes an appetite in video series [online] http://www.luxurydaily.com/hermes-gives-orange-boxes-an-appetite-in-video-series/ [accessed August 2014]

MAC cosmetics Aids Fund [accessed August 2014] http://www.macaidsfund.org/

Mackenzie, Dorothy (2013) Integrity: A key component for a successful sustainable organization, *Dragon Rouge* [online] http://www.dragonrouge.de/blog/integrity-key-component-successful-sustainable-organisation [accessed May 2013]

MailOnline (2007) Queen of Green Roddick's unfair trade started when she copied Body Shop formula, *Mailonline* [online] http://www.dailymail.co.uk/femail/article-482012/Queen-Green-Roddicks-unfair-trade-started-copied-Body-Shop-formula.html [accessed August 2014]

Malcolm, Hadley (2013) Lululemon lovers buy into healthy lifestyle, *USA Today*, 19 March

Manjoo, Farhad (2014) What the Beats deal says about Apple: it loves tastemakers, *New York Times*, 30 May

Martin, Richard (1995), *Contemporary Fashion*, St. James Press, London

McCann [accessed August 2014] http://mccann.com.au/about/the-mccann-story/

McDonald, Duff (2011) Red Bull's billionaire maniac, *Businessweek* [online] http://www.businessweek.com/magazine/content/11_22/b4230064852768.htm [accessed July 2014]

Meck, Georg (2014) Bier oder Champagner, *Frankfurter Allgemeine Sonntagszeitung*, 10 August

Method (a) [accessed August 2014] http://methodhome.com/methodology/our-story/

Method (b) [accessed August 2014] https://www.themuse.com/companies/method/office

Miller, Matthew (2009) Billionaire Acrobatics, *Forbes*, November [online] http://www.forbes.com/2009/03/11/laliberte-cirque-du-soleil-rich-billionaires-2009-billionaires-cirque.html [accessed August 2014]

MINI fan site [accessed August 2014] http://www.mini2.com/forum/second-generation-mini-cooper-s/160620-hello-expectant-mini-cooper-s-owner.html

Mini Menzies Stirling [accessed April 2014] Mini Finance Offer [online] https://www.facebook.com/OfficialMINIMenziesStirling/posts/313766908751155

Moleskine (a) [accessed August 2014] http://www.moleskine.com/us/news/bruce-chatwins-notebooks

Moleskine (b) [accessed August 2014] http://www.moleskine.com/us/news/bruce_chatwins_unpublished_letters

Moleskine [accessed July 2014] http://www.moleskine.com/us/moleskine-world

Montblanc [accessed August 2014] https://press.montblanc.com/corporate/montblanc-montre-sa/index/58/Montblanc-Montre-SA-in-Le-Locle-Switzerland

Moses, Lucia (2011) Vogue casts 1000 'Influencers' for network, *Adweek* [online] http://www.adweek.com/news/advertising-branding/vogue-casts-1000-influencers-network-133299 [accessed April 2014]

Muller, Joann (2013) In bankrupt Detroit, Shinola puts its faith in American manufacturing, *Forbes.com* [online] http://www.forbes.com/sites/joannmuller/2013/07/26/in-bankrupt-detroit-shinola-puts-its-faith-in-american-manufacturing/2/ [accessed May 2014]

Musk, Elon (2006) The secret Tesla Motors master plan (just between you and me), *Tesla Motors* [online] http://www.teslamotors.com/blog/secret-tesla-motors-master-plan-just-between-you-and-me [accessed August 2014]

Myarchitecturalmoleskine [accessed August 2014] http://architecturalmoleskine.blogspot.com/2011/12/roman-colosseum.html

Mycoskie, Blake (2012) *Start Something that Matters*, Virgin Books

Nalley, Richard (2013) Brunello Cucinelli: life by design, *Forbes Life* [online] http://www.forbes.com/sites/richardnalley/2013/03/28/brunello-cucinelli-life-by-design/ [accessed June 2014]

NBC News (2006) Ben & Jerry back to roots [online] http://www.nbcnews.com/id/13819483/ns/business-us_business/t/ben-jerry-back-roots-seeking-social-change/#.U-Dl8Sj6QeE [accessed August 2014]

Nespresso commercial (2013) *YouTube* [online] https://www.youtube.com/watch?v=pw6ZfPQypBg [accessed August 2014]

Nestle-Nespresso.com [accessed November 2014] Facts and Figures [online] http://www.nestle-nespresso.com/about-us/facts-and-figures

North American Motoring [accessed May 2014] http://www.northamericanmotoring.com/

Numerology.com [accessed May 2013] http://www.numerology.com/numerology-numbers/7

O'Connor, Clare (2014) Bain deal makes TOMS shoes founder a $300 million man, *Forbes* [online] http://www.forbes.com/sites/clareoconnor/2014/08/20/bain-deal-makes-toms-shoes-founder-blake-mycoskie-a-300-million-man [accessed August 2014]

O'Flaherty, Mark C (2012)] The stuff of fables, *Financial Times* [online] http://howtospendit.ft.com/health-grooming/7224-the-stuff-of-fables [accessed 14 October 2012]

Olmsted, Larry (2013) Scotch whisky preview: new Johnnie Walker platinum hits stores this month, *Forbes* [online] http://www.forbes.com/sites/larryolmsted/2013/08/20/scotch-whisky-preview-new-johnnie-walker-platinum-hits-stores-this-month/ [accessed August 2014]

Orsini, Patti (2010) Ben & Jerry's AR app, *JWT Intelligence* [online] http://www.jwtintelligence.com/2010/07/ben-and-jerrys-ar-app/#axzz39qjicwWY [accessed August 2014]

Oscarprgirl [accessed January 2015] http://oscarprgirl.tumblr.com/

Outside magazine editors (2011) The Power List – 1. Dietrich Mateschitz, *Outside* [online] http://www.outsideonline.com/outdoor-adventure/celebrities/1-Dietrich-Mateschitz.html [accessed May 2014]

Oxford Dictionaries [accessed May 2013] http://www.oxforddictionaries.com/us/definition/american_english/myth?q=myth

Packard, Vance (1957/1987) *Die Geheimen Verführer*, Ullstein, Berlin

Page, Antony and Katz, Robert (2012) The truth about Ben & Jerry's, *Stanford Social Innovation Review*, Fall [online] www.ssireview.org/articles/entry/the_truth_about_ben_and_jerrys [accessed May 2014]

Patagonia [accessed August 2014] http://www.repreve.com/products/Patagonia.aspx

Pine, Joseph and Gilmore, James (1999) *The Experience Economy*, Harvard Business School Press, Boston

Prestige Volkswagen [accessed March 2014] Volkswagen Beetle vs Mini Cooper http://www.prestigevolkswagen.com/Volkswagen-Beetle-vs-Mini-Cooper

Rapaille, Clotaire (2006) *The Culture Code*, Broadway Books, New York

Redbullbcone.com [accessed July 2014] Announcing Seoul Top 16 [online] http://www.redbullbcone.com/en/news/official/announcing-seoul-top-16/

Riesman, David (2001) *The Lonely Crowd*, Yale University Press

Ross, Geoff (2001) *Every Bastard Says No: The 42Below story*, Random House, New Zealand

Ryan, Eric and Lowry, Adam (2011) *The Method Method: Seven obsessions that helped our scrappy start-up turn an industry upside down*, Penguin, New York

Safranski, Ruediger (2007) *Romantik: Eine deutsche Affäre*, Carl Hanser Verlag, Munich

Salinger, J D (1951) *Catcher in the Rye*, Little, Brown

Sartre, Jean-Paul (1947) *Huis Clos*, Editions Gallimard, Paris

Schulz, E J (2014) Watch Mila Kunis' debut for Jim Beam, *Advertising Age* [online] http://adage.com/article/news/watch-mila-kunis-debut-jim-beam/291760/ [accessed August 2014]

Schulze, Gerhard (1992) *Die Erlebnisgesellschaft: Kultursoziologie der Gegenwart*, Campus, Frankfurt

Selfridges [accessed 2014] http://style.selfridges.com/whats-on/no-noise-selfridges

Silverstein, Michael J and Fiske, Neil (2003) *Trading Up*, Penguin, New York

Simonet, Paul and Virgile, Carlos (2013) Luxury brand marketing: the seamless consumer journey, *Admap*, November

Sinek, Simon (2009) *Starting With Why*, Penguin, New York

SKII Rituals (2012) *YouTube* [online] https://www.youtube.com/watch?v=2VXJptlX82g [accessed August 2014]

Slywotzky, Adrian with Weber, Karl (2011), *Demand: Creating what people love before they know they want it*, Crown Business

Sneyd, Ross (2006) Ice cream activists target nukes Ben & Jerry's campaign is American pie, Madison.com [online] http://host.madison.com/business/ice-cream-activists-target-nukes-ben-jerry-s-campaign-is/article_11aa38fd-cb00-5baf-88fe-c06978887f34.html [accessed August 2014]

Spence, Roy (2009) *It's Not What You Sell, It's What You Stand For*, Penguin, New York

Stengel, Jim and Garbe, Benoit (2011) Discuss the Best Brands Study 2011, *millwardbrown.com* [online] http://www.millwardbrown.com/global-navigation/insights/media-gallery/videos/best-brands-study-2011[accessed May 2014]

Stevenson, Seth (2012) Patagonia's founder is America's most unlikely business guru, *Wall Street Journal* [online] http://online.wsj.com/news/articles/SB10001424052702303513404577352221465986612 [accessed May 2014]

Stories [accessed July 2014] http://www.stories.com/gb/About

Story, Louise (2007) Seaweed Clothing Has None, *New York Times*, 14 November

Story, Richard David (2013) Hermès En Famille, *Departures Magazine*, November

Swansburg, John (2012) Where fashion is the F-word', *slate.com* [online] http://www.slate.com/articles/life/fashion/2012/03/patagonia_yvon_chouinard_s_company_makes_technical_climbing_gear_how_d_it_catch_on_with_the_rest_of_us_.2.html [accessed May 2014]

Szmydke, Paulina (2011) Bernard Arnault vows to keep LMVH's upmarket drive, *Women's Wear Daily*, 11 April

Thomas, Dana (2007) *Deluxe – How luxury lost its luster*, Penguin Books, New York

Thomas, Dana (2013), Chanel, self-appointed guardian of Paris's artisan workshops, *New York Times Style Magazine*, 11 November

Tomlinson, Richard (2002) L'Oreal's global makeover, *Fortune* [online] http://archive.fortune.com/magazines/fortune/fortune_archive/2002/09/30/329290/index.htm [accessed August 2014]

Trei, Lisa (2008), Price tag can change the way people experience wine, study shows' *Stanford News Service* [online] http://news.stanford.edu/pr/2008/pr-wine-011608.html [accessed August 2014]

Tungate, Martin (2011), *Branded Beauty: How marketing changed the way we look*, Kogan Page, London

Van Laer, Tom, de Ruyter, Ko, Visconti, Luca and Wetzels, Martin (2014) The extended transportation-imagery model: a meta-analysis of the antecedents and consequences of consumers' narrative transportation, *Journal of Consumer Research*, **40** (5) pp 797–817

van Rensburg, D J (2014) In-sourcing disruptive brands as a corporate entrepreneurship strategy, *International Entrepreneurship and Management Journal*, **11**, DOI 10.1007/s11365-014-0309-4

Veblen, Thorstein and Banta, Martha (ed) (2009) *The Theory of the Leisure Class*, Oxford, New York

Voight, Joan (2013) Absolut's iconic design is its ticket to younger consumers, *Adweek*, 16 September

Waldmeir, Patti (2012) Luxury brand makes links with China's past, *Financial Times* [online] http://www.ft.com/cms/s/0/d82d1a58-6f49-11e1-9c57-00144feab49a.html#ixzz3EN8YfRj3 [accessed May 2014]

Warc (2013) *Trends Toolkit*, Warc

Watzlawick, Paul, Beavin, Janet H. and Jackson, Don D (1969/1985) *Menschliche Kommunikation*, Verlag Huber, Bern

Weil, Jennifer (2014) Reaching for the heights, *WWD Beauty Inc* [online] http://www.wwd.com/beauty-industry-news/beauty-features/reaching-for-the-heights-marc-puig-7670352 [accessed January 2015]

Welles, Edward (1992) Lost In Patagonia: Yvon Chouinard's ambitious social mission, *Inc Magazine* [online] http://www.inc.com/magazine/19920801/4210.html [accessed May 2014]

Wendlandt, Astrid and Denis, Pascale (2013) Hermès tests European appetite for its young Chinese brand, *reuters.com* [online] http://www.reuters.com/article/2013/09/11/us-hermes-shangxia-idUSBRE98A11X20130911 [accessed May 2014]

Wheelan, Hugh (2011) Alpha for 'high sustainability' companies, *Responsible-Investor.com* [online] https://www.responsible-investor.com/article/harvard_lbs/P0/ [accessed January 2013]

Whole Foods Market [accessed August 2014] Whole Story: The official Whole Foods Market Blog [online] http://www.wholefoodsmarket.com/blog/truth-about-farmed-salmon-whole-foods-market

Wooldridge, India (2013) 10 truths about advertising, *Admap*, June, pp 14–15

www.brunellocucinelli.com [accessed June 2014], The Solomeo School [online] http://www.brunellocucinelli.com/en/school

www.wikiluxurybrands.com Hermès [accessed August 2014] http://www.wikiluxurybrands.com/listings/hermes/

Xu Xiao (2010) Mini branding for youthful market – and young at heart, *China Daily* [online] http://www.chinadaily.com.cn/cndy/2010-12/23/content_11742389.htm [accessed April 2014]

Yuan Soap Video [accessed August 2014] *YouTube* [online] https://www.youtube.com/watch?v=brWtxZ025aA

Yuan Soap website [accessed August 2014] http://www.yuansoap.com.my/index.php?main_page=page&id=12

Yuan, Jada (2007) Still doing the hustle, *New York Magazine*, 24 October

problem

tour /

Product
Message

1 — Message out
2. Live up to hype
3. Be Magnetic

Digital
jery tour
ads?
free cards
press

Flavors	perfection
pints	every
Sammies	time
onvo	
feel good	something
	to come
	back for

get LA up first

Umbrellas in LA.
   ☒ or orange stools along wall
   to draw attention.
Reduce flavors permanently to allow
   for more variety

   put line through the pint
change Sammie to packed cookie

INDEX

Note: The index is filed in alphabetical, word-by-word order. Numbers within main headings are filed as spelt out; acronyms are filed as presented; 'Mc' is filed as 'Mac'. Page locators in *italics* denote information contained within a figure or table; locators as roman numerals denote material contained within the Preface.

CPSIA information can be obtained at www.ICGtesting.com
Printed in the USA
BVOW08s1203110515

399847BV00003B/6/P